Leaps of Faith

leaps of faith

*Science,
Miracles, and the Search for
Supernatural Consolation*

NICHOLAS
HUMPHREY

BasicBooks
A Division of HarperCollins*Publishers*

Published by BasicBooks,
A Division of HarperCollins Publishers, Inc.

First published in the United Kingdom in 1995 by Chatto & Windus.

Library of Congress Cataloging-in-Publication Data
Humphrey, Nicholas.
    Leaps of faith : science, miracles, and the search for supernatural
consolation / Nicholas Humphrey.
        p.   cm.
    Includes bibliographical references and index.
    ISBN 0-465-08044-8
    1. Parapsychology—Controversial literature.   I. Title.
BF1042H88   1996
133—dc20   95-44537
                                                                          CIP

96 97 98 99 RRD 9 8 7 6 5 4 3 2 1

Glendower
I can call spirits from the vasty deep.

Hotspur
Why, so can I, or so can any man;
But will they come when you do call on them?

Henry IV, Part One, III, i

Contents

Acknowledgements

While working on this book I held a Senior Research Fellowship at Darwin College, Cambridge, funded by the Perrott and Warrick Fund. The Fund was set up to sponsor research into phenomena suggestive of the existence of psychic powers in human beings. I am grateful to the College and the Electors to the Fellowship for allowing me to interpret my duties in my own way. Darwin College has provided an exceptionally warm and stimulating environment, and I have been very happy there.

Among many who have helped with the book, I am especially indebted to my friends Charlotte Grant and Ruth Brandon for reading and criticising the final manuscript, and to Jenny Uglow for her meticulous and intelligent editing. Above all I have depended in untold ways on my wife, Ayla Kohn.

That Hypothesis

'I have no need of that hypothesis.' So said the mathematician Pierre Simon de Laplace to Napoleon, when he was asked what part God played in his picture of the universe. Earlier calculations made by Isaac Newton had seemed to show that there were irregularities in the movements of the planets which would require the direct intervention of God to set them right. Laplace had now proved that every last detail could be accounted for by gravitational attraction. No additional *ad hoc* assumptions were necessary.

Laplace was referring in particular to the workings of the solar system. But the implication was that he would have no need of 'that hypothesis' in general. By the end of the eighteenth century, men of science had persuaded themselves – if not yet everybody else – that across the whole of nature the God-hypothesis was *de trop*. Admittedly, no one would deny that God the Creator might have played a part in the beginning. But even if he was responsible for bringing the universe into being, he had long since ceased to take an active interest in its progress. He had originally chosen a few simple and beautiful Laws of Nature. He had filled the void with matter. He had seen that it was good. But then he had left his creation to its own devices.

Some might imagine that God did at least continue to watch over developments with fatherly concern. Yet even this could hardly be expected of him. Knowing the disposition of all the atoms of the universe at the start and knowing the laws, he should already know exactly what would happen till the end of time. Laplace himself evoked the image of such a super-intelligence: 'Nothing for it would be uncertain, and the future as well as the past would be present to its eyes.'[1]

Even if God were somehow to have got it wrong and were to disapprove of how things were in fact progressing, he would presumably be too high and mighty to become involved. He would never, for example, suspend the Laws of Nature, or arrange for super-natural miracles to happen. To do so would not only be an admission of error at the time of the original creation, it would – if one dare say it – be rather vulgar.

Whatever all this meant for ordinary people, the prospects for the scientific project were bright. If once natural philosophers could discern the basic Laws by observation and experiment – a project on which Newton and others had made such an excellent beginning – they should find in them a sufficient explanation for everything that is or might be. Not only should there be no need to postulate an interventionist deity, there should be no need to introduce any other messy hypotheses to 'save the appearances' for science. No need for a life-force, or *élan vital*, to explain the difference between dead and living matter; no need for a human soul to explain the difference between consciousness and unconsciousness; no need, still less, for magical powers of action or perception at a distance to explain the so-called miracles that superstitious people still made claims for.

The behaviour of the whole – even the very special wholes that constitute our own bodies and minds – would be bound to be the sum of the behaviour of the parts. Hence nothing would or could happen to us or by us that exceeds the powers we possess by virtue of our material constitution. As Julien de La Mettrie had written in *L'Homme-machine*: 'The soul is, then, an empty symbol . . . Given the least principle of movement, animate bodies will possess all they need in order to move, sense, think, repeat, and behave, in a word, all they want of the physical; and of the mental, too, which depends thereon.'[2]

Two hundred years later this ambitious programme for a self-sufficient science has succeeded beyond the dreams of its inventors. Across great swathes of nature 'what was to be proved' has become 'what has been proved', 'explananda' have become 'explanata'. The major puzzles of existence have been pulled to pieces in the hands – or some would call it the maw – of all-conquering and -consuming scientific rationality. Indeed, the basic laws that govern everything have turned out to be fewer in number and, to those who understand them, simpler and more beautiful than anyone originally guessed. So successful has it been that many scientists would now say, and even fear, that there will soon be little left for them to do.

Yet equally, two hundred years later, the majority of ordinary people have remained as faithful as ever to the earlier ways of thinking. In the United States (the country to which those scholars of the Enlightenment looked before all for the revolution in ideology that would mark the escape from religious superstition) census data for the 1980s show that 95 per cent of the population still believe in an active God, 88 per cent in a human soul, and 71 per cent in the survival of the soul after bodily death. In Europe, 75 per cent believe in God, 61 per cent in a soul, and 43 per cent in survival after death.[3]

If these beliefs in God and the soul were merely tokens of a shallow faith in 'something over and beyond', such levels of credulity might not be so remarkable. However, other surveys show that this theism and soulism is paralleled in modern societies by the continuance of many more particular beliefs in what we may loosely call a 'counter-scientific reality': that is to say, beliefs in specific supernatural entities and powers for which science has discovered no empirical basis and whose existence would in many cases flatly contradict scientific theory.

It is found, for example, that in the developed world, between a third and two-thirds of the population still attest to the reality of such phenomena as telepathy, precognition, interaction with spirits of the dead, reincarnation and the paranormal effects of prayer.[4]

Typical of recent findings are those from a study of a representative cross-section of people in the town of Reading, England, which was commissioned for a television programme I made in 1987.[5]

Respondents were asked 'Do you think it true?' of a series of statements relating to paranormal phenomena. Excluding the small number of 'don't knows', the proportions of people who said definitely 'Yes' were as follows.

'It is possible to know what someone else is thinking or feeling even if they are out of touch by ordinary means' – 63 per cent. 'Dreams can foretell the future' – 71 per cent. 'Prayers will sometimes be answered' – 71 per cent. 'It is possible to make someone turn around just by looking at them' – 66 per cent. 'Some people can remember past lives that they have lived in other bodies' – 54 per cent. 'It is possible to get messages from the dead' – 37 per cent. 'Some houses are haunted by ghosts' – 69 per cent.

Despite the generally high level of belief, it could perhaps still have been the case that there was a substantial minority who were either unsure or did not believe in any of it. Not so: 88 per cent of the population said definitely 'Yes' to at least one of the statements, and 68 per cent said definitely 'Yes' to at least three of them. Further analysis of the background of those who were believers, comparing them with those (relatively few) who were not, showed that they did not differ either in social class or in educational attainment: a middle-class university graduate was as likely to be a believer as a shop-assistant who left school at fourteen. The only significant demographic variable found in this study (as in most others) was sex: 79 per cent of women said 'Yes' to three or more of the statements as against 57 per cent of men.

A survey in the USA did find that 'élite scientists and physicians', listed in *Who's Who*, generally have a much lower level of belief in paranormal phenomena.[6] But we should note that even among scientists, several have broken ranks and declared their fascination, and in several cases their open enthusiasm.

Who was it, for example, but Sigmund Freud who, while proclaiming himself 'not completely convinced, yet ready to be convinced', devoted a full chapter of his *New Introductory Lectures on Psychoanalysis* to a discussion of telepathy? He defined telepathy as 'a kind of psychic parallel to wireless telegraphy' and wrote that 'it may be the original archaic method by which individuals understood one another'.[7]

Who was it but the Nobel-prize winning physicist, Brian Josephson, who, along with three distinguished colleagues, professed in a letter to the *New York Review of Books* his unabashed belief in: (a) psychic metal-bending (to wit, 'the children produced large bending and stretching signals in metal objects equipped with strain gauges, without being in contact with the objects'), (b) psychokinetic effects on a random number generator ('two subjects ... could, by an effort of the will, cause the output of the generator to be non-random') and (c) clairvoyance ('several subjects were able to acquire significant amounts of information about ... targets blocked from ordinary perception by distance or shielding')?[8]

And who, at the somewhat zanier end, was it but a professor of psychiatry at Harvard University, John Mack, who wrote in a foreword to a new book on UFO abductions: '[It is] clear we are dealing with a phenomenon that has a hard edge, a huge, strange interspecies breeding program that has invaded our physical reality and is affecting the lives of hundreds of thousands of people and perhaps in some way the consciousness of the entire planet'?[9]

Yet, it does not take the endorsements of professors to make such paranormal ideas respectable and interesting. For it must be obvious that their real significance is at the grass-roots level, where they remain deeply embedded in our individual and our group psychology.

The celebration of the paranormal has long been woven into the fabric of Western culture.

Even if we put aside specifically Christian themes, we find paranormal happenings forming the leitmotif of much of our artistic heritage: in music, from Mozart's *Magic Flute* to Wagner's *Ring*; in painting, from Rembrandt's *Belshazzar's Feast* to Gauguin's *Nevermore*; in poetry, from Homer's *Odyssey* to Shakespeare's *Tempest*; in novels, from Bram Stoker's *Dracula* to Toni Morrison's *Beloved*; in film, from Lang's *Metropolis* to Spielberg's *E T*.

Our most impressive buildings, from Stonehenge to Chartres

Cathedral to Disney World, are monuments to paranormal ambitions and paranormal imagery. The memory of paranormal miracles – pagan as well as Christian – is the excuse for most of our public holidays: Christmas, Easter, Passover, Halloween. In bookshops the 'New Age' and 'Occult' sections – with titles such as 'The Unknown', 'The Unexplained', 'Beyond All Reason' – dominate the shelves. Stories about UFOs, hauntings, poltergeists, etc., are the stock-in-trade of popular journalism and television documentaries. And when it comes to children's literature, there is scarcely a straight story in the list. Spells, vanishings, levitations, clairvoyance are 'normal' in the worlds of Wonderland and Narnia.

Tour guides run regular trips round Haunted London. Elvis Presley's return is still eagerly awaited by a million fans. A Cambridge college establishes a Fellowship 'to investigate the existence of supernormal powers of cognition or action in human beings in their present life, or the persistence of the human mind after bodily death'.[10] Crowds gather beneath an Irish concrete statue of the Virgin Mary to see it rock its head. The police employ a psychic detective to catch a rapist. George Bush prays to God for success in the Gulf War. Saddam Hussein prays to God for success in the Gulf War. The British road authorities ban the number 666 from licence plates. NASA finances a costly research programme to explore the possibility of controlling spaceships by distant mind-power. A major mining company employs Uri Geller to dowse over a map of Malaysia for copper deposits. The Prince of Wales attempts to contact his uncle through table turning. The Princess of Wales consults a specialist in pyramid power. Etcetera, etcetera.

No doubt there are those among us who regard some of these practices as misguided or eccentric. Yet it is fair to say that most people see them as relatively normal human conduct. Nothing to write home about.

Could it be that the majority of people have simply not heard what science has done?

There are certainly some who not only prefer to remain

ignorant themselves, but do their best to keep everyone else in the same condition too. When, in the 1880s, the Bishop of Birmingham's wife received information that Charles Darwin was claiming that human beings were descended from monkeys, she is reported to have said to her husband, 'My dear, let us hope it is not true; but, if it is true, let us hope it will not become generally known.' The fact is, however, that you can run from science but you can't hide. Alas for the good lady, man's ancestry did become generally known. And it is of course almost inevitable that, in our truth-will-out, information-hungry culture, interesting ideas – be they welcome or not – soon enough become everybody's property. Each new success is trumpeted from the presses, analysed on television. Stewart Brand, founder of *The Whole Earth Catalog*, has even claimed that 'Science is now the only news. When you scan through a newspaper or magazine, all the human interest stuff is the same old he-said-she-said, the politics and economics, the same sorry cyclic dramas . . . Human nature doesn't change much; science does.'[11]

No, they have heard. Few adults in the modern world can actually be unaware that there are now physicalist explanations for most if not all natural phenomena, not excluding the workings of the human mind. And yet many people – including some of those who are themselves the messengers – continue to ignore the message. Indeed, it sometimes seems that the more that people hear, the less they want to know. In contemporary Russia, for example, with a population that under Communism must have been better educated in science than any other in the world, alternative beliefs – ranging from Christian fundamentalism to black magic – are flourishing to an extent that even the USA can hardly match.[12]

The reason is transparent. Scientific materialism is regarded by many, even by some of its own prophets, as deeply unsatisfying: scary, bewildering, insulting, demeaning, dispiriting, confining. John Keats, in 1819, reacting to the march of so-called natural philosophy, voiced the common horror: 'Do not all charms fly / At the mere touch of cold philosophy?'

7

Philosophy will clip an Angel's wings.
Conquer all mysteries by rule and line,
Empty the haunted air, and gnomèd mine –
Unweave a rainbow ... [13]

Perhaps, these days, poets might use a more contemporary metaphor. Science, with its chain-saws and bulldozers of reason, has felled the tropical rain forests of spirituality. It has wreaked ecological destruction on fairyland. It has extinguished the leprechauns, the elves and goblins. It has caused a global change in the weather of imagination. It has made a dustbowl of our Eden, and created an inner drought. And all this, not to bring greater peace or happiness, but to satisfy people's hunger for the Big Macs of technology.

Vaclav Havel, the Czech president, has written: 'Modern thought – based on the premise that the world is objectively knowable, and that the knowledge so obtained can be absolutely generalised – has come to a final crisis. This era has created the first technical civilisation, but it has reached the point beyond which the abyss begins.' He recommends instead the cultivation of 'soul, individual spirituality, and above all, trust in one's own subjectivity as one's principal link with the world.'[14] Only a cynic, surely, would point out that there have been others, less admirable than Havel, who have anticipated this call for a return to earlier values. Adolf Hitler, for example: 'We stand at the end of the Age of Reason. A new era of the magical explanation of the world is rising.'[15] The fighters for a cause cannot always choose their comrades on the barricades.

Laplace, maybe, did not need 'that hypothesis' (although even with him we cannot be sure he really meant it). But there can be no disputing that others, with a broader register of anxieties and questions, still need it desperately.

This book takes these anxieties and questions as its beginning point. In the first part I trace the history of how people have attempted to allay them: with the help of revealed supernatural systems such as are offered by religions, by naïvely optimistic scientific study of the natural world, or eventually by attempting to create a science of supernature. In the second part I discuss the search – which has become increasingly frantic as people's faith in these supernatural systems has grown weaker – for a variety of miraculous phenomena to set in opposition to materialist philosophy. And in the last part I undertake a critique of modern parapsychology and its claims to have proved the reality of paranormal psychic powers.

I shall not be attempting to represent every position on these issues, let alone to balance them. I shall be trying instead to develop my own line. This line will be closely argued and scientifically supported where appropriate, but I shall not stick entirely to matters that are academically respectable. The book will sometimes move casually between the sublime and the ridiculous, because so do the human beings whom it concerns. It may seem, particularly in the early chapters, that I make freer use of literary quotation than is called for. The purpose will be to allow these human beings – especially the more articulate and poetic ones – to have their say about matters that are *theirs*.

2

Who Needs It?

'Tell us, doctors of philosophy, what are the needs of a man?' John Dos Passos asked in his novel *The Big Money*. 'At least a man needs to be notjailed notafraid nothungry notcold not without love, not a worker for a power he has never seen that cares nothing for the uses and needs of a man or a woman or a child.'[16] The truth is, however, that men and women have more positive spiritual needs also, and all great supernatural belief systems – indeed, all philosophical systems, up till now – have catered to two central ones: the need for a rational understanding of the surrounding world, and the need for emotional security within it.

'D'où venons nous? Que sommes nous? Où allons nous?' The famous questions were scrawled in the corner of Paul Gauguin's 'final' painting. 'Where have we come from? What are we? Where are we going?' People want *explanations* in answer to the first two questions; they want *reassurance* in answer to the third. That is, they want – from doctors of philosophy or doctors of divinity or witch-doctors or Dr Watson – a reading of life's symptoms that makes sense.

There has to be a reasonable diagnosis of what presently exists – an explanation, especially where obvious natural explanations are lacking, of the pains and aches, flushes, stars in the eyes, strawberry rashes of the present world. There has to be an acceptable prognosis of what lies ahead – an assurance, especially where natural assurances are lacking, that life is worth living.

Why *has to be*? Because otherwise, to put it bluntly, we might as well be dead. Albert Camus thought so. 'There is but one truly serious philosophical problem and that is suicide. Judging whether life is or is not worth living amounts to answering the fundamental question of philosophy.'[17] And if we answer the question negatively – if, on the basis of the diagnosis, the prognosis looks too bad – the remedy is obvious. Gauguin thought so. Having finished his painting, 'a philosophical work on a theme comparable to the Gospel' as he called it, he swallowed a bottle of arsenic. Although, to his own chagrin, he survived – and went on painting – he made his point.

Human beings cannot stop the world. But they can always make a personal decision to get off. 'How thin the line between the will to live and the will to die,' Susan Sontag suggested. 'How about a hole . . . a really deep hole, which you put in a public place, for general use. In Manhattan, say, at the corner of Seventieth and Fifth . . . A sign beside the hole reads: 4 PM–8PM / MON WED & FRI / SUICIDE PERMITTED. Just that. A sign. Why, surely people would jump who had hardly thought of it before.'[18]

'But one must live somehow,' it was said. 'Je n'en vois pas la nécessité,' came the reply ('I don't see the necessity for that').[19] It is by no means obvious that staying alive is worth the effort. Most people have probably imagined ending it. Indeed, in the USA recent studies show that about 60 per cent of teenagers report that they have considered suicide at some time, 26 per cent within the last year.[20]

Blaise Pascal, in a celebrated passage from his *Pensées*, expressed the common feeling of existential isolation. 'When I consider the brief span of my life, absorbed into the eternity before and after, the small space I occupy and which I see swallowed up in the infinite immensity of spaces of which I know nothing and which know nothing of me, I take fright and am amazed to see myself here rather than there: there is no reason for me to be here rather than there, now rather than then. Who put me here? By whose command and act were this time and place allotted to me? . . . The eternal silence of these infinite spaces terrifies me.'[21]

People are bound to dream of a less threatening, less lonely and more obviously ordered world. It may be a world that in their innocence they once believed was theirs already. For it is likely that in everybody's life there was once a time when it seemed there would always be someone ready to take care of them . . . to lighten the darkness, to fence off the beckoning hole. 'So runs my dream,' said Tennyson:

> So runs my dream: but what am I?
> An infant crying in the night:
> An infant crying for the light:
> And with no language but a cry.[22]

Pascal's own sad reflection on his plight is itself recognisable at another level as the anxious cry of a small child. When Daniel Stern, the psychologist, described in his *Diary of a Baby* how it must feel to be a left-alone infant whose mother eventually rescues him and puts him to her breast, he echoed Pascal's words: 'At once the world is enveloped. It becomes smaller and slower and more gentle. The envelope pushes away the vast empty spaces.'[23]

I simplify, perhaps; but not, I think, misleadingly, and certainly with no intention to disparage. There is no shame in people having childlike needs nor in their seeking familiar childish ways of satisfying them. That is the kind of people that we humans are. Fine pieces of work, for sure. The paragon of animals, maybe. Noble in reason, and so on. But never other than pieces of work that were born between the two legs of a woman, helpless creatures, dreadfully needy; pieces of work that scarcely in their lives achieve more than token independence of their own and other people's fragile bodies; pieces that, even if they sing about it, too often reflect that 'nobody loves me, everybody hates me, think I'll go and eat worms'.

No wonder that, in these scary circumstances, people hark back to a time when things were better: to that time in each of their lives when most did indeed have *parents* to look after them – caring adults who would, at any rate in fantasy, act as founts of both wisdom and compassion. Was explanation needed? Hopefully, those parents would act as consultants and teachers, trusted providers of answers to the Whences, Whats and Whys. Was assurance sought? Those same parents would be their protectors and guides, guarantors of a safe passage to the Whither.

No surprise, therefore, that if people have once experienced – or even imagined – this comprehensive solution to their needs, they seek again in later life a *singular* philosophy to live by; or that the appeal of the world's great religions has always been, at least in part, that they minister to the desire for an idealised parent figure who is *all in one*.

God, in the Christian tradition for example, is both Wisdom and Love. To know him is to have the world both explained and made secure for us. The Christian God is both the God of the means and the God of the ends. And the same holds for successful rivals to religion, such as Marxism. The Hegelian Idea of Progress, or the Goddess of History for Marxists, is both our instructor and our nurse. We sit in her lap, we play at her feet. She has made us what we are, she is taking us on to a Utopian future.

Correspondingly the sacred texts – the Bible, the epics of Gilgamesh and Enkidu, the Upanishads, *Das Kapital*, even *Mein Kampf* – all run from a Beginning to a Middle to an End. Where from? From Genesis. What now? Now Acts. Where to? If we are good children, on to the Book of Revelation.

So, yes, honk if you love Jesus. Honk if you love the Maharishi, Moses, Marx, Mary or Muhammad. Tell them you need that womb-like envelope your parents once provided.

Carl Jung wrote: 'Among all my patients in the second half of life – that is to say over thirty-five – there has not been one whose problem in the last resort was not that of finding a religious outlook on life.'[24] And equally, an ex-nun, Karen Armstrong, speaking for those in the first half, said: 'At adolescence, when you are so bogged down in misery about your own confusions, the idea of losing yourself in God and finding an enhanced self seems enormously attractive.'[25]

In a recent survey conducted by the European Values Study Group, it was found that, of those Europeans who believed in God (70 per cent of the total), a full half (35 per cent of the total) agreed with the statement that 'Life is meaningful *only* because God exists.'[26] Simply interpreted, this would suggest that as many as one in three would find life 'meaningless' if they were to be robbed of their belief. And this general picture of the saving effect of supernatural belief has time and again been both confirmed and illuminated by the testimony of writers, poets and philosophers.

Elizabeth Barrett, for example, in the year of her marriage, 1846, spelt out in a letter to her future husband, Robert Browning, what would be the consequences of *loss* of faith: 'Miss Bayley told me that she was a materialist of the strictest order, & believed in no soul & no future state. In the face of these conclusions, she said, she was calm & resigned . . . What resistless melancholy would fall upon me if I had such thoughts! – & what a dreadful indifference. All grief, to have itself to end in! – all joy, to be based upon nothingness! – all love, to feel eternal separation under & over it! Dreary & ghastly, it would be! I should not have the strength to love you, I think, if I had such a miserable creed.'[27]

Søren Kierkegaard, the brave philosopher of individualism, secretly cried out in his Journal: 'If man had no eternal conscious-ness, if, at the bottom of everything, there were merely a wild, seething force producing everything, both large and trifling, in the storm of dark passions, if the bottomless void that nothing can fill underlay all things, what would life be but despair?'[28]

And Robert Burns, otherwise the merriest of poets, wrote in a letter to a friend: 'There are two great pillars that bear us up, amid the wreck of misfortune and misery. The ONE is composed of the different modifications of a certain noble, stubborn something in man, known by the names of courage, fortitude, magnanimity. The OTHER is made up of those feelings and sentiments . . . which connect us with and link us to, those awful obscure realities – an all-powerful and equally beneficent God; and a world to come, beyond death and the grave. The first gives the nerve of combat, while a ray of hope beams on the field: – the last pours the balm of comfort into the wounds which time can never cure.'[29]

Surveys show that in general the degree of belief in supernatural forces is highest amongst the most vulnerable members of society – the poor, the sick, the socially marginalised. Predictably it comes to the fore at times of personal stress, as, for example, in athletes before a competition, students before examinations, women during pregnancy, people who are recently divorced or bereaved, soldiers on the battlefield, and whole nations in times of political and economic chaos such as 1930s Germany and present-day Russia.[30]

Several recent studies have specifically compared the mental health of religious believers with that of non-believers, and found that, as might be expected, the former show many fewer symptoms of psychological disturbance. John Schumaker, who has reviewed the evidence, cites two studies in particular.[31] In his own study of a group of undergraduates at an American university, he found that irreligious individuals had 45 per cent more symptoms of mental disturbance than their religious counterparts. In a study, by Handal and others, of a group of black women from Missouri, they found that irreligious individuals had 63 per cent more symptoms. Although such correlational data may have to be interpreted with caution, they all point to the remarkable effectiveness of supernatural belief systems in combating feelings of worthlessness, lifting depression and calming fears.

Evidently the packages of nurturance and explanation that religions and quasi-religions offer can provide remarkably effective medicine for orphaned minds. Jung again: '[They] give a human being that sense of wholeness, which he had as a child, but loses when he leaves his parents.'[32]

These packages may in fact be even more effective than the child's real parents. For in some ways they seem to work as what ethologists would call 'super-stimuli', whose power exceeds that of the natural example of a parent that most people have once known. In the laboratory it is quite possible to construct 'super-parents' for young birds, simply by exaggerating the most attractive features of the natural parent – a red beak, say, and clucking sounds – and then combining them in an artificial model. When it is done right, the young bird will direct all its filial responses to this model.

Arguably, the effect if not the explicit intention of the founders and promoters of religious systems has been to play a very similar trick on human beings. And their special art has been to discover or invent a way of looking at the world that, like the ideal parent, delivers on *both* fronts at the same time: combining a reasonable explanation of the present with a comforting picture of the future.

There is, however, more to it than this. It would be impressive enough if all that these systems were able to offer their believers were a package in which assurance comes along with explanation. In fact what they offer is something still more attractive and seemingly reliable: namely, a package in which assurance *follows on* from explanation as a predictable consequence. The real world (so their story goes) is such that, once we have arrived at the correct understanding of 'what we are', we shall no longer have to worry about 'where we are going' because we shall be able to see that what is true now pretty much guarantees that what is coming later will be all right.

It is as if these systems are offering something that the ethologist could never offer with his artificial model: a super-parent that not merely has a red beak and clucks, but clucks *by virtue of* having a red beak.

3
Preparing for the Best

The art of religions and quasi-religions, I wrote in the previous chapter, has been to offer a way of looking at the world in which explanation and assurance are part of a single integrated package. Yet the claim made by believers is, of course, that this is not a matter of 'art' but of truth. No doubt it will take some specialist skill, they say, to reveal exactly what the world is presently like and to provide the one and only proper explanation – but, once this has been done, there will be no question about what follows (or might follow) as a consequence.

This claim, it can be said, is usually a fair one. Most religious systems actually are, in this respect, quite rational (or at least genuinely try to be). They fall back on an argument, which in essence goes like this. If, in order to explain the present state of things, P, we have to posit an explanatory principle, E, and if the truth of E is sufficient to ensure that we are moving towards an agreeable future, F, then the fact of P entails the fact of F. So we can confidently say that the very fact that we are living in *this* present means we can look forward to *that* future.

This, at any rate, is the most straightforward and strong version. In other weaker, if more plausible, variants assurance would not follow inevitably from explanation but at least would be made possible by it. If, in order to explain the present, P, we have to posit an explanatory principle, E, and if the truth of E is necessary but not in itself sufficient to ensure an agreeable future, F, then P at least permits F even if it does not guarantee it. In this case, we can still confidently say that the very fact that we are living in this present means we have a hope of going forward to that future.

The strong version is presumably what the best of all possible belief systems should deliver. But in reality it is the weaker version that is more commonly on offer – and that in practice seems to have the greater intuitive appeal. As we shall see, the belief systems that most people seem prepared to settle for typically work in such a way as to give believers reasonable grounds for hope rather than absolute certainty of winning through. Or – since this is often the more salient issue – they work so as to give them reasonable grounds for not despairing, rather than absolute certainty of avoiding disaster.

This applies even with a highly elaborated religion such as Christianity. But it is especially true of the more open-ended systems of belief which I shall be discussing later in the book. I shall be arguing, in particular, that the idea that human beings possess psychic powers is as attractive as it is because many people reckon that the existence of such powers is a necessary precondition for there being any worthwhile future for mankind, even if not a guarantee of it. The minimum that people are inclined to ask for is assurance that 'where we are going' will not necessarily be so bad as we might fear, because 'what we are' is not so deficient as we might think.

I shall come back to this later. But my point for now is that, whether in the strong or weak version, the attraction of supernatural belief systems lies in the reasonableness with which things fit together. They must – and typically do – offer a package in which the theses relating to explanation and assurance are logically connected: connected as premise to conclusion, as diagnosis to prognosis.

This is undoubtedly one of the reasons why religions often have such strength and staying power. Why do arches stand, while single columns fall? Because their parts mutually support each other. Why do skulls survive on the plains of Africa while long bones disappear? Because there is no way for predators to get a hold of them, their teeth slip off.

It is one thing, however, to grant that explanation and assurance really do hang together in these systems, but another to grant that they hang together in the order that they are standardly supposed to do.

The way it is generally told is, of course, that explanation comes first, with assurance being derived from it. You start with past and present facts and then work your way towards the future. Past, present, future, in that order. This is the way the argument is presented in the sacred books. It is probably the order in which people read the books, and it may even be the order in which they were written. We can be sure however that seldom is this the way in which the argument has come to mind originally. Instead, when thinking in religious ways, people almost always start with the future and then work their way backwards to the present and the past. They begin at the end, and go on till they have come to a suitable beginning.

The reason they do so is that they always have an asymmetry of interest. It may well be the case that they want *both* assurance *and* explanation, to know *both* where they are going *and* where they have come from and what they are. But it is never the case that they are concerned equally with both halves of the package. Nor would it make any human sense for them to be so. As Kierkegaard noted, '[although] life must be understood backwards . . . it must be lived forwards'.[33] As Marx noted too, while philosophers interpret the world, the point is to change it. Nobody (much) is or should be interested in explanation of present facts *per se*; but everybody is and should be interested in what this explanation bodes for them. The future takes precedence in people's fantasies. And because the future comes first it inevitably drives the argument.

Pascal in his gloomy way remarked: 'We are so unwise that we wander about in times that do not belong to us, and do not think of the only one that does [i.e. the present moment].'[34] But in real life this is the opposite of being unwise. For it is precisely the time that does not yet belong to us that excites our anxiety and hope. Hence we set up goals and try to change the facts to meet them. We decide what we want (or perhaps what we do not want), work out what would be required to deliver it (or stop its being delivered), and then attempt to find it (or prevent it). When we are hungry, for instance, and want to obtain food, we do whatever we can now do to procure it. When we are in love and want to bring about a consummation, we say whatever seems suitable now to bring it about . . . And so on. This kind of constructive thinking is what our brains are best at. The whole panoply of human intelligence is concerned with, and has evolved for, laying such plans.

We change things in the realm of action by manipulating present facts to deliver the actual future that we hope for. So, then, why not try to do it in the realm of thought? Why not manipulate our *theory* of present facts to deliver the *theoretical* future that we hope for? If beginning with the end seems out of order, the order can always be reversed in the telling of it.

It is, I suppose, obvious why not, or at least why we should be very careful about it: namely, that when and if we do this we are in danger of losing touch with reality and becoming cocooned within a circle of self-delusion. Still, cocoons are relatively comfortable places (so would-be butterflies have been heard to say). And, whatever the risks of circularity, there is no denying that this way of construing the present in order to construct the future may be an effective psychological technique.

Plato, long ago, remarked on how well it can be made to work at the level of social propaganda. In the *Republic* Socrates discussed the role of what he called 'convenient myths' (sometimes translated as 'noble lies') that might, he thought, be introduced by a benevolent despot to make people generally more accepting of their fate. Let us tell the citizens, he suggested, an origin myth that will help them make sense of what is to become of them (and why some have a more promising future than others): to wit, that future rulers are made from gold, soldiers from silver and everyone else from iron – so that everyone, once their own case has been explained to them, will have no doubts about where they best belong. 'Do you think there is any way of making people believe it?' Socrates asked. Well maybe 'not in the first generation but you might succeed with the second and later generations'.[35]

It may work even better at the level of the individual. In today's world analytic psychotherapy provides perhaps one of the clearest examples of how effective this kind of explanatory myth can be. The therapeutic strategy is for doctor and patient to conspire to bring the patient to a future state of health by uncovering the memories of past events and appropriate explanations to go with them. Is there any way of making the patient believe it? Not in the first session, but in later sessions it not infrequently succeeds.

The point is that religions and quasi-religions all too often and obviously adopt just this kind of reconstructive strategy, shamelessly writing facts and explanations into history so as to deliver the prognosis that their clients want. In the case of the Christian Bible, for example, we know that the text was in fact revised continually so as to bring the earlier chapters into line with changing idealisations of the future. In the USSR the joke used to be that the works of Lenin were still being written many years after his death. Yet, so effective can it be, that all that people see now is the beauty of the final construction. In fact it may succeed to such a degree that, just as with stories told in therapy, the mythical history may easily become established as the false memory of real events.[36]

There is indeed truth in these systems as well as art – the truth of a self-validating argument. The earnest young evangelists who knock on our doors with the promise that, if we will only give them a few minutes, they will demonstrate by the Book that the events described therein *prove* that God loves us are by no means totally deluded. The premises, once accepted, do lead to the conclusion – as so they should, since that is what they were designed to do.

But there is art as well as truth – the art of begging the question. It is the art of a sculptor who sees the finished figure in the block of marble before he sets to work, the art of a Hollywood screenwriter whose first scene lays the ground for the happy ending . . . the art of putting the cart before the horse.

Suppose, however, we were to *leave out* the art. Suppose, in the naïve belief that the way the story is presented is literally the way it should be done, we were to try to write the Book of Nature genuinely forward. Suppose, in a spirit of pure research, we were innocently to start scratching at the block of marble to see what is 'really' there inside. Well, then we would be engaged in a radically different enterprise. We would be taking the approach that was at first called 'natural philosophy' and, later, 'science'.

Science does not, it should be said, dispense with *a priori* notions altogether. No scientist would know how to do this even if he aspired to it, and in any case there would be little point. As Charles Darwin remarked, 'all observation must be for or against some view if it is to be of any service ... About thirty years ago there was much talk that geologists ought only to observe and not to theorize; and I well remember someone saying that at this rate a man might as well go into a gravel-pit and count the pebbles and describe the colours.'[37]

'Reason', Immanuel Kant declared, 'must approach nature in order to be taught by it. It must not, however, do so in the character of a pupil who listens to everything that the teacher chooses to say, but of an appointed judge who compels the witnesses to answer questions which he has himself formulated.'[38]

But compelling a witness to answer a pre-formulated question is not the same thing as compelling a particular answer. When the Bishop asked his page, 'Who is it that sees and hears all we do, and before whom even I am but as a crushed worm?' he did not expect to be told 'Your wife, my Lord.'[39] When Little Red Ridinghood asked the creature in her bed, 'Why do you have such big teeth, Grandmother?' she was not looking forward to the answer she actually received.

When we do science we are, for sure, going to get *an* explanation of the present, and from this explanation we are certain to get *a* future. But we are living dangerously. The explanation may not be what we were anticipating, and the future that follows from it may no longer be the one for which we hope.

4

A Ministry of Science

For Isaac Newton, 'We must believe there is one God or supreme Monarch . . . We must believe that he is the father of whom are all things, & that he loves his people as his children that they may mutually love him & obey him as their father. We must believe that he is the παντοχρατωρ [pantocrator] Lord of all things with an irresistible & boundless power . . . & that we may expect great rewards if we do his will.'[40]

We *must* believe it? For years people had believed it largely on biblical authority. But by the seventeenth century in Europe the founders of the new science were becoming so bold as to argue that, by directly cross-questioning nature as to what the present facts are, they would find out even more about God's ways and his master plan. These first scientists, devout believers to a man, did not think they were doing anything dangerously radical, let alone subversive. They took it for granted that the world is God's creation and that, if put to the test, it could only provide further living proof of his wisdom and munificence.

Francis Bacon expressed the general faith in 1612: 'I had rather believe all the fables in the Legend, and the Talmud, and the Alcoran than that this universal frame is without a Mind . . . It is true that a little [natural] philosophy inclineth man's mind to atheism; but depth in philosophy bringeth men's minds about to religion: for while the mind of man looketh upon second causes scattered, it may sometimes rest in them, and go no further; but when it beholdeth the chain of them, confederate and linked together, it must needs fly to Providence and Deity.'[41]

A little science, as Bacon recognised, might be a dangerous thing. But deep science could only lead men further on the path of right and righteousness. Science itself could be a form of worship.

Its purpose would always be to tell more of the sacred story, never to undermine it.

Several of the Renaissance scholars actually combined study of natural phenomena with study of biblical texts, as if they were indeed parts of the same enterprise. John Napier, the sixteenth-century mathematician who invented logarithms, held that his most important work was the book *A Plaine Discovery of the Whole Revelation of Saint John*. Newton himself devoted as much energy to the study of the prophetic books of the Bible as to optics and mechanics. In the words of one of his early biographers, 'he had been a searcher of the Scriptures from his youth, and he found it no abrupt transition to pass from the study of the material universe to an investigation of the profoundest truths and the most obscure predictions of Holy writ'[42] – or vice versa.

Nonetheless, even if there were still seams to be tapped in the Scriptures, it was in the Book of Nature, as yet largely uncut, that the first scientists hoped to find still richer ore. And so they delved deeper, and deeper.

They should perhaps have known. It was curiosity not care that killed the cat. Some mysteries are better left alone. However wonderful a child may think his parents are for giving him his life, it is probably not wise for him to creep into the bedroom to try and get a closer view of the creative act.

The Bible itself, in the story of the Fall, contains an early warning against wanting to learn more than is good for you. Many other cautionary tales tell of what happens to people who show too much zeal for knowledge. Pandora was told not to open the box that Zeus had given her, but she did – and out flew a swarm of evil sprites, all the bodily and mental ills that have ever since tormented the human race. Oedipus was warned by Tiresias against inquiring too deeply into his origins, but he did – and we know what a shocking discovery awaited him.

Still, the enthusiasm of the scientists drove them on. The quest for discovery was an appetite not to be resisted. As with Bertrand Russell, three centuries later, 'With ... passion I have sought knowledge. I have wished to understand the hearts of men. I have wished to know why the stars shine.'[43] As with Ivan Pavlov, 'Remember, science requires your whole life. Even if you had two lives to give it would still not be enough. Science demands of man effort and supreme passion.'[44] Newton's laboratory assistant, who saw his master working in a frenzy, said of him, 'What his aim might be, I was not able to penetrate into, but his pains, his diligence at these times, made me think he aimed at something beyond the reach of human art and industry.'[45]

William Derham, Newton's contemporary and Fellow of the Royal Society, argued that it would be blasphemous *not* to make science one's first priority. God, like any other artist, demanded an audience for his works, and would be upset if people took them too much for granted. There was no reason to worry: 'For the more we pry into, and discover of [God's works], the greater and more glorious we find them to be, the more worthy of, and the more expressly to proclaim their great *Creator*. Commendable then are the Researches, which many amongst us have, of late Years, made into the Works of Nature. And therefore when we are asked, *Cui Bono*? To what Purpose such Enquiries, such Pains, such Expense? The Answer is easy . . . It is to follow and trace him, when and whither he leads us, that we may see and admire his Handywork our selves, and set it forth to others.'[46]

Pain and expense were unavoidable. There were indeed already martyrs in the cause. Archimedes had famously died at the hand of a Roman soldier, while contemplating a mathematical diagram in the sand. Galileo only just escaped with his life. Bacon himself met his end as the result of catching cold when stuffing a hen with snow in order to observe the effect of freezing on the preservation of flesh (the first – but by no means the last – experimental scientist to die in active service).

Whatever the personal cost, however, it would not have occurred to any of these pioneers that their discoveries could possibly bring spiritual or even material costs to mankind as whole. No one, yet, could have imagined the time coming when, like Einstein, they might have to say, 'If I had known, I would have been a watchmaker.'[47]

*

In principle their programme *could* have worked. The problem was not that scientific inquiry was (or is) bound to fail to bring assurance. It was just that, unlike religious inquiry, it was not (and is not) bound to succeed.

Thus, to skip on to a later phase, the scientific study of human thought and action, undertaken by psychologists, *could* have shown that it is necessary to postulate that human beings have an immaterial soul which interacts non-physically with their bodies – with all that this would imply about the possibility of an afterlife, etc. The study of natural history, undertaken by biologists, could have shown that there is no way of accounting for the obvious evidence for adaptation and design in the structures of plants and animals without postulating a divine designer – with all that this would imply about his purpose in putting us on earth, etc. Even the study of physical chemistry could have shown, as Newton himself hoped, that in order to explain certain chemical reactions it is necessary to postulate the existence of subtle spirits and assume a 'principle of sociability', indeed that 'it will first be necessary to understand the *anima*, and investigate the laws which are observed in these operations of the spirit, the powers and actions of the electrical spirit which pervade all bodies'[48] – with all that this would imply about the possibility of mystical union with nature, etc.

If proof is needed that it could have worked, we have only to turn to the claims made by a few modern scientists that it actually has worked (or at least very shortly will do). Rare as they may be, there are certain unconventional thinkers who are still prepared to argue that, in order to explain the present in strictly scientific terms, we really do need to postulate explanatory principles that, when extrapolated forwards, more or less guarantee a happy future.

The biologist Rupert Sheldrake, for example, has made a skilful case to the effect that in order to explain certain present facts such as the crystallisation of salts and the nest-building habits of birds, we are required to postulate the operation of a principle he calls 'morphic resonance', whereby patterns in nature get preserved and communicated across the aether. From the play of morphic resonance Sheldrake deduces all sorts of promising outcomes.

Combining it with the Gaia hypothesis, for example, he argues that it means that the development of the Earth as a whole is essentially purposeful – with everything tending towards an evolutionary goal (whose nature, admittedly, we human beings are not yet privileged to understand).[49]

A still stronger pitch has been made by the theoretical physicist Frank Tipler. He notes that in order to explain certain elementary properties of matter such as radioactive decay we are (as everyone would agree) required to postulate the principle of quantum indeterminacy. From quantum indeterminacy Tipler moves to the so-called 'many-worlds hypothesis' and the 'strong anthropic principle'. And on this he builds the most wonderful castle in the air, whose glories he hints at in the following passage: 'I present the Omega Point Theory, which is a model for an omnipresent, omniscient, omnipotent, evolving, personal God who is both transcendent to spacetime and immanent in it, and who exists necessarily. The model is a falsifiable physical theory deriving its key concepts not from any religious tradition but from modern physical cosmology and computer science; from scientific materialism rather than revelation ... I show that the Omega Point theory suggests a future universal resurrection of the dead very similar to the one predicted in the Judeo-Christian-Islamic tradition. The notions of "grace" and the "beatific vision" appear naturally in the model.'[50]

It could have worked. Some observers still believe it has done. But, since science is by its very nature investigative rather than prescriptive, since it lacks the internal logic of religion, it was not bound to work as people hoped. And hardly had the scientific enterprise got under way before it began to give cause, to many who watched from the sidelines, for increasing dismay.

'O Rose,' William Blake would soon be writing, 'thou art sick!'

> The invisible worm
> That flies in the night,
> In the howling storm,
>
> Has found out thy bed
> Of crimson joy:

And his dark secret love
Does thy life destroy.[51]

In the picture that accompanies his poem, the worm that has been carried in on the wind of scientific materialism is crawling into the heart of the rose, and the spirit of joy is being extruded.

In the next chapter I shall begin to look at what went wrong.

5
The Howling Storm

Think back to the formula I gave in Chapter 3. If, in order to explain the present P, we have to posit an explanatory principle E, and E either guarantees or at least permits a future F, then the very fact that we are living in this P allows us to look forward to that F.

The crucial issue over which science and religion were destined to break ranks was – and is – the question of exactly what kind of explanation we do *have to* posit in order to explain the present state of things. Rarely if ever is there only one possible way of explaining any given set of facts: it depends on how ingenious we are prepared to be.

Let us consider a simple mathematical example.[52] Given the sequence 2, 4, 6, 8, what rule would you guess is operating to generate the series? There are several theoretically possible answers. One would be the relatively simple rule: take the last number, x, and compute x + 2. But equally valid for these data would be the much more complicated rule, take the last number, x, and compute $-1/44 \, x^3 + 3/11 \, x^2 + 34/11$.

Or, let's have a more human example. Suppose a child finds a £10 note lying at the foot of her bed on Christmas morning. What explanatory story ought she to tell herself? It might occur to her that any one of the following explanations could in principle make sense: that the note was left by Father Christmas, or by her own parents, or by an absent-minded burglar who was in a hurry.

Would there be some rational way for the child to choose which one of these she 'has to' adopt? Suppose that, on the evidence available, none of these candidate explanations could either be excluded altogether or confirmed beyond a shadow of a doubt. In that case the question of 'has to be adopted' would boil down to which is 'most plausible' or 'best'.

Now, if the child were in fact arguing in what I characterised earlier as the religious mode, she might well equate 'best' with 'most promising'. Then, assuming the world would be likely to turn out to be a nicer place if the explanation lay with Father Christmas than with her parents, let alone with a burglar, she would likely prefer the former explanation to either of the latter. Suppose, however, the child is arguing in scientific mode, and that therefore she is eschewing this kind of future-driven reasoning. In that case there would be three overlapping criteria that she might use, and that are central to the scientific method:

Frugality. Work with what you have already got. Try to explain things in terms of previously established principles, rather than by introducing new ones on a purely *ad hoc* basis. If you have already established the existence of your parents and burglars, but you have no independent evidence for Father Christmas, the latter explanation – being introduced purely to explain this new phenomenon – is relatively extravagant.

Elegance. Go for the explanation which does the job most neatly. Try to explain things with a minimum of special pleading. If both Father Christmas and your own parents would be behaving entirely in character by leaving a banknote on Christmas night, but a burglar would have to be a special sort of burglar – a peculiarly absent-minded one – then the burglar explanation is relatively inelegant.

Probability. Prefer the probable to the improbable. Try to explain things in whatever way seems least unlikely. If your parents were already in the house, whereas Father Christmas would have had to get down a narrow chimney and a burglar would have had to open a locked door, both the Father Christmas and burglar explanations are relatively improbable.

From which it would follow that, all in all, the parental explanation is the solution to be favoured.

These criteria (and other related ones) can be summed up under the famous rule now generally known as Occam's Razor: 'Entia non sunt multiplicanda praeter necessitatem', or, roughly translated, 'No more things should be presumed to exist than are absolutely necessary.' This elementary rule of scientific method, named after William of Occam, a fourteenth-century Franciscan monk, was the time bomb that was destined to blow up under religion and the supernatural in general.

René Descartes, the seventeenth-century philosopher, perhaps did most to lay the fuse. Descartes was motivated by a peculiar mixture of scepticism and piety. His scepticism told him that philosophers should believe only in things that they cannot legitimately doubt without getting into contradiction. His piety told him that whatever laws of nature God had laid down must be worthy of their author, very simple and written in the language of pure mathematics.

It was on this basis that Descartes had the temerity to argue in the 1640s that the best explanation for almost *all* the phenomena of nature must be that they result merely from matter in motion, the rubbing and bumping of material particles against material particles. In short the whole universe – on every scale, from the solar system to an anthill – should be conceived of as just one huge machine, a mechanical automaton governed by ineluctable and changeless mathematical laws. Not only did Descartes consider it otiose to suppose that non-living things contain subtle spirits (the idea that Newton was still playing with years later), he considered it unnecessary to suppose that living animals did so either.

Only in the case of human beings did Descartes admit that some additional explanatory principle might indeed be required. The mental powers of human beings so far exceed anything that he could then imagine as being within the capacity of a mechanical device, that he graciously allowed that the human body must have a rational soul contingently associated with it. But 'contingent' was the operative word. No body could ever have a soul *by virtue* of its material constitution. While a person's soul might indeed interact via a channel in his brain with his material body and so move it from its course, the soul as such would not be part of the material world and would belong to an entirely different realm.

No doubt Descartes thought that by thus separating soul and body, and by arguing that animals other than humans are essentially soulless, he was not only emphasising the gap between animals and human beings but actually helping to place human beings nearer to God. In demeaning everything else he was at least enriching man. His philosophy might, therefore, make people feel relatively good about themselves. This was not, however, the way it went down with most of those who heard of it. To those who took it seriously, the message that came through most strongly was not that man's own state had been illuminated, but that the lights had gone out all over the rest of nature.

The world that most people had thought themselves to be living in – 'a world rich with colour and sound, redolent with fragrance, filled with gladness, love and beauty, speaking everywhere of purposive harmony and creative ideals' – was crowded now into minute corners in scattered human brains. And the rest was 'hard, colourless, silent and dead; a world of quantity, a world of mathematically computable motions in mechanical regularity'.[53] Keats was right: Descartes had emptied the haunted air and gnoméd mine.

It was too much for most of Descartes's contemporaries, even the scientists. The Cambridge philosopher Henry More expostulated in a letter to Descartes: 'There is nothing in your opinions that so much disgusts me, so far as I have any kindness or gentleness, as the internecine and murderous view which you bring forward . . . which snatches away life and sensibility from all the animals.'[54] And, later, in his *Immortality of the Soul*, More flatly rejected Descartes's premises: 'Mere impact of one particle on another cannot account for all the phenomena of nature, but a directing *Spirit of Nature*, the great quarter-master-general of Providence, must needs intervene.'[55]

William Derham fulminated still more vehemently. It could only be a 'Sign a Man is a wilful, perverse Atheist, that will impute so glorious a Work, as the Creation is, to any Thing, yea, a mere

Nothing (as Chance is) rather than to God.' It would be, he thought, 'a great Argument of the infinite Inconvenience of those Sins of Intemperance, Lust, and Riot, that have made the Man abandon his Reason, his Senses, yea I had almost said his very human Nature, to engage him thus to deny the Being of God.'[56]

It was too much for Newton too. Having been an initial enthusiast for Descartes's 'mechanistical philosophy', he later dissociated himself from its strongest conclusions. Indeed by 1684 he could not even bear to write Descartes's name. He could take comfort from the fact that Descartes himself was not much of an observer, and certainly never dirtied his hands with the kind of alchemical experiments that he himself engaged in. Nonetheless Newton, unlike More or Derham, was too clever not to realise that it was only by the skin of its teeth that science could escape confirming Descartes's vision or even worse. Maybe 'mere impact of one particle on another' could not, *as yet*, account for all the phenomena of nature. But it would all depend on what precisely those phenomena turned out to be.

In addition to his opinions about the role of subtle spirits in chemical reactions, Newton still believed, on the basis of current information, that divine intervention was necessary to keep the solar system stable. Almost everyone in the seventeenth century still believed that God must have been responsible for perfecting life on earth. And absolutely everyone believed, along with Descartes, that human thought and consciousness must involve non-mechanical spiritual powers. But what would science show next?

I shall not dwell in any detail on what science showed next. We know the outcome. The principle of not multiplying entities unnecessarily turned out, when rigidly applied, to be a way of decreasing them inexorably. Occam's razor turned out to be a butcher's knife. In fact it was an instrument that scientists would eventually turn on human beings themselves, as they became, in Friedrich Nietzsche's memorable phrase, 'their own vivisectional animals'.[57]

In cosmology, the supervisory deity was cancelled as unnecessary. In natural history, the evolutionary designer was cancelled as unnecessary. In psychology, the non-material mind was cancelled as unnecessary. For a long time human consciousness held out, but even this came under siege.

In every sphere, mechanism and materialism were increasingly triumphant. Franz Gall, founder of phrenology (the science of reading character from skull shape), expressed the general confidence in scientific explanation in 1825. 'The physiology of the brain is entirely founded on observation, experiments, and researches for the thousandth time repeated, on man and brute animals ... All is connected and harmonious; everything is mutually illustrated and confirmed. The explanation of the most abstruse phenomena of the moral and intellectual life of man and brutes, is no longer the sport of baseless theories; the most secret causes of the difference in the character of species, nations, sexes, and ages, from birth to decrepitude, are unfolded; ... man, finally, that inextricable being, is made known; organology composes and decomposes, piece by piece his propensities and talents; it has fixed our ideas of his destiny, and the sphere of his activity.' Following which, in the manner of a robber who leaves a thank-you note behind him, he had the gall to add: 'Surely, these are so many guarantees of the truth of the physiology of the brain – so many titles of gratitude to HIM, who has made them known to me!'[58]

Blake's howling wind was blowing all before it. And by the time it was done the landscape had completely changed. 'Man's destiny', as Arthur Koestler wrote, 'was no longer determined from "above" by a super-human wisdom and will, but from "below" by the sub-human agencies of glands, genes, atoms, or waves of probability. The shift of the locus of destiny was decisive ... A puppet of the Gods is a tragic figure, a puppet suspended on his chromosomes [or he might have said his brain bumps] is merely grotesque.'[59]

Grotesque indeed. Even so, Koestler was still taking as given that these puppets were suspended from *something* – the world still had some sort of puppet-master in control. Yet one of the most devastating discoveries of the new science was that in many instances there may be nothing in control at all. Even those things we see as being most obviously patterned and purposeful may in reality have been shaped by purely accidental processes.

From earliest times it had been a central function of religious explanation to assure people of precisely the opposite: that little if anything in the world is truly accidental. 'Chance has its reasons', as Petronius said, even if it is not vouchsafed to men to know them. In fact so strong was the conviction in both classical and medieval Europe that everything that happens must have some sort of deeper meaning, that accidental events could even be taken to the law courts to prove they were not really accidents at all but rather someone or something's criminal responsibility.[60]

A Saxon text, relating to a trial that took place at the village of Hawarden in Wales in the year 946, illustrates dramatically how folk wisdom assumed there had to be a reason behind everything.[61] It tells how there was a terrible drought in the locality and all the villagers prayed for rain, addressing their prayers to a wooden statue of the Virgin Mary in the loft of the village church. One day, with still no sign of rain, the Lady of the castle was praying long and hard when tragedy befell: the statue toppled from its loft, landed on her head and killed her. When news of this unprovoked assault on the good Lady spread, there was uproar in the village. The authorities decided to bring the statue of the Virgin to trial before a jury on a double charge: for the wilful murder of the Lady and for not answering the people's prayers. Accordingly the statue was brought to court, and after evidence had been heard on both sides, the statue was declared guilty on both counts. It was condemned to be hanged. But, in consideration of the fact that it was indeed an image of the Virgin Mary, the jury agreed that this sentence should be commuted to a lighter one. They decided therefore to place the statue on the sandbanks of the river Dee, to see what would become of it. In the event, the tide came up and 'carried the said statue to some low land near the walls of the city of Chester where', to everyone's satisfaction, 'it was found next day drowned and dead'.

How would *this* kind of reasoning (which at one level or

another still characterises many modern people's thinking) fare under the scientific regime? The questions would remain: Why should the statue have fallen at that moment, on that head? Why, to begin with, should there have been no rain, and why should the villagers' prayers have been so ineffective? Yet the new answer would be that, like as not, there is no interesting answer to be given.

In some areas – crucial areas – of human experience, explanation itself had been cancelled as unnecessary. The best explanation would now be that there is *no* explanation. As if, when the truth be known, 2, 4, 6, 8 were just a random set of numbers, or as if the £10 note had accidentally been blown in through the open window by a freak gust of wind. In a church in Maryland in May 1993, a statue of the Virgin Mary fell on a four-year-old boy and killed him – and the court's verdict in this case was indeed the meaningless one of 'accidental death'.[62]

The implications were – and are – unsettling. If, in order to explain the present, we are not required to postulate any explanation at all, *then* what about the future? Jacques Monod, author of *Chance and Necessity*, said what. 'Man must at last wake out of his millenary dream and discover his total solitude, his fundamental isolation. He must realise that, like a gypsy, he lives on the boundary of an alien world; a world that is deaf to his music, and as indifferent to his hopes as it is to his sufferings and his crimes.'[63]

What would it be like – what is it like – to subscribe to such a brave new vision of man's place in nature? What would we now have to believe if we were to declare, with Elizabeth Barrett's friend Miss Bayley, that we have become converts to 'materialism of the strictest order'?

It would mean accepting that we human beings – body and mind – really are made of matter and nothing else, in a world where matter merely knocks up against other matter for ever and ever. That we are in essence no more than soft machines, designed by no designer, placed on this planet by accidental forces, sputtering briefly into life before tiring and being dissipated. That there is nothing more to being ourselves than we can see reflected in the looking-glass of natural science: that physics and chemistry can show us what we are, biology and psychology can show us how we are and why we are, and that their answers, while containing so little to assure us, contain everything there is.

It would mean subscribing to the thesis that, while we live, all our human powers and sensitivities, our thoughts and consciousness, originate in our bodily machinery. That every influence we have upon the outside world has to begin with physical changes occurring at our body surfaces. That bodies can move things, hold them, kick them, spit at them, set the air vibrating in their voice-boxes, reflect light from their faces, secrete odours from their armpits, tear their hair, roll their eyes, waggle their arses ... but that this is all, in principle, that they can do. That any further impression we make on our surroundings can only be a secondary effect of these poor causes. That when and if our bodily activity is inadequate to have the secondary effects we may desire, there is precious little we can do about it. That we can achieve nothing at all external to us by means of purely inner unexpressed mentation. That thoughts without causally sufficient action by the body must inevitably fail in their ambitions. That we have no magic powers. That prayer and spells are ineffective. That we shall accomplish nothing whatsoever that we crave simply by the 'best will in the world'.

It would involve the realisation that other people are as limited as we are. That all our intercourse, our words, our loves and hates are directed only towards other transiently existing packages of flesh and blood, and that we receive love only from the same. That we are totally debarred by our and their embodiedness from communicating with our fellow human beings directly, mind-to-mind. That not even in the deepest crisis will our needs be known to absent friends. That, since the inner qualities of our experiences have no surface translation into speech or bodily behaviour, we are unable to share crucial aspects of our consciousness even in the closest of encounters.

It would require the acknowledgement that not only are we lonely and limited in our effects, but worse still our loneliness in space does not even have the compensation of depth in time. That we can neither commune with others far away, nor do we even have the prospect of communing with those close to us for long to come. That being locked into our mortal bodies we are inexorably locked out of eternity – and hence, it seems, locked out of any wider frame of meaning. That if we suffer now, we shall have no later pleasures to set against it; if we strive for perfection, we shall receive no reward; if we do harm, we shall not come to judgement … That the entire history of our individual presence in the universe will, when all is said and done, have been the trail left by this little human comet that burned so prettily but insignificantly and – like all the others – finally burned out.

What would people be getting in return for losing their hoped-for future? Bertrand Russell elegiacally said what. 'That man is the product of causes which had no prevision of the end they were achieving; that his origin, his growth, his hopes and fears, his loves and beliefs, are but the outcome of accidental collisions of atoms; that no fire, no heroism, no intensity of thought and feeling, can preserve an individual life beyond the grave; that all the labours of the ages, all the devotion, all the inspiration, all the noonday brightness of human genius, are destined to extinction in the vast death of the solar system … Only within the scaffolding of these truths, only on the firm foundation of unyielding despair, can the soul's habitation henceforth be built.'[64]

What did Jonathan Swift's hero, Cassinus, get when he sneaked into the privy to check up on what his mistress had been doing there? He got an eyeful of reality.

> No wonder how I lose my wits.
> Oh! Caelia, Caelia, Caelia shits.[65]

6

Jam Today

When I was eight years old I was sent away from home to a boarding school in Sussex. On my arrival the first day I was introduced to an older boy, Hugh Stewart, and told that he was to be my helper and look after me. I said I was not in need of 'looking after', and he went away. But I lied. I needed it like anything, only not from him.

Every night before lights-out in the communal dormitory the Matron, Miss Chard, would stand in the doorway with an open notebook and ask each boy in turn, 'Have you managed properly today?' Each of us regularly said, 'Yes, Miss Chard.' But in the early days, when I was missing my mother particularly badly, sometimes I said, 'No, Miss Chard.' Usually nothing happened. But once I said 'No, Miss Chard' two nights in a row. Then I was asked to present myself in Matron's room and was given a large spoonful of castor oil. It was only many weeks later that I discovered what Hugh Stewart might have told me, that her concern was with whether I had moved my bowels that day, not with whether I had been moved to tears of loneliness.

It was a good school, where we learned during the day the difference between latitude and longitude, how to decline Greek verbs, and even why the stars shine and something about the hearts of men (though not of women). 'To be learning something is the greatest of pleasures,' Aristotle said, 'not only to the philosopher but also to the rest of mankind.' At school we were getting learning in full measure and many of us found it passably pleasurable. But we were lacking something else. There was nothing in these lessons to help us make sense of our own situation. Like Pascal, we wanted to know why we were 'here rather than there'. The highlight of the week for all of us was 'own jams day', when at teatime we were allowed the jar of jam that we had each brought from home – the one reminder that someone somewhere cared for us. Most nights (and especially on the nights of own jams days) many of us wept into our pillows.

Little had changed at the level of small boys' true needs since an eleven-year-old wrote this letter on his second day at Westminster school in 1775. 'MY DEAR DEAR MOTHER, If you don't let me come home, I die – I am all over ink, and my fine clothes have been spoilt – I have been tost in a blanket, and seen a ghost. I remain, my dear dear Mother, Your dutiful and most unhappy son, FREDDY. P.S. Please remember me to my Father.'[66]

'With passion', Russell wrote, 'I have sought knowledge.' But with equal passion 'I have sought love . . . I have sought it because it relieves loneliness – that terrible loneliness in which one shivering consciousness looks over the rim into the cold unfathomable lifeless abyss. I have sought it . . . because in the union of love I have seen, in a mystic miniature, the prefiguring vision of the heaven that saints and poets have imagined.'[67]

But, as we saw earlier, these two human passions – for knowledge and for love – cannot be expected to operate with equal strength. In the ideal world pictured by traditional religions – where the more you know, the more you can feel sure of being loved – the two passions complement each other. But in the world revealed by science – where the more you know, the less you can feel sure – they pull instead in opposite directions. Where once it was love *through* knowledge, now it is love *or* knowledge. And, when people have to choose between one or other of these staples, it is pretty obvious what their priorities will be.

In the 1950s the American psychologist Harry Harlow conducted some famous experiments with infant monkeys, in an attempt to discover *their* priorities when the two things that a mother monkey would traditionally offer them were put in conflict.[68] If baby monkeys had to choose between obtaining *either* material nourishment *or* loving bodily contact, which would they prefer?

Harlow gave the baby monkeys a choice of two 'surrogate

artificial mothers'. One was made of bare wire, with a nipple attached to it at breast level, through which the baby could suck milk. The other was made of comfortable terry-cloth that felt and smelt more like a monkey, but had no nipple. The test revealed that even though the babies were getting all their physical nourishment from the wire mother, they would spend almost all the time when they were not actually feeding in contact with the cloth mother 'clinging and cuddling on her pliant terry-cloth surface'.

Harlow then investigated how these babies would behave in situations of anxiety when they needed emotional support. 'We exposed them to a room that was far larger than the cages to which they were accustomed. In the room we had placed a number of unfamiliar objects such as an artificial tree, a crumpled piece of paper, a folded gauze diaper, a wooden block and a doorknob. If the cloth mother was in the room, the infant would rush wildly to her, climb upon her, rub against her and cling to her tightly. Its fear then sharply diminished or vanished ... If the cloth mother was absent, however, the infants would rush across the test room and throw themselves face-down on the floor, clutching their heads and bodies and screaming their distress ... The bare wire mother provided no more reassurance in this "open field test" than no mother at all.'

The experiment provides a telling metaphor for how people dealt with the dilemma posed by scientific progress. People who had been brought up to believe that knowledge and love, explanation and assurance, would go together now had to decide which to cling to: the wiry rationality of scientific truth – the choice that fed their intellects – or the comfortable cloth of traditional religion – the choice that still felt and smelled right.

Pascal himself had been an innovative scientist, philosopher and scholar. He made original contributions to mathematics, was one of the first to provide experimental proof of the possibility of vacuums and was the inventor of the barometer and the syringe. He had perhaps as strong a commitment to knowledge as any of his generation. Yet, when he died, there was found sewn into the lining of his jacket a paper on which was written, 'God of Abraham, God of Isaac, God of Jacob, not of the philosophers and scholars. Certainty, certainty, feeling, joy, peace . . . Greatness of the human soul . . . Everlasting joy in return for one day's effort on earth. Amen.'[69]

Some others wavered. There were then (as there are now) revisionist theologians, people who called themselves 'deists' rather than 'theists', who were quite prepared to make their peace with science by granting God the role of prime mover and creator, but then sidelining him to the position of a disinterested spectator rather than an active player. This 'natural religion', which later became the rationalist rarefied religion of Hume, Voltaire and Rousseau, was an ingenious if somewhat arid compromise – that would allow its adherents to have their religious cake without having to eat it. But for most people it was, in effect, no religion at all. Traditionalists wanted none of this intellectualised non-interactive God. They wanted the old man with the beard, the terry-cloth version.

'When I consider . . . the small space I occupy and which I see swallowed up in the infinite immensity of spaces of which I know nothing and which know nothing of me, I take fright.' In this open field, which is the common experience of so much of mankind, only the familiar theist God could satisfy. The deist God provided no more reassurance than no God at all.

'You, O Deists . . . are the enemies of the human race and of universal nature,' Blake wrote later. Natural religion could only be 'an opinion of fatal and accursed consequence to man, as the ancients saw clearly by revelation, to the entire abrogation of experimental theory'.[70]

> Mock on, mock on, Voltaire, Rousseau:
> Mock on, mock on: 'tis all in vain!
> You throw the sand against the wind,
> And the wind blows it back again . . .
>
> The atoms of Democritus
> And Newton's particles of light
> Are sands upon the Red Sea shore,
> Where Israel's tents do shine so bright.[71]

And so the anti-science reaction set in with a vengeance, appealing to the best and the worst in the human heart and head.

Maybe people could avoid the issue simply by ignoring science? Maybe if they resolutely did not see the signal it would go away. Maybe if they shut their eyes they could pretend they were still back at home and it was 'own jams day' every day? Or maybe, if it was not available from Matron, they could find the jam within themselves? As we used to sing at school (declining the present tense of the Latin *sum*):

> Sum I am a pot of jam
> Es thou art a clot, etc.

Do not 'jam' and 'I am' have a common root in language? No, they do not. Nonetheless, as poets have continually insisted, what 'I am' is open to negotiation. 'I am the gardener and the flower,' wrote the Russian poet Osip Mandelstam, 'In the dungeon of the world I am not alone.'[72] 'I am the doubter and the doubt,' wrote the American Ralph Waldo Emerson.[73] 'I am the batsman and the bat,' wrote the Scotsman Andrew Lang, 'I am the bowler and the ball, / The umpire, the pavilion cat, / The roller, pitch, and stumps, and all'.[74]

'I am: yet what I am none cares or knows, / My friends forsake me like a memory lost, / I am the self-consumer of my woes,' wrote the Englishman John Clare, '. . . and yet I am, and live.'[75]

Who was to say what 'I' am really? As the nineteenth century got under way, it was becoming increasingly hard to dispute that science had got the measure of the stars and planets. But perhaps it could still be argued that science would never get the measure of the human psyche.

Were people obliged to take seriously Gall's seemingly preposterous claim that 'man, that inextricable being, has been made known' by brain physiology? Would it ever be necessary to accept statements such as this by the modern philosopher John Searle: that 'even the most cursory investigation' shows that 'mental phenomena are as much a result of electrochemical processes in the brain as digestion is a result of chemical processes going on in the stomach and the rest of the digestive tract'?[76] Or this by the scientist Francis Crick: that ' "You," your joys and your sorrows, your memories and your ambitions, your sense of personal identity and free will, are in fact no more than the behaviour of a vast assembly of nerve cells and their associated molecules.'[77]

Alfred Tennyson was sure it would never be so. As he commented searingly in *In Memoriam*:

> I think we are not wholly brain,
> Magnetic mockeries . . .
> Not only cunning casts in clay:
> Let Science prove we are, and then
> What matters Science unto men?[78]

Tennyson may have had particular reasons for wishing to disparage science. Among other provocations he had been the recipient of a letter from the first of all computer engineers, which ran: 'Sir, In your otherwise beautiful poem ("The Vision of Sin") there is a verse which reads – "Every moment dies a man, Every moment one is born." It must be manifest that if this were true, the population of the world would be at a standstill . . . I would suggest that in the next edition of your poem you have it read – "Every moment dies a man, Every moment 1 $\frac{1}{16}$ is born." . . . The actual figure is so long I cannot get it onto a line, but I believe the figure 1 $\frac{1}{16}$ will be sufficiently accurate for poetry. I am, Sir, yours, etc., Charles Babbage.'[79]

Yet, even without such goading, many sensible people reacted much as Tennyson did. Like King Canute they simply took up positions on the shoreline and defied science to roll over them. The obvious danger was that, as happened to the statue of the Virgin Mary in Hawarden, the tide would come up and carry the said people to some low land where they would be found the next day (or the next decade), drowned and dead.

7
Another Think Coming

Imagine how it felt for those who stood out for the traditional values. Or, rather, imagine how it *feels*, because the discussion is still very much a part of our contemporary culture. 'I just want to know who I am and why I'm alive.' It's the cry of people everywhere. Everything can seem so frustrating. Our intellectual understanding of creation, nature, life and death, is so limited.' So reads the front page of the *Jesus Revolution Streetpaper* that was pushed through my door in Cambridge this evening.[80]

What is the problem? The problem is actually *not* that our intellectual understanding is so limited. Anyone who cares to do so can read up on creation, nature, life and death, any day they please. And they will get a much fuller and better understanding than has ever been available before. Rather, the problem is that this modern scientific understanding neither entails – nor, in all honesty, can even be said to be consistent with – the future people yearn for. They will not find from science that, as the *Streetpaper* goes on, 'the only real answer is to allow our spirits to rise beyond ourselves, to rise to God in faith, love and worship. We are all God's children.'

Would it be possible, as Tennyson and others hoped, simply to face science down? Or to argue at least that it has no special claim on our attention?

There have been several philosophers in recent years who, eager to play to the anti-scientific gallery, have tried to argue that science is really nothing but a paper tiger. Leading the attack, Paul Feyerabend has denied that scientific rationality has any unique claim to be a path to truth. 'The appeal to reason to which [the scientist] succumbs', he has stated, 'is nothing but a *political manoeuvre* . . . It is clear that the idea of a fixed method, or of a fixed theory of rationality, rests on too naïve a view of man and his social surroundings . . . There is only *one* principle that can be defended under *all* stages of human development. It is the principle: *anything goes* .'[81]

This argument may have gone down well with a privileged group of modern intellectuals. But it is hard to see how it could ever provide other than cold comfort to ordinary people. A philosophy that manages to deny that science has all the right answers only by denying that there is any such thing as 'a right answer', is hardly going to be much help to those who are earnestly seeking, like Pascal, 'Certainty, certainty, feeling, joy, peace'. The last thing the street people need is to be told that 'anything goes'.

But in any case, the argument, however superficially persuasive, is light-weight. To take the famous example, we have probably all had it impressed on us that we can see Figure 1 either as a duck or as a rabbit. Both, it will be said, are equally 'true' readings of the evidence. It just depends on what your game is. Yet even the most dedicated relativist would have to agree that, in the real world, no object could actually *be* both a duck and a rabbit. And, if in fact alternative readings are possible, this can only be because we do not yet have sufficient information to make a better judgement.

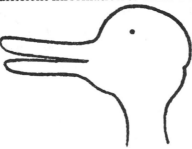

Figure 1

Suppose our game is to know whether the object in question is going to quack or not – or, more pertinently, whether it is going to lay a golden egg or not? Then what? In some circumstances (not perhaps these) too much depends on our making the correct prediction about what it is we are dealing with for it to be permissible to play fast and loose with truth. If anything goes, some things obviously go more than others. And when it comes to discovering what does go and what does not go, the scientific method has repeatedly proved itself terribly convincing.

Yet, if people cannot dismiss the methodology of science, might they still be able to ignore its conclusions on the grounds that they are too difficult to follow? No, this will not do either. For the problem is that scientific explanations are generally not so very difficult to follow. Notwithstanding the jibes of its detractors, science has in most areas made the world much less of a mystery than it was in the past, and its explanations are sometimes almost alarmingly straightforward.

Admittedly, there is also sometimes a deceptive simplicity about religious explanations. 'For often we talked of my daughter, as died of the fever at fall,' sighed Tennyson's Village Wife. 'And I thought 'twere the will of the Lord, but Miss Annie she said it were drains.'[82] Here the good mother could be forgiven for thinking the religious explanation, 'the will of the Lord', is actually simpler and more attractive than the semi-scientific one, 'drains'. And since no one could say that it is obviously false – indeed here, as in other cases, the two explanations are not necessarily incompatible – if she finds the former the more comforting, who is to say she should not stay with it.

Yet even here it has to be said that, if and when it is the future we are interested in, there is no question about which explanation would be the better guide. In terms of its elegance and its predictive power the theory of drains (and their associated microbes) must win hands down over the theory that God is taking sick children back into his bosom.

In general, every time religious and scientific explanations have met on the same field, history shows that it has been the scientific explanation that has come off best. As Denis Diderot wrote: 'If nature offers us a difficult knot to untie, let us . . . not use to untie it the hand of a being who immediately becomes a fresh knot, harder to untie than the first.'[83]

*

The problem, it seems, is precisely that when science has looked at the very same facts that our forefathers previously looked at, it has regularly come up with explanations that are too good – or at least too much better than the religious ones – not to be taken as the best approximation to the truth.

The problem is therefore that these facts – at any rate these particular *standard* facts about the world – no longer either require or in all honesty can even be said to allow the explanations on which our forefathers based their hopes for salvation. Therefore the problem in general would seem to be that we have run out of excuses.

Or so it seems. Yet maybe in this very phrasing of the problem is also the beginning of an answer, offering a window of opportunity for the traditional outlook. For who says that these standard facts *are all the facts there are*?

Perhaps, if we only pry a little bit further, we shall find new facts that science has yet to take on board – non-standard facts that may, with luck, still force a revision of the scientific picture? Indeed perhaps such facts have been knocking on the door for ages, only to be told by science to go away?

To illustrate, let me return to the numerical example I gave in Chapter 5. Imagine again that someone is presented with that series of numbers, 2, 4, 6, 8, and is looking for the explanation, in the form of a rule that connects the numbers. As we saw, there would seem to be two possible rules (assuming the sequence is not random). Either take the last number and compute $x + 2$, or take the last number and compute $-1/44\, x^3 + 3/11\, x^2 + 34/11$.

For the data as given so far, the first is unquestionably the better of the two. And if someone were to maintain that, since they both work equally well, he was going to make a personal choice of the second, we would surely be right to think he was being deliberately obscurantist or silly.

But suppose this person were to say: 'I bet if we look a little further we shall find I was right in my choice all along.' And suppose, when we do look further, we find to our surprise that the next number in the sequence is not 10, but 8.91 and the next after that not 12 but 8.67, i.e. the sequence we actually discover goes 2, 4, 6, 8, 8.91, 8.67. Then what had previously seemed the best rule would no longer fit the facts at all. Yet – surprise, surprise – the second rule would still fit nicely. In this case we should now be forced to admit that obscurantism had won the day. (Only, if we had any shame, we should now call it not obscurantism but prescience.)

This sort of forced rewriting of the rules does in fact happen every so often, even within conventional science.

Consider, for example, how classical physics was obliged to give way to quantum theory. So long as physicists worked only with the data drawn from large-scale phenomena such as apples falling from trees, the comparatively simple Newtonian laws of mechanics did the job perfectly well, and there was no call to replace them with the much more complicated rules of quantum mechanics (if anyone had thought of them). But once physicists came up against certain peculiar phenomena at the atomic level, such as the photo-electric effect, they had no alternative. Only the complicated theory could now meet all the facts.

Or consider an example of a more controversial kind. The conventional scientific theory of how human memory works assumes that people's memories are stored as physical traces in their individual brains. Almost all the data are, of course, consistent with this. Nonetheless for some time there have been other, more outré theories doing the rounds. These suggest that memories are actually not stored in the physical brain at all but rather in non-physical 'fields' outside the brain to which individuals 'tune in' when occasion arises. Rupert Sheldrake's theory of 'morphogenetic fields', which I mentioned briefly earlier, is one version; but there have been several others.[84]

The field theory (if someone were ever to spell out just how it works) would certainly be much more complicated than the brain theory. Since the facts as known at present do not demand it, most scientists would say there is no reason whatever to take it seriously. Sheldrake, however, maintains that if and when we look in the right places in nature, we shall find new evidence (in fact he says he has already found it) that completely undermines the brain theory: evidence, for example, of memories being transferred between different individuals who have had no form of physical contact.[85] If it were really to be so, he would be right that the field theory would then be the only one left in contention.

Scientific theories themselves undoubtedly do change and grow in response to new evidence and human insights. An accepted theory can be proved wrong and even turned on its head when more facts come to light. J. B. S. Haldane, the Marxist biologist, admitted: 'The world is much queerer than we realise; in fact, I think it is queerer than we *can* realise.'[86] T. H. Huxley, the evolutionary theorist who coined the word agnosticism, considered that absolute atheism is absurd 'when the possibilities of nature are infinite'.[87] There is always room for further change in the world outlook, and therefore – for those who do not like the current scientific picture – room for hope.

Furthermore, brilliant minds do sometimes come up with revolutionary ideas before their time. It has often been said that the mark of genius is to be able to see the revolution coming, to sense that something is wrong with a received idea even while other people are still celebrating its rightness. As Diderot wrote: 'Our great investigators in the field of experimental science . . . have watched the operations of nature so often and so closely that they are able to guess what course she is likely to take . . . to *smell out*, so to speak, methods that are still to be discovered, new experiments, unknown results.'[88] These scientific innovators possess what Diderot called *l'esprit de divination*.

But why should the new methods and unknown results – especially in the areas that most matter to us – have to be uncovered by the scientists themselves? Could not a Blake or a Tennyson claim to have as good a nose as any for smelling out new truths about the human mind and its potential? While scientists have, for sure, taken it on themselves to watch the operations of nature often and closely, the poets and mystics have arguably watched *human* nature more often and more closely than anyone.

Maybe they could already legitimately claim to know something the scientists do not.

Maybe, when it comes to it, most Toms, Dicks and Harrys might claim this too. Or better still most Annes, Kates and Marys, since it is women who arguably have the greater sensitivity to human personal relationships – and who, as every contemporary survey shows, tend to be surest that the scientific picture of the world is incomplete.[89]

For those who would resist the drift towards materialism, there might therefore be an intellectually honourable way forward. Rather than ignoring or deriding science, the better way could be to try to beat science at its own game.

We want a particular future state. We cannot expect to get to it unless we have good reason to posit a special explanation of present facts. As things stand, however, contemporary scientific doctrine tells us this special explanation is not required. Then our strategy, should perhaps, be to go out and uncover new facts that *do* require it: facts that prove the current doctrine wrong.

Indeed, maybe this is exactly the strategy that members of other cultures, less bothered by scientific scruples than we moderns are, have always had. Andrew Lang, the poet of bats and balls whom I quoted in the previous chapter, was the author in 1894 of a more serious work on the origins of supernatural belief among our 'savage' ancestors. There he wrote: 'The savage, it is said, started from normal facts, which he misinterpreted. But suppose he started, not from normal facts alone, but also from abnormal facts, – from facts which science does not yet recognise at all . . . "Spirits" may not exist, – but the universal belief in their existence may have had its origin, not in normal facts only, but in abnormal facts. And these facts, at the lowest estimate, must suggest that man may have faculties, and be surrounded by agencies, which physical science does not take into account in its theory of the universe and of human nature.'[90]

8

Uncommon Sense

The search for extraordinary facts was on. A search uniting the Jesus street people at one end, laboratory based parapsychologists at the other, in pursuit of any such facts as might force a revision of the prospects for mankind.

It was the shocking success of scientific explanation that gave this search new urgency and new direction. But I should stress, so as to set the parapsychological campaign in context, that it was by no means an entirely novel enterprise. Indeed, it should probably be seen as representing a continuation by other means of a much older campaign against the threat posed by 'normality'. As Lang noted, similar searches had in fact been going on throughout the course of human history – for similar reasons. While the new science was undoubtedly providing a serious challenge to people's hopes for their own future, the truth is that common sense had always done so too.

Some commentators might object to the drawing of any parallel between common sense and science, arguing that before science was 'invented' most human beings never thought in anything like the scientific mode. The embryologist Lewis Wolpert, in his book *The Unnatural Nature of Science*, has recently claimed that the scientific method was an intellectual breakthrough that flew in the face of more traditional ways of making sense of things.[91] Mark Ridley, the evolutionary theorist, has gone further still in saying that 'No doubt our ancestors needed some rational skills to survive, but . . . the human brain evolved more as a religious than a rational organ . . . Rational science is a minority interest . . . It is likely therefore that the first human brains evolved to impose symbolic meaning on the external world, and the scientific virus later infected a minority of their descendants, where it now flourishes in nerve circuits that originally evolved to carry other ideas.'[92] In this respect both these authors are unexpectedly at one with the anti-science campaigner Brian Appleyard, whose intemperate attack on science, in *Understanding the Present*, has accused it of being some kind of cuckoo in the nest of more homespun – and humane – ways of interpreting the world.[93]

Such arguments, however, greatly exaggerate the supposedly unscientific and irrational character of the pre-scientific mind. *Chambers Dictionary* defines science, broadly but quite appropriately, as 'knowledge ascertained by observation and experiment, critically tested, systematised and brought under general principles'.[94] But just such is the typically human way of gaining knowledge. So much so that, by these criteria, all human beings are almost from birth inveterate 'minor natural scientists' – keen observers of the universe, collectors of facts, framers of hypotheses, investigators of the as yet unexplained.

It is true that Science, once it became institutionalised, introduced more rigorous procedures for gathering data, stricter rules about how to argue from the particular to the general, new standards for what counts as a good explanation and how to test one explanation against another. But an unnatural way of thinking? an alien virus? Never. On the contrary, science is an extension of a natural faculty that was long ago firmly implanted in human heads because it works in practice to deliver knowledge of the kind that people have always needed in order to survive in daily life. Even if minor natural scientists is not *all* that people are – they do of course also sometimes employ other less reliable (and less effective) ways to gaining knowledge – it is what they *all are*.

It follows that, far in advance of 'science' as such, people, using their native intelligence, must have discovered for themselves many of the ordinary facts and basic laws of nature – if not at the level of abstract theory, then certainly at the level of descriptive generalisation. Although it may have taken Newton to explain *why* apples regularly fall, it did not take Newton to realise *that* they regularly fall. Indeed, much of what we now call scientific knowledge – in the areas of physics, biology, psychology, and so on – was there for the taking long before it was dignified under these titles.

People must have known as a matter of course the *general rule* that, for example, no one can be in two places at one time, that thoughts cannot travel directly between human minds, that it is not given to human beings to read the future, that spoons will not bend because we tell them to, and so on. They must have known, of course, that miracles hardly ever happen, that (other things being equal) people cannot walk on water, cannot make seven loaves feed four thousand, cannot conceive babies without sexual intercourse, cannot rise from the dead, etc., etc. They must have known the dreadful truth that materialism is to all intents and purposes the fact of life.

They must have known these sobering truths because time and again they and their fellow human beings must have come slap up against the evidence for them. *Try* walking on water (do the experiment, if that is what you want to call it) and you will sink. Try bending a spoon by saying 'bend, bend, bend' and it will not. Try choosing a lottery ticket by divining the winning number and you will (in all probability) lose your money.

Most telling of all, *take a look* at the body of a human being and you will not find there anything more indicative of special creation or soulfulness than you would find in the body of a dog. It is simply not the case, as St Paul claimed, that 'All flesh is not the same flesh: but there is one kind of flesh of men, another flesh of beasts'.[95] Any butcher could have told him. Joseph Heller's hero, Yossarian, in the novel *Catch-22* – no scientist he – read the message in the entrails of his dying friend Snowden as countless people must have read similar messages before: 'He gazed down despondently at the grim secret Snowden had spilled all over the messy floor. It was easy to read the message in his entrails. Man was matter, that was Snowden's secret. Drop him out of a window and he'll fall. Set fire to him and he'll burn. Bury him and he'll rot like other kinds of garbage ... "I'm cold," Snowden said. "I'm cold." "There, there," said Yossarian. "There, there." '[96]

*

Of course people will still dream about and hope for other possible worlds more to their liking – where men and women live for ever, wishes are reliably granted, God is in his heaven and all is right with the world. But, as psychologists have shown, even small children know well the difference between reality and fantasy: the difference for example between a 'pretend' event and an actually occurrent one.[97] A child of four is quite capable of realising – indeed almost all do – that merely imagining, for example, that there is a biscuit in a box, does not make it real.[98] And it must always have been obvious to anyone who has grown up with his or her feet upon the ground that, even if there is no absolute necessity for things to be the way they mostly are, they mostly are.

Indeed, no matter what people have said they believe about the possibility – in principle – of a counter-factual world (and have written in their fables or recounted to impressionable anthropologists), their actions in the area of everyday events have always shown that, when and where it matters, their view of the world they inhabit is considerably more mundane. Most people most of the time actually behave as if they were thoroughgoing materialists. And they do so – whether or not they have had any scientific education – for the simple reason that it would be impractical and stupid to do otherwise. No one can sensibly run their lives on the basis of hopes and expectations that run counter to commonsense experience; and no one sensibly does.

A substantial number of people in our own society, for example, say they believe in the possibility of telepathy: nonetheless, when they themselves want to communicate with a distant friend, they play safe and write or call them. They say they believe in the power of mind-over-matter: but, when they themselves want to achieve a physical effect, they make sure of using physical means. They say they believe in survival after death: but (in contemporary Europe anyway) they make no practical allowance for the deceased returning when they put them finally to rest.

There are of course exceptions. It is not unknown for individuals to jump from bridges in the expectation that a band of angels will lift them up, or to refuse nourishment when they are convinced God will provide, or to gamble their entire resources on the say-so of a gypsy at the fair. But the rareness of such actions – even among those who have never heard of science – confirms the general rule that most people know only too well how things stand.

This is confirmed too by people's sense of wonderment when and if their commonsense expectations are confounded. When a 'psychic' does apparently move a distant object by pure mind-power or is able to divine the contents of a secret message, anyone who witnesses it is likely to be greatly – even if pleasantly – surprised. If someone finds that he himself has done something by magic his first reaction is probably to disbelieve it.

Are pre-scientific cultures different from our own modern one in this regard? Anthropologists used to claim so. But more recent and sensitive studies have shown that so-called primitive peoples are by no means the unsophisticated thinkers they were once thought to be. In most respects they are in fact as commonsensical in their actions and as rational in their expectations as we moderns are. Pascal Boyer, who worked with the Fang tribe in Africa, has written: 'The people concerned find stories of flying organs and mysterious witchcraft killings fascinating as well as terrifying, precisely because they violate their expectations of biological and physical phenomena.' Even if, with the Fang, '[these stories] are certainly taken as accounts of real events . . . they are not taken as accounts of ordinary real events.'[99]

It is certainly not the case, Boyer insists, that such tribal people are so steeped in 'magical thinking' that somehow they simply do not notice the difference between the ordinary and the extraordinary. On the contrary, even though, for example, 'it is accepted as plausible, among the Fang, that some cases of illness are caused by witches flying about on banana leaves and throwing poisoned darts at their victims . . . [nonetheless] such Fang causal judgements are considered attention-demanding by virtue of their intuitive unnaturalness; to say that some Fang people entertain them as plausible does not imply that their counter-intuitive nature is not recognized.'[100]

*

Thus human beings, without the benefit of science, have probably always known more or less what they were up against. They have known, if not the full picture that science would later reveal, at least sufficient of it to indicate how limited their options are. And it is precisely because they have known this that they have everywhere courageously sought evidence of exceptional events so as to prove their own commonsense intuitions wrong.

In every culture and every era this appetite is evident. Counter-intuitive phenomena have always been news. Not, maybe, always and unmitigatedly good news. People, being only human, are quite capable of being alarmed by the very thing that promises them freedom – and like caged birds may sometimes show considerable ambivalence about what lies beyond the open door. Nonetheless, with their heads in the air, even if with their hearts sometimes in their boots, they have sought such evidence as they can find that there are more things in heaven and earth – but especially more things on earth – than are dreamt of in common-sense philosophy. They have gone all out to establish the seemingly outrageous proposition that anomaly rules.

This somewhat anarchic programme for human liberation became, as we shall see, a major influence on the theory and practice of parapsychology from the nineteenth century on. But it had already found its institutional outlet in traditional religions.

David Hume wrote of Christianity: 'The Christian religion not only was at first attended by miracles, but even at this day cannot be believed by any reasonable person without one. Mere reason is insufficient to convince us of its veracity: and whoever is moved by faith to assent to it, is conscious of a continued miracle in his own person, which subverts all the principles of his understanding, and gives him a determination to believe what is most contrary to custom and experience.'[101]

Although Hume's words sound like – and surely were meant to be – an indictment of Christianity, he might have done better to have seen the Christian emphasis on miracles as a testament to the fact that Christianity was doing its proper job. Given that it is avowedly the purpose and the duty of religions to nurse people's hopes of transcending physical reality, it makes perfect sense that they should seize – as they so effectively have done – every opportunity to discover, collate (and, if need be, manufacture) palpable evidence that there is more to life than common sense suggests. A religion that stayed with custom and experience might in rationalist terms be a magnificent achievement, but it would not be much of a religion.

As Pascal, who knew as well as any what the problems are, observed: 'Miracles are more important than you think.'[102] When people are drowning, they do not want a lifebelt made of water, they want one that helps them rise above the waves.

Admittedly there do exist modern believers – even modern Christians – who bravely maintain that *their* conception of religion does not involve anything so vulgar as paranormal miracles: that they are happy to render unto common sense the things that are common sense's, while reserving for religion the things that are religion's – which latter need have nothing to do with anything that goes contrary to natural law.

Well, let them have this advanced conception if it suits them – provided they acknowledge that in that case their position is *in every practical respect* no different from that of those who openly espouse materialism. But in reality few if any would go so far. And even if they did so it would almost certainly be disingenuous.

This is not to say that it would be a contradiction in terms for someone to be both a religious believer (of sorts) and a materialist: only that there can be scarcely a one who deep down is so. I have, for example, yet to meet any Christian, Jew or Muslim who does not every so often – and especially at times of danger to himself or others – give himself over to immaterialist fantasies about the possibility of supernatural forces intervening.

But then my larger point here is that I have yet to meet a single human being, of any faith or none, who really deep down does not entertain such thoughts. Even for someone who claims to deride all paranormal phenomena as nonsense, it would, as Ernest Hemingway said, 'be pretty to think otherwise'.

Thomas Hardy, remembering the traditional belief that farm-yard cattle go down on their knees at midnight on Christmas Eve in homage to the Christ Child, wrote:[103]

> So fair a fancy few would weave
> In these years! Yet, I feel,
> If someone said on Christmas Eve,
> 'Come; see the oxen kneel
>
> 'In the lonely barton by yonder coomb
> Our childhood used to know,'
> I should go with him in the gloom,
> Hoping it might be so.

There are, I think, few people who are not, at some time, tempted to go hand in hand with the believers. Hardy may or may not have intended a play on words with the phrase 'in the gloom'. But I shall say it for him: it is especially when in gloomy mood that we cannot but hope – maybe against better judgement – that the paranormal miracle may be so.

9
The World of a Difference

Miracles are *as* important as we think. They become even more important when the miraculous events that common sense has already told us are unlikely to happen are declared by a newly authoritative science to be unable to happen. The search for extraordinary facts becomes a crusade to retake the present on behalf of the future. And yet exactly what kind of extraordinary facts might do the trick?

What people wanted – and still want – was, above all, to get their *souls* back from science. For it was and still is their possession of a soul that most people have relied on as their ticket to a better world. The immediate task therefore had to be to seek out whatever facts could be counted as firm evidence in favour of the soul's existence.

As we saw in Chapter 1, almost everybody believes – or at any rate hopes – that they themselves do possess a soul. Nonetheless, when it comes to looking for evidence, the problem is that the soul is not an entity that many people would know how to define in practical or instrumental terms.

Perhaps most would, if asked, claim to *know* what a soul is even without being able to *say* what it is. Perhaps, as Louis Armstrong said of jazz, 'if you gotta ask, you're never going to get to know'. Maybe belief in the soul has always been one of those beliefs which, as the social philosopher Dan Sperber wrote, 'does not lend itself to a final, clear interpretation. Part of the interest of religious beliefs for those who hold them comes precisely from this element of mystery . . . their very mysteriousness makes them "addictive".'[104]

But if people were now to set about proving that the soul exists, in the face of science but by the methods of science, the concept could not be allowed to remain too mysterious. Even though they might not know quite what a soul *is*, they would need to have a fairly clear idea about where and how it can be expected to *come into play*. And the answer, albeit somewhat circular, would have to be that it comes into play in those areas of their lives where human beings do in fact prove in *material* ways their *immaterial* nature – their freedom to escape the constraints that science suggests their bodies and selves would otherwise be subject to.

As the anthropologist Claude Rivière, writing of the concept of the soul in tribal communities, has insisted: 'The essence of the soul is power.'[105] What power? At the very least such power as will prove beyond dispute that there is a practical difference between *this* piece of work, that is a man, and that other lesser piece, *l'homme machine*.

The task of revealing this power might not be altogether easy. Although Descartes himself had never questioned the soul's efficacy, his followers, as we have seen, had been pressing the materialist philosophy to what they took to be its logical conclusion: namely, that even if the soul does exist, it makes no difference *in this world* at all.

Diderot, for instance, writing in his *Elements of Physiology* in 1774, scorned the very idea that the addition of a soul to a machine could contribute anything to the machine's practical capabilities. 'A tolerably clever man', he wrote, 'began his book with these words: *"Man, like all animals, is composed of two distinct substances, the soul and the body."* I nearly shut the book. Oh! ridiculous writer . . . you do not know what it is that you call soul, less still how they are united, nor how they act reciprocally on one another.'[106] 'What difference', he asked testily, 'between a sensitive and living pocket-watch and a watch of gold, of iron, of silver and of copper? If a soul were joined to the latter, what would it produce therein? If the union of a soul to a machine is impossible, let someone prove it to me. If it is possible, let someone tell me what would be the effects of this union.'[107]

Diderot, by then himself a total sceptic, was evidently expecting the answer to his rhetorical question to be: None. The addition of a soul to a watch (and by implication to a human being) would, he implied, make no interesting difference either to the watch itself or to our own attitudes towards it.

Yet Père Bougeant, Diderot's Jesuit compatriot, in his *Amusement Philosophique*, had already made, as he thought, a cogent case that even so humble a mechanism as a watch would, once granted a soul, no longer be quite the watch it was before. 'Imagine how it would be for a man to love his pocket-watch as one loves a dog, & to stroke and caress it because he feels himself loved by it, being persuaded that when the watch shows one o'clock it is doing so out of friendly sentiment for him.'[108] A watch with a soul might at least have reason to feel less lonely and more cared for.

Bougeant hinted at the possibility of there being some sort of miraculous *psychic* interaction between the watch and human minds. It might be said, indeed, that he was anticipating the remarkable mind-over-watch phenomena that two centuries later were to become one of the most celebrated paranormal feats of Uri Geller. Here is Geller, in the 1970s, performing on the radio: 'Yes, now, hold your watches in your hands, broken watches, and start stroking them very gently, very, very gently. Just want the watches to start working. Say "work, work" in your head . . . really believe that even if the springs are broken, parts are missing, the watch will start ticking.'[109]

The fact remains, however, that a watch could never be considered other than a very simple-minded machine, and we should probably not expect too much of it even if it were to have a soul. But, to jump forward to the more obvious contemporary analogy, a modern digital computer would be a different matter. If the union of a soul to a computer were to be possible, what sort of miraculous difference might we hope or even expect *that* to make?

For an answer in one special area we can turn to Alan Turing, the founder of the science of artificial intelligence. In his famous paper on 'Computing machinery and intelligence', Turing made a surprising proposal, albeit a hesitant one, as to how experimental scientists might be able to distinguish once and for all between an ordinary computer and a human being.

Turing was convinced that ordinary computers should in

principle be capable of 'thinking' very much like human beings, perhaps even of being conscious. Yet he was persuaded that human beings, unlike any conceivable computer, have an additional capacity that goes beyond mere thinking. 'I assume that the reader is familiar with the idea of extra-sensory perception, and the meanings of the four items of it, viz., telepathy, clairvoyance, precognition, and psychokinesis ... [In humans] the statistical evidence, at least for telepathy, is overwhelming.'[110]

With this in mind, he imagined a version of the 'imitation game' (better known now as the Turing Test), as follows. A human being and a computer, which would be doing its best to *imitate* a human being, would be placed out of sight behind a screen, and an interrogator would be given the task of trying to work out which is which by asking questions of them. As Turing imagined it, the interrogator would try all sorts of conventional tests, and in every case the human being and the computer would give equivalent answers. But then at last he would decide to test for *psychic power*, and to do so he would conduct an experiment in card-guessing. In Turing's words, anticipating a successful outcome, 'The interrogator can ask such questions as "What suit does the card in my right hand belong to?" The man [behind the screen] by telepathy or clairvoyance gives the right answer 130 times out of 400 cards. The machine can only guess at random, and perhaps gets 104 right, so the interrogator is able to make the right identification.'

The difference, Turing implied, between (soulful) human beings and (soulless?) digital computers might lie precisely in this: that we but not they can transcend the mechanical limitations of our bodies and communicate directly mind-to-mind.

'These disturbing phenomena', Turing wrote, 'seem to deny all our usual scientific ideas.' And this was of course spot-on. For it is just these usual scientific ideas that fence us in and from which we are so eager to be free.

It is *paranormal* powers we seek: powers that by definition exceed the usual limits, powers that demonstrate beyond dispute that, while we human beings are evidently *in* the world of physical machines, we are not entirely *of* that world. As John Beloff, the leading contemporary theoretician of parapsychology, has written: 'The significance of the paranormal is precisely that it signals the boundary of the scientific world-view. Beyond that boundary lies the domain of mind liberated from its dependence on the brain. On this view, parapsychology, using the methods of science, becomes a vindication of the essentially spiritual nature of man which must forever defy strict scientific analysis.'[111]

Defy, deny, disturb . . . that has to be the way it goes. It is not just that, with Tennyson, we *think* we are not wholly brain, it is that we are quite determined that we cannot be – and require practical evidence of our potential freedom. If the existence of a soul is to be the answer to our prayers not to be merely machines (even conscious, intelligent machines), it *must* manifest itself through the potential it gives us for exercising, even if only occasionally, these non-machine-like supra-scientific paranormal powers; it *must* allow us, from time to time, to escape the limits of our bodies and bring about events that run counter to the 'normal' course of nature.

I advisedly say 'must', where others might say 'might'. For it has to be obvious, to all who have thought it through, that if the soul does *not* manifest itself this way, there would be nothing to it. If the soul were to have only normal powers, we would be back where we started. If it had no powers at all, we would equally be back where we started. There could be no point in having a purely epiphenomenal soul: a soul outside the chain of physical causation, a soul that like Wittgenstein's beetle-in–the-box 'cancels out, whatever it is'.

If the soul exists, we *must* be able to know it by its works; and its works *must* exceed the usual – normal – limits on what human beings might otherwise achieve. If there are still some people who say that the questions of soulfulness and paranormal power are *independent* issues, I would suggest to them that anyone who does indeed profess to believe in a soul while not believing in the soul's potential for paranormal action, should be asked to have another think about just what it is they really do believe in.

None of this is to say that, even assuming the soul does have these special powers, we should expect the evidence to be constantly before us. In fact even the most optimistic of us should probably expect sometimes to be disappointed. It may be typical (it may, as we shall see later, even be definitive) of paranormal powers, that they are not available to order but are somewhat wayward and inconstant. Even if we modern human beings, as much as the 'primitive man' whom Rivière discussed, like to think of ourselves as being in principle 'unlimited with regard to our physical potentialities', in reality it could be true that 'the soul never appears as a pure essence but is identified through props and manifestations. Its power can vary from individual to individual, and even in the same individual in the course of his life.'[112]

We human beings may propose, but perhaps something not quite under our control disposes. The soul, when it comes to it, may prove to be some kind of a trickster, not operating at all in the way that we would choose. And the results may sometimes take us unawares. The soul's props and manifestations may appear to be surprisingly trivial, even crass; its presence may indeed be revealed in nothing more uplifting than card-guessing or psychic watch-mending. How narrow the line, a cynic might remark, between the wonderful and the absurd.

Yet, granted that the soul may not always deliver quite what we want quite when we want it, we ought at least to be happy to have evidence that the soul undoubtedly exists. Provided that we can demonstrate that *any sort* of paranormal phenomena attend on human beings, then, to Diderot's question about what difference the soul makes, we should be able to counter the answer 'None' with 'This!'

No matter, then, if the phenomena are disappointingly scarce and take surprising forms. Indeed, once we have realised what we are dealing with, the fact of the soul's unreliability, so far from being a cause of theoretical embarrassment, might even be interpreted as evidence in favour of its existence. Perhaps this very unreliability would be still further proof that the soul's powers are in a different league from the material body's.

In the commonsense world of physics, repeatability is the

norm: given the same circumstances, the same thing will regularly happen. Suppose, however, that once the soul has got involved, given the same circumstances, *different* things happen, or something happens *only sporadically*, or maybe even happens *only once*? Would this not be just the kind of thing we should expect?

Boyer has emphasised how, among tribal societies, people generally do have low expectations of there being any orderly pattern to the world of spirits. When it comes to the behaviour of everyday objects, the Fang think in terms of generalities and rules – antelope typically behave like this, water behaves like that, fire like that, and so on. But they do not expect ghosts, for example, to behave in such typical ways. And therefore in discussing the behaviour of ghosts they use something more like 'case law', based on particular instances. As Boyer has put it: 'Many religious representations do not consist of general principles, but of memories of singular episodes.'[113]

Maybe this is part of what Pascal meant when, having carefully defined what miracles are, viz. 'My view is that any effect is miraculous when it exceeds the natural powers of the means employed,' he added unexpectedly: 'Miracles are no longer necessary because we have already had them.'[114]

10

Breaking the Law

The search – this age old search – was on. But we should note a considerable paradox which runs through the story from here on. Those scientists who took up the cause of searching for the soul were, at first at least, keen to discover evidence of regular behaviour. In 1885, one of the founders of the Society for Psychical Research, Frederick Myers, coined the word 'supernormal' to be applied to 'phenomena which are beyond what usually happens' and went on: 'By a supernormal phenomenon I mean one . . . which exhibits the action of laws, higher, in a psychical aspect, than are discerned in action in everyday life.'[115] And the *Oxford English Dictionary* has defined 'paranormal' as 'applied to observed phenomena or powers which are presumed to operate according to natural laws beyond or outside those that are considered normal or known'. These laws may indeed be 'higher' or 'beyond' what is already known, but the assumption is nonetheless that the phenomena are in their own way lawful.

This would seem also to have been Newton's assumption in relation to miracles. 'For miracles are so called . . . because they happen seldom and for that reason create wonder. If they should happen constantly according to certain laws impressed upon the nature of things, they would no longer be wonders or miracles but might be considered in philosophy as part of the phenomena of nature notwithstanding that the cause of their causes might be unknown to us.'[116] And the poet John Donne had already made much the same point in one of his Sermons, although the other way around: 'There is nothing that God hath established in a constant course of nature, and which therefore is done every day, but would seem a miracle, and exercise our admiration, if it were done but once.'[117] The corollary of this is precisely Newton's

67

point: every one of those things that God has apparently placed outside the constant course of nature, and which therefore is done only occasionally, would cease to seem a miracle, and would no longer exercise our admiration, if it were done every day.

It is perhaps significant that, while Newton the natural philosopher imagined the possibility of miracles becoming frequent and therefore relatively commonplace, Donne the poet imagined the possibility of commonplace phenomena becoming infrequent and therefore relatively miraculous – an early example of the difference in attitude of the 'two cultures' of science and art. Both, however, were clearly of the opinion that, while paranormal phenomena might never be assimilated to existing laws, they could certainly coexist with them – in other words, that while these phenomena would be outside the law, they would not be intrinsically lawless.

Yet John Beloff, in the passage quoted in the previous chapter, seemed to be taking a much more radical line. For him paranormal phenomena 'must forever defy scientific analysis.' And by 'defy' he did not, presumably, mean that these phenomena must be merely extra-scientific or contingently beyond the scope of science – because perhaps they happen so infrequently and apparently unpredictably that even if they are lawful scientists never get the chance to pin them down. No, he meant (as is confirmed in his other writings) that they must be contra-scientific and therefore necessarily beyond the scope of science – either because they are actually unlawful or because whatever laws they do obey make a mockery of the existing laws. Beloff's aim for parapsychology has not been simply to extend our understanding into new areas as yet untouched by science, it has been to make science itself eat humble pie.

There is, I think, a real tension here – which we shall find running through the discussion from now on. It is the tension between, on the one hand, the positive urge to legitimise an alternative welcome reality and, on the other, the negative urge to delegitimise an existing unwelcome reality.

I have been suggesting all along that people's primary motivation for seeking out paranormal phenomena has generally been positive rather than negative. There is something people want of the world, namely the prospect of a better future than the one currently on offer. Hence they seek for new facts that can only be explained by means of new principles that lead on in the new direction: a new P that requires a new E which leads to a new F. The same reasoning might however issue in a much more negative stratagem. There is something people do not want of the world, namely the prospect of the actual future that is currently on offer. Hence they seek for new facts that are strictly incompatible with the currently accepted principles and hence reduce the chances that this is where things will lead: a new P that excludes the old E which therefore with luck excludes the old F.

If and when the positive motive is uppermost in people's minds, we should not expect to find them searching promiscuously for any sort of weird and wonderful facts. Only some weird facts – relatively few – could actually help to make the constructive case for a more promising future. But if the negative motive is uppermost, then indeed we might expect to find people welcoming weird facts simply for the sake of weirdness.

Early in the history of Christianity, St Paul himself acknowledged that, when it came to promoting the positive content of the Christian message, there were just a few specific miracles that could be said to really count. Of these Christ's resurrection was obviously the most significant. For this reason Paul insisted again and again on the importance of the resurrection as an underpinning of faith. If Christ as a man *had* risen from the dead, mankind in general might be able to do likewise (there might in fact be a general law of resurrection.) But, on the other hand, 'if Christ be not risen, then is our preaching vain, and your faith is also vain . . . For if the dead rise not, then is not Christ raised: And if Christ be not raised, your faith is vain, ye are yet in your sins . . . If in this life only we have hope in Christ, we are of all men most miserable.'[118]

Yet the truth is that across the Bible as a whole many – indeed most – of the recorded miracles were simply not in this class. They were, for sure, demonstrations that flew in the face of common sense, but not demonstrations that in themselves would have brought anyone closer to salvation. This was especially true of the Old Testament miracles, many of which would seem to have been little more than one-off paranormal curiosities: a stick being turned into a serpent, an iron axe being made to swim, a widow's oil being multiplied, and so on. And many of the New Testament miracles were hardly more illuminating: water being turned to wine, a coin showing up in the mouth of a fish, the cursing of a fig tree, and so on.

In contrast to the resurrection, the latter might be considered pure 'wow! factor' miracles with little positive to offer. Nonetheless, the historical record shows that they were well received by those who witnessed them. And it goes to show that even in those days there was an eager audience for demonstrations that did not so much help to confirm a new spiritual reality as *merely* help to destroy the existing temporal and physical one.

It may even have been that those who gathered round the biblical prophets, as they have gathered round countless other miracle-workers before and since, came like spectators at a bullfight simply to watch their hero vanquish the black beast of normality. What they were getting from Moses or Jesus may not have been so different from what the crowds that packed into the music-halls two thousand years later were getting from Houdini.[119]

As I stressed in the previous chapter, beggars can hardly be expected to be choosers. Not surprisingly, therefore, the common pattern has been for people to be content with negative evidence. They are bound to make the best of what there is. And it is always going to be easier to find evidence *against* something than evidence *for* something else – the obvious reason being that there are always many more ways of being wrong than of being right.

Consider again our earlier arithmetical example. Given the sequence 2, 4, 6, 8 . . . , there are many numbers, e.g. 19 or −3, that if they came next could *discredit* the simple rule of adding 2, but only one number, namely 8.91, that could actually *support* the alternative rule based on $-1/44\ x^3 + 3/11\ x^2 + 34/11$. By the same token there must always be many extraordinary facts that could potentially discredit the conventional world-view, but relatively few facts that could provide positive support for a specific alternative. The project of doing down science was therefore always more likely to make headway than the project of bolstering a new kind of parascience.

But we should not ignore the risks that come with conducting a negative campaign. When we examine these risks, we may be able to judge just how far they have been heeded.

11

Anything Goes?

It is a familiar story in other spheres of life. People begin with a bang, and end with a whimper. They start off with high ambitions to be millionaires, and settle for whatever keeps them off the streets. They begin with grand ideas about being perfect parents and end like the television star Roseanne, admitting: 'I figure if the children are still alive when my husband gets home I've done my job.'[120]

Parapsychology at its inception was, as Beloff said, meant to be 'a vindication of the essentially spiritual nature of man'. But as time passed it became more a case of providing evidence that man's essential spirit was still showing any signs of life at all. The search for specific evidence in favour of a new reality became instead a search for anything that tells against the existing one.

Yet why *not* make the best of what there is? When scientific materialism has been identified as the soul's enemy, *anything* that tells against it must surely be counted the soul's friend. When the word going round is that man himself is an automaton, *any* evidence of his transcending mechanical limitations will help refute this calumny. If 'the essence of the soul is power', why not welcome even the most minor and peculiar miracles as confirmation of this power?

No reason why not, except the rather good one that – once you conduct the investigation on these terms – you are in danger of being sold a pup. Once you accept that, instead of actively looking for specific evidence in favour of a new reality, you are going to be receptive to anything that goes against the existing one, you no longer have critical control. Remember the words of Kant I quoted in Chapter 3: we must not approach things 'in the character of a pupil who listens to everything that the teacher chooses to say, but of an appointed judge who compels the witnesses to answer questions which he has himself formulated'. The problem is not just that, if you let the investigation be conducted on the soul's own terms rather than your own, you have fatally lost the initiative. It is that, if you accept in advance that the soul's mode of operation may be as idiosyncratic as I have described in previous chapters, you have unilaterally made normal criteria of validity redundant.

What have you done to your own critical faculties if you admit that the phenomena you are in search of are by their very nature likely to be not merely paranormal but unpredictable, unrepeatable, temperamental, shy, highly context dependent, droll, evanescent, dreamlike? What have you done when you positively affirm – for all the good reasons I described – that the soul is likely to play tricks?

What you have done, even if you do not acknowledge this explicitly, is to admit that you expect the soul to behave in ways which in any other situation you would regard as diagnostic of chance or psychological illusion or human deceitfulness. And once you have done so – once you have admitted that it is all too likely that the soul will behave in the way a clever conman or illusionist or deceiver and/or self-deceiver would behave – then, if and when it does behave like this, you can have no idea what you are really dealing with. If it behaves like a conman, how do you know it is not actually a conman? (Because it says it isn't? That won't get you far!)

The dilemma – it is a genuine dilemma – has uncomfortable parallels with theatrical farce. On stage, say, a young belle is told that her lover will come to her disguised as a footman; and indeed a footman turns up and climbs into her bed. But how is she to tell the difference between her lover disguised as footman and a real footman disguised as her lover disguised as a footman? (The parallel is not far-fetched. At a reincarnation centre in California a few years ago, bereaved people were told that the ghosts of their dead husbands or wives would materialise as white-sheeted bronze-skinned young hippies. Maybe the police were wrong to accuse the managers of the centre of running an unlicensed brothel, but . . . .)

In the theatre we can recognise, sympathise with and laugh at the impossible situation the heroine is in. But how should we react if the same dilemma confronts the actors in the paranormal drama? Unfortunately the answer will in most cases be obvious. If it appears that someone or something is playing paranormal games with us, we had better assume that the party responsible is a normal human prankster rather than a paranormal spiritual one.

We had better assume this because of the asymmetry of what we already know. We have independent evidence – from many other contexts – of human trickery and human error of the kind that could produce just such surprising phenomena as the soul apparently displays. We know for a fact that it is within the normal powers of human beings to bamboozle others and themselves. But we have no *independent* evidence of the soul behaving in any of these ways. We do not know for a fact that it is within the paranormal powers of the soul to bam or boozle its way into the lives of anyone at all.

If we explain something by means of the soul hypothesis we have therefore, in Occam's phrase, 'multiplied entities'. We have been well warned against this when there is no 'necessity'. Here, however, the lack of necessity would be especially serious. For, as I stressed earlier, the whole point of the search for the paranormal has been that we should discover a set of facts that *requires* us either to adopt a wonderful new explanation or at the very least to throw over any conventional one. The goal is, ideally, that the soul should emerge from this search as the only hypothesis still standing. If it does not, if it emerges merely as a somewhat quaint – and superfluous – alternative to a more normal explanation, nothing has been gained.

It would be wrong, however, to rush to judgement on this. The problems I have just drawn attention to arise once we make allowances for the soul's reputedly unruly character. And yet, while we may be forced by the facts to make such allowances, we should not necessarily concede this in advance. Even if there are reasons for thinking that the soul will sometimes behave like a trickster, this need not mean that it will always behave this way. The question of how it actually behaves is – at least it ought to be – an empirical matter, to be decided by the evidence of when and where paranormal phenomena actually show up.

If the evidence suggests that supposedly paranormal phenomena show up *only* in what we might call fishy circumstances, the case for these phenomena being genuinely paranormal would be difficult to sustain. But if it indicates that sometimes at least they show up in sweet and fresh conditions, the case would be comparatively strong.

It is important, however, that we play this fairly and do not load the dice against the paranormal. In particular, we must be careful not to prejudge the issue of 'fishiness' by presuming that the very fact that a paranormal phenomenon would contravene normal laws is proof that it cannot really have occurred and that, therefore, human trickery *must* have been involved. While this fact ought certainly to alert us and make us sniff around, it should not be taken as a sure sign of their being something fishy.

The philosopher David Hume, in his *Essay on Miracles* in 1748, put forward a famous argument against ever taking paranormal phenomena at their face value which in this respect was not wholly fair.

Hume's argument was based on probabilities. It stands to reason, he said, that when we have to decide between two rival hypotheses to explain something, to each of which we can assign an antecedent probability, we are obliged to accept the most probable as the best explanation.

Suppose, for example (though not Hume's example), we know that someone has drawn a black ball from one or other of two bags, each of which contains a mixture of black and white balls. We do not know which bag the ball was drawn from. But we know that bag A contains at most 1 per cent black balls, while bag B contains at least 50 per cent. If we now have to say which bag we *think* the ball was drawn from, we can and must confidently say bag B.

Now, if someone tells us they have witnessed an apparently paranormal phenomenon, the situation is similar. We know their testimony could have originated either from an objective fact about the world that was genuinely paranormal or from a propensity on the observer's part to make up a story. That is, it could have come, as it were, either from the 'Objective Fact bag', OF, or from the 'Human Invention bag', HI. In many cases we do not actually know which. We know however that the probability of finding a paranormal phenomenon in bag OF is very low indeed: otherwise the phenomenon would not be considered paranormal – indeed, years have gone by and the chances are that we ourselves have seldom if ever come across clear examples of paranormal phenomena in our own experience. We also know that the probability of finding such a phenomenon in bag HI is relatively high: otherwise human observers would have to be paragons of honesty and reliability, which we know they are not – indeed, every day of the week we have come across examples of people lying, exaggerating, misperceiving, misremembering, saying things for effect, and so on, and no doubt we have done it ourselves on some occasion. Hence, Hume argued, when we are required to choose one or other hypothesis about where the testimony has come from, we ought always to assume bag HI.

It is true, Hume acknowledged, that in some circumstances we might be very unwilling to draw this conclusion. We might find it hard to believe that *this* person in *this* case could be capable of such invention. But even when the person involved is a close friend or even ourself, our understandable astonishment at this evidence for human folly ought to be much less than our astonishment at what would otherwise be evidence for natural laws being overturned.

'The plain consequence is,' Hume wrote, ' "That no testimony is sufficient to establish a miracle, unless the testimony be of such a kind, that its falsehood would be more miraculous, than the fact which it endeavours to establish" ... When anyone tells me [for example] that he saw a dead man restored to life, I immediately consider with myself, whether it be more probable that this person should either deceive or be deceived, or that the fact, which he relates, should really have happened. I weigh the one miracle against the other.'[121] No matter how remarkable and apparently incontrovertible the evidence, 'I would still reply that the knavery and folly of men are such common phenomena, that I should rather believe the most extraordinary events to arise from their concurrence, than admit to so signal a violation of the laws of nature.'[122]

Hume's argument, so far as it goes, is perfectly solid. Given what we know about the world we live in, he must be right that the *balance of probability* is always going to be against evidence for the paranormal being what it seems to be. Nonetheless, cogent as it is, there are good reasons for not taking this argument to be the knock-down argument Hume meant it to be.[123]

We must recognise that an argument based on probabilities can never be more than that – a *probabilistic* argument. While it can provide a rule of thumb that tells us how the plausibility of one explanation compares with another, it surely cannot provide an absolute guarantee of where the truth lies.

In the case of the black and white balls, it is true that the best bet has to be that the black ball came from bag **B**. But unless we have reason to believe that there were *no black balls at all* in bag **A**, we can never be absolutely sure that it did not come from bag **A**. The relative proportions of black and white balls in the two bags is of course a relevant consideration. But even if all the balls in **B** were black and almost none of them in **A** were, the black ball chosen *could* still have come from **A**.

Likewise, in the case of someone testifying to a paranormal phenomenon, the best bet has to be that it came from bag **HI** and is a case of human invention. But unless it can be separately proved that paranormal phenomena are not just highly improbable in fact but impossible in principle – in other words, that the probability of finding one in bag **OF** is zero – we cannot rule out that this is where it came from. The question of how frequently people make up stories is certainly something we should take into account. But even if we had reason to believe that people tell such stories constantly, we would still have to allow that the reported event might on this occasion have been genuine.

*

The danger of arguing Hume's way is of course that we shall refuse to believe something is true when it actually is true – because we make the Humean calculation and reckon, correctly, that on balance it is more than likely to be false.

There is the cautionary tale of Matilda, who everybody knew was never to be trusted.[124] 'Matilda told such dreadful lies, / They made one gasp and stretch one's eyes.' When Matilda screamed out that her house was on fire (an unlikely event), the neighbours did indeed have every reason to assume she was making up the story (a likely one). Hence 'every time she shouted "Fire!", / They only answered "Little Liar!" ' But, this time, believe it or not, the house really was on fire: and 'therefore, when her Aunt returned, / Matilda and the house were burned'.

John Locke, in a different vein, told the story of the King of Siam who, when informed by a Dutch ambassador that 'the water in his country would sometimes in cold weather be so hard that men walked upon it, and that it would bear an elephant if he were there', refused on Humean grounds to believe him. 'Hitherto,' the King replied, 'I have believed the strange things you have told me, because I look upon you as a sober, fair man; but now I am sure you lie.'[125]

The King, wrongly as it happens, refused to accept the facts of ice. Likewise in real life there have been notorious examples of people wrongly refusing to accept the facts of meteorites, the facts of continental drift, the facts of evolution, the facts of child abuse, the facts of acupuncture, the facts of Nazi genocide, and so on. In every case people presumed they knew enough about the world and about human fallibility to be safe in concluding that these facts could not be genuine and they were wrong.

It may be instructive if we put your own presumptions to the test right now, using a relatively neutral example of an unlikely fact. If I tell you that I have numerological evidence that Shakespeare's birth was anticipated in the Bible, I expect that (unless you know what I am about to say) you will be inclined to think either that I am pulling your leg or that there is some subterfuge involved. The idea of there really being such evidence is antecedently absurd.

Yet I am not pulling your leg, and, whatever it is, it is not a subterfuge.

William Shakespeare was born on 23 April 1564 and died on 23 April 1616. Two 23s make 46. There are 46 letters in the words 'Twenty third of April in fifteen hundred and sixty four'. Moreover Shakespeare was 46 years old when the King James Version of the English Bible was completed in 1610. With all these 46s, the number 46 is presumably a pointer. Which book of the Bible should we turn to? If we examine possible anagrams of WILLIAM SHAKESPEARE, we find the letters spell out a clear message: HERE WAS I, LIKE A PSALM. We should turn then to the Book of Psalms – and, in particular, to Psalm 46. Now, if we count to the 46th word from the beginning of the 46th Psalm we find the word is 'shake', and if we count back to the 46th word from the end we find the word is 'spear'.[126]

I do not want to make more of this than it deserves. But it does surely illustrate how unwise it may be to rush to judgement about the truth of antecedently improbable facts. This is not to say that it would be wrong to be *suspicious* of any such improbable fact. Indeed if I were you, I would – just to be on the safe side – check your Bible, and while you are at it check my spelling. People have been known to tell lies even in books (and the fact that I myself am saying this does not mean I am not doing it – I might be double-bluffing).

But to be suspicious is one thing, to close one's mind to the very possibility of such a highly improbable fact being true at all – as Hume in effect recommended – is another. As John Stuart Mill said: 'If we disbelieved all facts that have the chances against them beforehand, we should believe hardly anything.'[127]

As mentioned above, it would of course be an *entirely* different matter if the fact in question were not just to have the chances heavily against it but were to have a zero probability – if the OF bag were to contain no such facts at all. Suppose, in the extreme case for example, it were to involve a logical impossibility. In *that* case, there could be no two ways about it. Anyone who attests to the truth of a logically impossible fact has to be telling a witting or unwitting lie. Thus, if I were to tell you that I have discovered evidence in the Bible that Shakespeare's birthday occurred before his mother's, you would know what to do with this claim of mine without further consideration.

However, this case of logical impossibility is not – at least, not so far as we have yet established – the case that we are dealing with in relation to the paranormal. Perhaps someone someday will mount an argument to show that certain sorts of paranormal phenomena such as life after death or telepathy or psychokinesis are not merely contrary to the laws of worldly physics as we know them but contrary to some truly incontrovertible higher-level 'laws of mind'. I myself shall try out such an argument later in this book. But Hume himself certainly did not mount such an argument.

If we did have such an argument about the absolute impossibility of miracles, Hume's argument about the relative probability of human folly would in any case become redundant. As Sherlock Holmes sensibly said to Dr Watson: 'When you have eliminated the impossible, whatever remains, however improbable, must be the truth.'[128]

We have to conclude that the probabilistic argument really cannot do the work that Hume intended. This does not mean that the problems Hume raised can be ignored. Like it or not, knavery, folly and plain muddle-headedness are unquestionably such common phenomena that they should always be any investigator's first thought. It means, however, that Hume's argument in and of itself cannot give sceptics the excuse they have sometimes seemed to want, simply to sit back and close their minds to the stories they are hearing.

The question remains: where and when should we regard any particular bit of evidence in favour of the paranormal not just as improbably fishy, but as unconscionably and inordinately fishy? If the paranormal interpretation is not to be rejected merely on the basis of its *a priori* probability, what better criteria for rejection might we use?

The answer, I think, is that in assessing any particular piece of evidence we must consider what *else* the paranormal explanation of this evidence would lead us to expect. Assuming the phenomenon in question is the soul's work on this one occasion, we ought to ask how and where else we might expect the soul to show its hand. And if, in this wider context, we find that the patterns of phenomena we actually observe are really not at all what we might reasonably have predicted, we must of course ask *why*. Especially we must ask why the phenomena are manifest *only* in certain curiously mundane situations and *only* take certain curiously mundane forms. For I take it that, however unpredictable the soul may be, nothing in paranormal lore or paranormal logic suggests that the soul will do only such things as positively stink of *earthy* limitations on its powers.

Designed Too Far

The clue to whether we are dealing with the paranormal or the normal might lie, I am suggesting, not so much with what the soul does achieve as with what it does not achieve. We ought to examine the soul's preferred style of working and the peculiar patterns it slips into. We ought to look for evidence of unanticipated lacunae and silences, the sound of dogs that do not bark. If the soul does *not* exist perhaps we shall know it by the *restrictions* on its works.

But rather than merely throwing around the words 'fishy' and 'suspicious', as I did in the last chapter, it will be preferable to state the argument in more general and less value-laden terms. The criterion I suggest we should employ is one that, echoing the famous 'Argument from Design', I have elsewhere called the 'Argument from Lack of Design'.[129] But this name was not quite right for it. I would have done better to have called it, as I shall do now, the 'Argument from Too Much Design of the Wrong Sort' or maybe the 'Argument from Unwarranted Design'.

Essentially it goes like this. If a phenomenon shows signs of being unduly restricted in its form and manner of occurrence, so that our theory of its underlying cause provides us with no principled reason why it should take just the peculiar form it does, then we should suspect that the true cause of the phenomenon lies elsewhere. That is, if the theory cannot tell us either 'why *this* in particular' or 'why not *that* in general', we should take it that there is an alternative theory to be found which – if we were to know it – *would* tell us why.

The rationale for this argument is, I think, intuitively obvious. But let me illustrate it with several relatively straightforward examples.

Suppose you have a theory that the underlying reason someone sends you chocolates is that he loves you. In practice, however, all he does is to send you three After Eights on the second Thursday of each month, and he fails to come through in the other ways you might expect. Then, whatever this is, it is surely not what you would expect of 'love' – and there is no way of redefining 'love' that would accommodate it.

Suppose you have a theory that the reason the parrot talks to you in English every time you pass its cage is that it has mastered the English language. But in practice the only two things it ever says are 'Who's a pretty boy then?' or 'Strike a light!' Whatever this is, it is not what you would expect of 'English comprehension', and there is no way of redefining 'English comprehension' that could meet the case.

Suppose you have a theory that the reason someone says he is Lord Lucan, who mysteriously disappeared in 1974, is that he *is* Lord Lucan. But in practice the only part of Lucan's life he seems to be familiar with is the part serialised in the newspaper, and he gives a start whenever someone says 'Come off it, Jones.' Whatever this is, it is not what you would expect of normal 'human identity'.

Figure 2

Or, to take a rather more puzzling example, suppose you have a theory that what you are being shown in Figure 2 is an accurate drawing of a solid triangular object. But when you ask to be shown other views of it, you are told this is the only angle from which the object likes to be photographed and that it goes to pieces if anyone doubts its word. Whatever this is, it is not what you would expect of an ordinary 'solid object'.

Let us see how the argument might apply to a real-life example much closer to the paranormal.

Clever Hans, as everyone knows, was a German horse living at the turn of the century who could apparently solve arithmetical problems, and would respond to questions put to him by tapping out the answer with his hoof. Suppose you have a theory – as many did to begin with – that the explanation for the horse's skills was that he possessed the ability to do mental calculation. But when you investigate further, as psychologist Otto Pfungst did, you discover that Hans's performance has several major peculiarities: among them that Hans would perform correctly only if his owner or other members of the audience themselves knew the answers and were within sight when he responded, and that he did best of all when his owner was wearing a particular hat.[130]

The tell-tale signs of there being more design than is called for would be obvious. The 'calculation theory' might perhaps explain why Hans could do what he could do, but it would throw no light at all on why he could do it only under those conditions. Nor is there any way of redefining 'calculation' that could possibly meet the case. Calculation is simply not a fitting explanatory concept to do justice to the specificity of the observed phenomena. Calculation has nothing to do with hats.

On these grounds alone, therefore, you could – and ought to – reject the calculation theory without more ado. But note that in rejecting it you would not be relying on the Humean argument that for a horse to be able to calculate would be too improbable. Even though it clearly is highly improbable – indeed, it might mean acknowledging that Hans was the one and only calculating horse the world has ever seen – it might still be true in fact. However, for a horse or anyone else to have *this* kind of calculating ability would not only be improbable but conceptually absurd. What deals the knock-out blow is not so much factual probability as theoretical propriety.

*

It is important to recognise that this Argument from Unwarranted Design would give us a good enough reason for rejecting the calculation theory even if we could not come up with any more plausible alternative. No one could argue that it would be better to retain such an inappropriate theory than to have no theory at all. And the same goes for the other illustrative examples above.

With all these examples there are, as it happens, more or less obvious alternative theories which, unlike the theory first considered, *could* take the observed limitations in their stride. (I imagine you will be able to decide in each case – and with the help of Figure 3 – what the alternatives might be.) But the point is that we do not need to have any clear idea of what is the right explanation in order to recognise what is the wrong one. We can be sure it is *not* love, not language, not a triangular object, even if we do not have a clue what it really *is*.

Figure 3

This has, as we shall see, great relevance to assessing the status of phenomena that are supposedly paranormal. Again and again the argument is put forward by believers that a phenomenon *must* be paranormal if and when neither they nor anyone else can think of any normal explanation for it. It would be a weak argument at best. But it would collapse completely if the paranormal explanation itself should turn out to be quite unable to do justice to the facts.

*

Sceptics have often got themselves into unnecessary difficulties by unwisely promising to explain how everything that has ever occurred in the paranormal realm is in reality achievable by normal means. Even supposing they are right about the underlying normality, such a promise must be wildly over-confident. With many of the cases on record there is in practice no prospect of knowing what really happened – perhaps because there is insufficient information about the circumstances at this distance in time and space, or because investigation has been or is being blocked by interested parties, or simply because no one is clever enough to work it out.

The sceptic's position will be all the stronger if and when he *can* suggest how a particular effect was achieved, and stronger still if he can duplicate the phenomenon himself. But this challenge is not one that he should feel *obliged* to meet. Someday it is bound to happen that he will meet his match. And the danger is that when this happens, when he cannot say what normal explanation would make sense, this failure may be taken by the other side as positive evidence in favour of the phenomenon being paranormal by default.

James Randi, the American conjuror, has an impressive track record of simulating supposedly psychic phenomena. But he has made a tactical mistake by boasting that anything the psychics can do he can do at least as well. The case of Uri Geller's metal-bending is a case in point. Having myself witnessed at close hand both Geller and Randi bending spoons, I can vouch that Geller's performance has been altogether more elegant and mystifying. Does that mean – as several commentators friendly to Geller would argue – that, when Geller has done it, it has not been a trick but the real thing? No, the fact that some particular feat is para-Randi does not at all mean it is paranormal. More likely it simply means that with this trick, which Geller invented and made his speciality, he is a real star – better than Randi, and probably the best there has ever been.

But my point is that, if we adopt the Argument from Unwarranted Design, we have no need to get hung up on trials of strength between psychics and conjurors. What should make us quite convinced that Geller's spoon-bending is not paranormal, even if we do remain completely baffled by it, is that his performances have always seemed to be too bound around with irrelevant conditions – conditions that make no sense in terms of any paranormal origin.

If Geller *has* been able to bend a spoon merely by mind-power, without his exerting any sort of normal mechanical force, then it would immediately be proper to ask: Why has this power of Geller's worked only when applied to metal objects of a certain shape and size? Why indeed only to objects that anyone with a strong hand could have bent if they had the opportunity (spoons or keys, say, but not pencils or pokers or pound coins)? Why has he not been able to do it unless he has been permitted, however briefly, to pick the object up and have sole control of it? Why has he needed to touch the object with his fingers, rather than with his feet or with his nose? Etcetera, etcetera. If Geller really does have the power of *mind* over *matter*, rather than *muscle* over *metal*, none of this would fit.

It may be thought that by running on with these examples I am being prematurely gloomy about the prospects for paranormal phenomena in general. It is surely not a foregone conclusion that all the cases we may ever come across will show such patently obvious signs of there being something wrong.

It may be true, as we have seen already, that paranormal phenomena are likely to be troublesome and odd, and that the soul may not play by the rules we would expect. But oddness in itself is not the issue here. Mere irregularity as such would certainly not constitute evidence of unwarranted design. What would do so would be regularities of the wrong kind.

The new question will therefore have to be, not just, does the soul behave in unexpected ways, but does it behave consistently in inappropriate ways? Are there *unfitting* limitations on what the soul (or its sub-agents) can do?

Without knowing in advance what we shall find, it would seem prudent to focus attention on two areas, which in practice often overlap.

*

Material constraints

There might turn out to be surprising limitations on the physical props and manifestations that the soul makes use of.

For example, it would seem reasonable to ask why, if it were indeed the case, psychic power should be capable of transforming a wooden staff into a serpent but not into, say, an icicle, why it should be capable of turning water to wine but not to honey, why of producing 'thought images' on photographic plates but not on other people's retinas, why of divining water in a natural landscape but not an artificial one, why of reading the faces of playing cards in Professor Rhine's laboratory but not in a poker game, etcetera, etcetera.

The apparent arbitrariness of such constraints should be enough to alert us to the likelihood that something other than paranormal forces is involved. But it would of course be particularly puzzling if the pattern should turn out to be such as to suggest that the soul can do by paranormal means only what, in other circumstances, a human conjuror can do by normal means. Nothing in our starting concept of the soul would have led us to expect *that* kind of design.

Psycho-social constraints

There might equally turn out to be surprising limitations on the psychological or social conditions under which paranormal phenomena typically occur, and on the psychological content of people's paranormally generated experiences.

It would seem reasonable to ask why, if it is so, people should be more likely to witness paranormal events when the viewing conditions are relatively poor, why they should be more likely to do so in company than when alone, why those who already believe in the powers of the soul should be more susceptible than sceptics, etc. And, more particularly, why messages from the dead should be so surprisingly vague, why poltergeists are particularly active around teenage children, why a statue of the Virgin Mary rocks her head at night but not during daylight, etcetera, etcetera.

Again the arbitrariness of such constraints should alert us. But all the more so if it should turn out that paranormal experiences typically occur under conditions that are known to be conducive, in other circumstances, to common-or-garden psychological dysfunction, illusion or mendacity. Nothing we know about the soul would have led us to expect *that* either.

Nothing we know about the soul would lead us to expect it? I realise this is perhaps to underestimate the ingenuity of theorists who belong to the soul's camp. If these patterns of constraint do occur, the riposte from believers might still be that the soul, trickster that it is, is in fact being doubly tricky by arranging things precisely so as to mimic events that are sometimes brought about by normal means. They might even want to argue that the soul is presenting people with a kind of challenge – deliberately arousing their suspicions in order to test their willingness to suspend disbelief.

This kind of argument has been employed quite often and effectively before now. The seventeenth-century Italian abbess St Veronica Giulani, for example, was notorious for her ability to go without food for days on end. Particular proof of her saintliness was, so people said, provided by the fact that she was several times seen sneaking into the kitchens of the convent during the course of her fasts. The point of these visits, her supporters argued, was to make it look to sceptics as if she was eating surreptitiously, while all she was really doing was putting herself to the extra trial of seeing food she could not have.[131]

On rather a different level, a similar defence was mounted by certain theologians in the nineteenth century as an answer to what looked like compelling evidence in favour of the theory of evolution – especially the awkward evidence of continuous progression in the fossil record. Their idea was that, when God created the world six thousand years ago, he mischievously planted just this evidence of evolution in the earth, so as to tempt people to doubt the Bible story of divine creation and hence prove their religious fibre. Only those whose faith was strong enough to enable them to resist the Darwinian heresy, however well it was

apparently supported by the facts, would be saved (thus providing, as it were, a kind of natural selection for Christian sheep over
Darwinian goats).

Such a way of arguing would, admittedly, effectively disarm the
Argument from Unwarranted Design. For there is no denying
that, by building into the theory of the soul the very pattern of
limitations that seems to pose the problem, believers could make
the problem go away. If it could be argued, say, that it is *of the
essence* of the soul to imitate a human conjuror, then we would
never expect the soul to do things that a conjuror could not. Fair
would be foul and foul fair, and all sceptical objections would be
beside the point.

For those who want to take this line, the trick might be to add in
theoretical constraints retrospectively. And there is one particularly specious way of doing this that would almost always work.
This would be to argue that, while the phenomena in question do
indeed have their origins in conceptually simple design processes,
what has happened is that some sort of 'filter' has got interposed
between the underlying process and its particular expression.

Take, for instance, what might be done with our own earlier
examples. Perhaps the man who sends After Eights on Thursdays
is genuinely in love but happens to live somewhere where no other
chocolates are available and Federal Express only collects on
Wednesdays? Perhaps the parrot is a true English speaker who
happens to have become grossly aphasic? Perhaps the Lord Lucan
claimant is the real Lord Lucan with a highly selective memory
block?

Likewise, *perhaps* the soul really is out to make monkeys of
potential sceptics? Thomas Mann, reporting on a spiritualist
seance, enjoined critics to recognise that the pursuit of truth
involves dealing with 'a great deal of filth and foolishness',
because here 'nature takes the field, and nature is an equivocal
element: impure, obscene, spiteful, demonic'.[132] Brian Inglis went
so far as to say of certain paranormal manifestations that 'they
sound bogus . . . they look bogus. And yet, paradoxically, this is a
powerful argument in favour of their being genuine.'[133] Kenneth
Batcheldor argued that the soul seldom if ever behaves in ways
that are unequivocally paranormal because if people were to be

confronted with indubitable evidence they would find it too disturbing. And William James summed up his experience with psychical research: 'I confess that at times I have been tempted to believe that the Creator has eternally intended this department of nature to remain *baffling*, to prompt our curiosities and hopes and suspicions all in equal measure.'[134]

It may be the case that we cannot absolutely discount this kind of sophistry. Einstein said, 'God is subtle but he is not malicious.'[135] Einstein might have been wrong. But it is in general clear that it would make a mockery of explanatory procedures to plead this explanation of phenomena that are apparently designed too far.

13
The Art of the Possible?

It is true that thoughtful people have always paid lip-service to Kant's maxim that 'we should compel the witnesses to answer questions we ourselves have formulated'. In the past the Catholic Church itself was not slow to challenge the evidence when claims were made for facts that it could not, at least not yet, assimilate to its own model of the world. And the same diligence the Church showed, for example, in prosecuting Galileo's extraordinary claims about the natural universe was also evident in the investigations it instituted into extraordinary claims about the supernatural. In the case of a candidate for sainthood, for example, when reports came in of miraculous events, the Church would set up an official inquiry. A *promotor fidei* would be appointed, better known as 'devil's advocate', whose job was to try to discredit the testimony and evidence of the saint's supporters (by asking difficult questions, for example, about visits to the kitchen). In these and other, more straightforward investigations of the paranormal, however, there was – and is – considerable confusion about what arguments ought to tell for and what against.

The Argument from Unwarranted Design can, I think, now be brought into the courtroom, to provide a criterion rather different from those commonly in play. We shall have to see just how relevant it is to particular cases. But, when the task is to compel the witnesses to answer questions, we do have a clear line to pursue. Question 1: 'What is your hypothesis to explain the phenomena in hand?' Question 2: 'If this hypothesis is right, what form would you have expected in advance that the phenomena would take?' Question 3: 'Given what has actually occurred – and what has not – are there signs of inexplicable constraints?'

*

We shall have plenty of opportunity later in the book to try out these questions on the kinds of evidence that modern parapsychology brings forward. But I shall make a start with some much more venerable evidence: namely, the testimony of the Christian Bible.

The miracles recorded in the Bible, especially those attributed to Jesus, have done more than anything else to set the stage for all subsequent paranormal phenomena in Western culture, outside as well as inside a specifically religious context. Modern philosophy is not quite, as has been said of it, merely footnotes to Plato, and modern parapsychology is not quite footnotes to the Bible. But undoubtedly many of the major themes of parapsychology stem from the earlier tradition. Thus, it is still essentially the Judaeo-Christian concept of the soul – or parts of it – that contemporary critics of materialism find themselves defending. And it is Jesus' paranormal powers (of which over two hundred instances are recorded in the Gospels) that in many quarters still stand as the primary exemplar of what a man who is more than a man-machine might do.

If Western society had continued to have a strong tradition of shamans and sorcerers, like most other societies in the world, Jesus' influence would not necessarily have been so central as it has been. But, given the almost complete dominion of Christianity, the fact was that, by relatively modern times when the need to seek an alternative to materialism had become pressing, Jesus was probably the only major paranormal practitioner whom most people in the West still knew much about. While as individuals they may have had little if any personal acquaintance with miraculous phenomena, as a collective everybody – from rich man in his castle to poor man at his gate, from illumined mystic to enlightened sceptic – had the Jesus story off by heart.

The effect, even on those few who were not themselves professing Christians, was – as arguably it still is – to suggest that if paranormal phenomena were to be demonstrable in modern circumstances, they would basically come from the same stable. Jesus' miracles provided the *type* for the new phenomena that people imagined and hoped that they might find. This did not necessarily mean that many people were expecting a repeat performance. But it meant that Jesus' miracles had set the ground rules: they had given people an idea of what a genuine paranormal phenomenon might look like *if* it occurred – suggesting the kind of themes, the kind of circumstances, and, let it be said, the kind of allowable excuses. What was good enough for Jesus should presumably be good enough for anybody else.

I am not proposing that, at this stage, we attempt a scientific study of events that occurred two thousand years ago. The biblical accounts of Jesus' life cannot of course be trusted to be historically accurate: they were written many years after the supposed events, and in any case they were the work of men who had an obvious interest in embellishing their stories. We cannot expect to be able to subject the reports of Jesus' miracles to the kind of cross-examination we might want to give a more reliable history.

Nevertheless, we can quite well consider what we should do with this testamentary evidence *if* we had reason to take it at face value. The exercise will, I think, help us sharpen our critical faculties, get some practice in applying the argument from unwarranted design, and perhaps learn more than a little about miracles and miracle-workers as a whole.

If we do take the accounts in the Gospels as authentic, it is clear that a perfectly up-front answer is being given to our Question 1 above. The explanation for Jesus' remarkable powers is that, as the son of God, he had the general capability to divert Nature from her course. In particular he was able, by the power of his mind alone, to make objects at a distance (including human bodies) undergo physical changes in the direction he desired. He could intervene in the normal chains of causation. He could form and transform matter. And all this in total contradiction of what common sense or later science would consider theoretically possible or what is practically possible for ordinary human beings in ordinary circumstances.

This capacity – an exceptionally strong capacity for what parapsychologists these days call 'psi' – was, by assumption, without trivial limitations on it. Nothing in our concept of what it would mean to be the son of God would suggest that Jesus would have been bound by convention or that he would have wanted – or still less been obliged – to follow popular precedents. Indeed, nothing would suggest that there should have been anything at all that Jesus could not have done if he had chosen to, or even that some kinds of paranormal feat should have come more easily to him than others did.

Admittedly, 'if he had chosen to' might be the operative words here, so that in practice the full range of his powers might not have been on open display. We should understand it if he was not always willing to perform at other people's bidding. We are told, for example, that when, in the wilderness, Jesus was tempted by Satan to show off what he could do – 'If thou be the Son of God, command that these stones be made bread'[136] – he did indeed choose not to comply, preferring to win the argument with a verbal put-down even if it left him hungry. But we should note there is no hint here that he refused to do what Satan asked because he did not know how to.

So, our Question 2 is: if Jesus did have this kind of general ability, what particular things might we reasonably expect him to have done with it? What does this hypothesis predict would have been the pattern of his miracles?

We have of course no good model to go on, nor can we know for sure just what Jesus' (or his father's) larger purpose might have been. But we do know that it was at least part of his purpose to persuade ordinary people to take his philosophical and social message seriously. He wanted them to believe he was the son of God. And to this end he did deliberately use his powers in a cajoling way – as propaganda. It is true that he continually admonished his followers for being over-impressed by his paranormal demonstrations – 'Except ye see signs and wonders, ye will not believe.'[137] But he clearly knew what would impress them: and he was, it seems, quite ready to do the business when it suited him.

What business, precisely, would we expect this to have been? Not surely such business as could easily have been mistaken for the same old business that a host of other itinerant magicians, holy men, soothsayers, prophets, had been doing for hundreds of years? Surely Jesus would not have gone about *mimicking* the standard feats of conjuring that, according to the Roman philosopher Celsus, were on display in every market-place throughout the ancient world?

Yet, remarkably – and here is the answer to our Question 3 – this *was* apparently the pattern. Many scholars have noted (to their dismay or glee, depending on which side they were taking) that Jesus' miracles were in fact entirely typical of the tradition of performance magic that flourished around the Mediterranean at that time.[138] Lucian, a Roman born in Syria, writing in the second century AD, catalogued the range of phenomena that the 'charlatans' and 'tricksters' could lay on. They included walking on water, materialisation and dematerialisation, clairvoyance, expulsion of demons, and prophecy. And he went on to explain how many of these feats were achieved by normal means. Hippolytus, too, exposed several 'pseudo miracle workers' who had powers uncannily similar to those of Jesus, including a certain Marcus who had mastered the art of turning the water in a cup red by mixing liquid from another cup while the onlookers' attention was distracted.

So close were the similarities between Jesus' works and those of common, lower-class magicians, that several Jewish and pagan commentators at the time simply took it for granted that there was little except style and zeal to distinguish Jesus from the others. In their view, while Jesus might have been an especially classy conjuror, he was certainly not in an altogether separate class.

Celsus claimed that Jesus had picked up the art during his youth in Egypt, where the Samarian magicians were the acknowledged masters. Having listed the tricks of the Samarians, such as expelling diseases, calling up spirits of the dead, producing banquets out of thin air, and making inanimate objects come to life, Celsus (according to the Christian writer Origen) went on to say: 'Then, since these fellows do these things, will you ask us to think them sons of God? Should it not rather be said that these are the doings of scoundrels?'[139]

*

Christian apologists were, early on, only too well aware of how their Messiah's demonstrations must have looked to outsiders. They tried to play down the alarming parallels. There is even some reason to think that the Gospels themselves were subjected to editing and censure so as to exclude some of Jesus' more obvious feats of conjuration and to· delete references to the possible Egyptian connection.[140]

The Christian commentators were, however, in something of a dilemma. They obviously could not afford to exclude the miracles from the story altogether. Whatever Jesus' other merits as a man of wisdom, his particular claim to divinity had to rest four-square on its being shown that he really did have some sort of paranormal powers. Play down the miracles too far and Jesus would look too much like an ordinary mortal. But play them up and he would look even more like one of the magical fraternity.

The somewhat lame solution, adopted by Origen and others, was to admit that the miracles would indeed have been fraudulent if done by anybody else, simply to make money, but not when done by Jesus to inspire religious awe. 'The things told of Jesus would be similar if Celsus had shown that Jesus did them as the magicians do, merely for the sake of showing off. But as things are, none of the magicians, by the things he does, calls the spectators to moral reformation, or teaches the fear of God to those astounded by the show.'[141]

To return to the question: what would we expect, in advance, that a man with Jesus' powers would have made of them? And why is it so surprising that, with these powers at his disposal, he in fact did what he did?

Consider the following, wholly blasphemous, analogy. If, today, a fairy godmother gave *you* such paranormal powers, what would you do with them? You would, I imagine, hardly know where to begin. But, given all the wondrous things you might contrive, would you consider for a moment using your powers to lay on magical effects of the kind that other people could lay on *without* such powers? Would you produce rabbits from hats, or make handkerchiefs disappear or even saw ladies in half? Would you turn tables, or read the contents of sealed envelopes, or contact a Red Indian guide? No, I imagine you would actually take pains to differentiate yourself from contemporary conjurors and small-time spirit mediums, precisely so as not to lay yourself open to being found guilty by association.

I am not suggesting that all of Jesus' miracles were quite of this variety (although water into wine, or the finding of a coin in the mouth of a fish, are both straight out of the professional conjuror's canon). But what has to be considered surprising is that any of them were so. Moreover that so few of them, at least of those for which the reports are even moderately trustworthy, were altogether of another order.

Why *this*, not *that*? It seems to have been a common question put to Jesus even in his lifetime. If you are not a conjuror, why do you behave so much like one? Why, if you are so omnipotent in general, are you apparently so impotent in particular? Why – and this seems to have been a constant refrain and implied criticism – can you perform your wonders there but not here?

One of the tell-tale signs of an ordinary magician would be that his success would often depend on his being able to take advantage of surprise and unfamiliarity. And so, when the people of Jesus' home town, Nazareth, asked that 'whatsoever we have heard done in Capernaum, do also here in thy country,'[142] and when Jesus failed to deliver, they were filled with wrath and suspicion and told him to get out. 'And he could there do no mighty work,' wrote Mark.[143] Note 'could' not 'would'. Textual analysis has shown that it was a later hand that added to Mark's bald and revealing statement the apologetic rider, 'save that he laid his hands upon a few sick folk, and healed them'.[144]

It would seem that the evidence of unwarranted design – of inexplicable constraints on what was and was not possible – looked odd even to Jesus' would-be followers.

The excuse given on this occasion in Nazareth was that Jesus' powers failed 'because of their unbelief'.[145] But this, it must be said, was an oddly circular excuse. Jesus himself acknowledged that people's belief was contingent on his showing them signs and wonders. How then could he blame the fact that he could not produce the miracles they craved for on the fact that they did not believe?

Did Jesus himself know the answer to that nagging question: why, while he could do so much, could he still not do all that others – and maybe he too – expected of him?

The taunts of the crowd at the crucifixion, 'If thou be the Son of God, come down from the cross . . . He saved others; himself he cannot save,'[146] hostile as they were, must have seemed even to him like reasonable challenges. We do not know how Jesus answered them. But the final words from the cross, echoing the Twenty-second Psalm, 'My God, my God, why hast thou forsaken me?', suggest genuine bewilderment about why he could not summon up supernatural help when he most needed it.

It suggests there is more to this story. Is it possible that, even though Jesus was regularly using deception and trickery in his public performances like any common conjuror, he actually *believed* that he was much more than a conjuror: believed that sometimes he could *genuinely* exert the powers he claimed?

14
Behold the Man

Let us suppose, for the sake of argument, that Jesus really had no more paranormal powers than any other human being, and that this means in effect that he had no paranormal powers at all. Why might he have been deluded into thinking that he did have them?

It is a question that goes far beyond the case history of this one man. But, though it will mean introducing issues that otherwise might have waited till later in the book, having raised the question with regard to Jesus, I want to enlarge on it now.

We should begin, I think, by asking what there was in Jesus' personal history that might provide us with a clue to what came later. For there is good reason to believe that Jesus' formative years were, to say the least, highly unusual. Everything we know about his upbringing suggests that even in the cradle he was regarded as and treated like a being apart. Whether or not he was born to greatness, he clearly had greatness thrust upon him from an early age.

Admittedly, it is the privilege of many a human infant to be, for a time at least, the apple of his or her parents' eyes. So that the fantasy of being a uniquely favoured human being is not uncommon among little children. For a good many it is a fantasy that, unless the world has been peculiarly unkind to them, is based in the reality of their family relationships. The psychoanalyst Ernst Becker wrote: 'The child lives in a situation of utter dependence; and when his needs are met it must seem to him that he has magical powers, real omnipotence. If he experiences pain, hunger or discomfort, all he has to do is to scream and he is relieved and lulled by gentle, loving sounds. He is a magician and a telepath who has only to mumble and to imagine and the world turns to his desires.'[147] Although most children must, of course, soon discover that their powers are not all that they imagined, for many the idea will linger. It is probably quite usual for young people to continue to speculate about their having powers that no one else possesses. And it is certainly a common dream of adolescents that they have been personally cut out to save the world.

Intimations of greatness might not, therefore, have distinguished the young Jesus from other children. Except that there were in his case other – quite extraordinary – factors at work to feed his fantasy and give him an even more exaggerated sense of his uniqueness and importance. To start with, there were the very special circumstances of his birth.

Among the Jews living under Roman rule in Palestine at the time of Jesus' birth it had long been prophesied that a Messiah, descended from King David, would come to deliver God's chosen people from oppression. And the markers – the tests – by which this saviour should be recognised were known to everybody. They would include: (i) That he would indeed be a direct descendant of the King: 'made of the seed of David'.[148] (ii) That he would be born to a virgin (or, in literal translation of the Hebrew, to a young unmarried woman): 'Behold, a virgin shall conceive, and bear a son, and shall call his name Immanuel.'[149] (iii) That he would emanate from Bethlehem: 'But thou, Bethlehem, though thou be little among the thousands of Judah, yet out of thee shall he come forth unto me that is to be ruler in Israel.'[150] (iv) That the birth would be marked by celestial signs: 'A star shall come forth out of Jacob, and a sceptre shall rise out of Israel.'[151]

We cannot be sure how close the advent of Jesus actually came to meeting these criteria. The historical facts have been disputed, and many modern scholars would insist that the story of the nativity as told in Matthew's and Luke's gospels was largely a *post hoc* reconstruction.[152] Nonetheless there is a reasonable possibility that the gist of the story is historically accurate. (i) Even though the detailed genealogies cannot be trusted, it is quite probable that

Joseph was, as claimed, descended from David. (ii) Even though it is highly unlikely that Mary was actually a virgin, she could certainly have been carrying a baby before she was married; and, if the father was not Joseph (several early sources pointed to his being a Roman soldier called Panthera), Mary might – as other women in her situation have been known to – have claimed that she fell pregnant spontaneously. (iii) Although Joseph himself came from Nazareth, the story that he and Mary were commanded to go to Bethlehem for a population census and that the birth occurred there is not implausible. (iv) Although the exact date of Jesus' birth is not known, it is known that Halley's comet appeared in the year 12 BC; and, given that other facts suggest that Jesus was born between 10 and 14 BC, there could have been a suitable 'star'.

Some sceptics have felt obliged to challenge the accuracy of this version of events on the grounds that the Old Testament prophets could not – unless they really *were* capable of precognition – have foretold what would happen many centuries ahead. But such scepticism misses the mark. For the point to note is that there need be nothing in itself miraculous about foretelling the future, provided the prophet has left it open as to when and where the prophecy is going to be fulfilled. Given that a tribe of, let's say, a hundred thousand people could be expected to have over a million births in the course of, let's say, three hundred years, the chances that one of these births might 'come to pass' in more or less the way foretold are relatively high. It is not that it would *have to* happen to someone, it is just that if and when it did happen to someone somewhere, there would be no reason to be too impressed.

The further point to note, however, is that even though there may be nothing surprising about the fact that lightning strikes somebody somewhere, it may still be very surprising to the person whom it strikes. While nobody is overly impressed that someone or other wins the lottery jack-pot every week, there is almost certainly some particular person who cannot believe his or her luck – somebody who cannot but ask: 'Why me?' For the winner of the lottery herself and her close friends, the turn of the wheel will very likely have provided irresistible evidence that fate is smiling on her.

So too, maybe, with the family of Jesus. Suppose that through a chapter of accidents – we need put it no more strongly than that – the birth of Jesus to Joseph and Mary really did meet the preordained criteria. Assume that the set of coincidences was noticed by everyone around, perhaps harped on especially by Mary for her own good reasons, and later drawn to the young boy's attention. Add to this an additional stroke of fortune (which, as told in Matthew's gospel, may or may not be historically accurate): namely, that Jesus escaped the massacre of children that was ordered by Herod, so that he had good reason to think of himself as a 'survivor'. It would seem to be almost inevitable that his family – and later he himself – would have read deep meaning into it, and that they would all have felt there was a great destiny beckoning.

The image a person has of himself is bound to have a crucial influence on his psychological development. Not only will it shape his choices as to what he attempts to make of his own life, but – because of that – it will frequently be self-confirming. The man who believes himself born to be king will attempt to act like a king. The man who knows himself to have been selected from all the possible Tibetan babies to be the future Dalai Lama will allow himself to grow into the part. Children of Hollywood parents who are pushed towards fame and fortune on the stage will sometimes be dramatically successful (provided they are not, by having too much of it, dramatically hurt).

This kind of moulding of a person's character to match an imposed standard can be effective even when the pressures are relatively weak. A surprising, but possibly apposite, example is provided by a recent finding in the area of astrology. When the psychologist Hans Eysenck looked to see whether there is any correlation between particular individuals' 'sun signs' and their personality, he and his colleagues discovered that people born under the odd numbered signs of the zodiac (Aries, Gemini, Leo, Libra, Sagittarius, Aquarius) do in fact tend to be more extrovert than those born under the even-numbered signs (Taurus, Cancer, Virgo, Scorpio, Capricorn, Pisces) – just as predicted by astrologers.[153] But the explanation for this curious finding is almost certainly not that people are being directly influenced by astral forces. A much more likely explanation is that enough people regularly read their horoscopes for the astrologers' predictions to have had a profound effect on what individuals *expect* about their own character and the ways they behave. Further studies by Eysenck showed that the correlation is, indeed, absent in those (relatively few) adults who profess to know nothing about their sun sign or what it 'ought' to mean for them; and it is also absent in children.[154]

Now, if an individual's psychological development can be influenced merely by reading a newspaper horoscope, imagine how it might affect a young man for him to have been born, as it were, under the 'sign of the Messiah'. It would be wholly predictable that, as the meaning dawned on him, it would turn his head to some degree.

The accounts of Jesus' youth do in fact tell of a boy who, besides being highly precocious, was in several ways somewhat full of himself and even supercilious.[155] According to the Book of James (a near contemporary 'apocryphal gospel', supposedly written by Jesus' brother), Jesus during his 'wondrous childhood' struck fear and respect into his playmates by the tricks he played on them. Luke tells the revealing story of how, when Jesus was twelve, he went missing from his family group in Jerusalem and was later discovered by his worried parents in the Temple 'sitting in the midst of the doctors, both hearing them, and asking them questions.' His mother said: 'Son, why hast thou thus dealt with us? behold thy father and I have sought thee sorrowing.' To which the boy replied: 'How is it that ye sought me? wist ye not that I must be about my Father's business?'[156]

Still, no one can survive entirely on prophecy and promise. However special Jesus may have thought himself in theory, it is fair to assume he would also have wanted to try his hand in practice. He would have sought – privately as well as publicly –

confirmation of the reputation that was building up around him. He would have wanted concrete evidence that he did indeed have special powers.

In this Jesus would, again, not have been behaving so differently from other children. Almost every child probably seeks in small ways to test his fantasies, and conducts minor experiments to see just how far his powers extend. 'If I stare at that woman across the street, will she look round?' (Yes, every so often she will.) 'If I pray for my parents to stop squabbling, will they let up?' (Yes, it usually works.) 'If I carry this pebble wherever I go, will it keep the wolves away?' (Yes, almost always.) But we may guess that Jesus, with his especially high opinion of his own potential, might also have experimented on a grander scale. 'If I command this cup to break in pieces . . . ,' 'If I wish my brother's sandals to fly across the room . . . ,' 'If I conjure a biscuit to appear inside the urn . . .'

Unfortunately, unless Jesus really did have paranormal powers, such larger scale experiments would mostly have been unsuccessful. The facts of life would soon have told him there was a mismatch between the reality and his ambitions. Jesus would, however, have had to be a lesser child than obviously he was if he let the facts stand in the way – accepting defeat and possible humiliation. In such circumstances, the first step would be to *pretend*. And then, since pretence would never prove wholly satisfactory, the next step would be to *invent*.

Break the cup by attaching a fine thread and pulling . . . Hide the biscuit in your sleeve and retrieve it from the urn . . . By doing so, at least you get to see how it would feel *if* you were to have those powers. But what is more, provided you keep the way you do it to yourself, you get to see how other people react *if they believe* you actually do have special powers. And since you yourself have reason to think – and in any case they are continually telling you – that deep down you really do possess such powers (even if not in this precise way on the surface), this is fair enough.

So it might come about that the young Jesus might have begun to play deliberate tricks on his family and friends and even on himself – as indeed many other children, probably less talented and committed than he was, have been known to do when their reputation is at stake. Yet, although I say 'even on himself', it hardly seems likely he could have successfully denied to himself what he was up to. In such a situation you may be able to fool other people most of the time, but not surely yourself. Pretending is one thing. Deluding yourself is another thing entirely. It is nonetheless your reputation in your own eyes that really matters. Jesus' position therefore would not have been an easy or a happy one.

Imagine what it might feel like: to be pretty sure that you have paranormal powers, to have other people acclaiming what you do as evidence that you do indeed have these powers, but to know that none of it is for real. The more that other people fell for your inventions, the more you would yearn for evidence that you could in fact achieve the same results *without* having to pretend.

Suppose, then, that one day it came about that Jesus discovered, to his own surprise, that his experiments to test his powers had the desired effect *without* his using any sort of trick at all. What might he have made of it then?

I speak from some experience of these matters (and surely some of you have had like experiences too). Not, I should say, the experience of deliberately cheating (at least no more than anyone else), but rather of discovering as a child that certain of my own experimental 'try-ons' were successful when I least expected it.

For example, when I was about six years old I invented the game of there being a magic tree on Hampstead Heath, about half a mile from where we lived. Every few days I used to visit the tree, imagining to myself 'what if the fairies have left sweets there?' Sometimes I would say elaborate spells as I walked over there, although I would have felt a fool if anyone had heard me. Yet, remarkably, not long after I began these visits, my spells began to work. Time after time I found toffees in the hollow of the tree trunk.

Or, to take another example, when my brother and I were a bit older we started digging for Roman remains in the front garden of our house on the Great North Road in London. Each night we would picture what we would discover the next day, although we had little faith that anything would come of it. Resuming the dig one morning we did find, under a covering of light earth, two antique coins.

Draw your own conclusions about these particular examples. I have, however, a still better case history to tell, which may arguably provide a closer parallel to Jesus' own story. It concerns a teenage boy, Robert, who had become famous as a 'mini-Geller', a child spoon-bender, and whom I met while taking part in a radio programme about the paranormal. I repeat it here as I wrote it up some years ago:[157]

He had come with his father to the studio to take part in an experiment on psychic metal-bending. He was seated at a table, on which was a small vice holding a metal rod with a strain-gauge attached to it, and his task was to 'will' the rod to buckle.

Half an hour passed, and nothing happened. Then one of the production team, growing bored, picked up a spoon from a tea-tray and idly bent it in two. A few minutes later the producer noticed the bent spoon. 'Well I never,' she said. 'Hey Robert, I think it's worked.' Both Robert and his father beamed with pleasure. 'Yes,' Robert said modestly, 'my powers can work at quite a distance; sometimes they kind of take off on their own.'

Later that afternoon I chatted to the boy. A few years previously Robert had seen Uri Geller doing a television show. Robert himself had always been good at conjuring, and – just for fun – he had decided to show off to his family by bending a spoon by sleight of hand. To his surprise, his father had become quite excited and had told everybody they had a psychic genius in the family.

Robert himself, at that stage, had no reason to believe he had any sort of psychic power. But, still, he liked the idea and played along with it. Friends and neighbours were brought in to watch him; his Dad was proud of him. After a few weeks, however, he himself grew tired of the game and wanted to give up. But he did not want people to know that he had been tricking them: so, to save face, he simply told his father that the powers he had were waning.

Next day something remarkable happened. At breakfast, his mother opened the dresser and found that *all* the cutlery had bent. Robert protested it had nothing to do with him. But his Dad said: How did he know – perhaps he had done it unconsciously . . . There was no denying the cutlery had bent. And how *does* a person know if he has done something *unconsciously*? It was then that Robert realised he must be genuinely psychic.

Since that time, he had received plenty of confirmation. For example, he had only to think about a clock in the next room stopping, and when his father went in he would find that it had stopped. Or he would lie in bed thinking about the door-bell, and it would suddenly start ringing. He had to admit, however, that he was not exactly in control. And the trouble was that people kept on asking him to do more than was psychically within his power. So just occasionally he would go back to using some kind of trick . . . He would not have called it cheating, more a kind of psychic 'filling-in'.

Such was the boy's story. Then I talked to his father. Yes, the boy had powers all right: he had proved it time and again. But he was only a kid, and kids easily lose heart; they need encouraging. So, just occasionally, he – the father – would try to restore his son's confidence by arranging for mysterious happenings around the house . . . He would not have called it cheating either, more a kind of psychic 'leg-up'.

This *folie à deux* had persisted for four years. Both father and son were into it up to their necks, and neither could possibly let on to the other his own part in the deception. Not that either felt bad about the 'help' he was providing. After all, each of them had independent evidence that the underlying phenomenon was genuine.

The purpose of my telling this story is not to suggest any exact parallel with Jesus, let alone to point the finger specifically at anyone in Jesus' entourage, but rather to illustrate how easily an honest person *could* get trapped in such a circle: how a combination of his own and others' well-meaning trickery *could* establish a lifetime pattern of fraud laced with genuine belief in powers he did not have.

Still, I cannot deny that, once the idea has been planted that Jesus became caught up this way, it is hard to resist asking who might conceivably have played the supporting role. His mother? Or, if it continued into later years, John the Baptist? Or, later still, Judas, or one of the other disciples? Or all of them by turns? They all had a great investment in spurring Jesus on.

I do not want to suggest any exact parallel with anyone else either. But there are, I think, several clues that point to the possibility that just this kind of escalating *folie* might have played a part in the self-development of several other recent heroes of the paranormal.

Many modern psychics – notably the Victorian spiritualist D. D. Home, and in our own times Uri Geller – have been childhood prodigies. In Geller's case it is reported that 'At about the age of five he had the ability to predict the outcome of card games played by his mother. Also he noted that spoons and forks would bend while he was eating . . . At school his exam papers seemed identical to those of classmates sitting nearby . . . Classmates also reported that, while sitting near Geller, watches would move forwards or backwards an hour.'[158] And the same precocity is evident with several of those who have gone on to be, if not psychics themselves, powerful spokesmen for the paranormal. Arthur Koestler, for example, 'as a boy was in demand for table-turning sessions in Budapest'.[159]

It is also significant that when, as has frequently happened, celebrated psychics have been discovered to be cheating by non-paranormal means, they have nonetheless maintained that they did not *always* cheat. And it is significant too that their supporters have found this mixture of fake and real powers plausible and even reasonable. Of Geller, Koestler said: 'Uri is certainly 25 percent fraud and 25 percent showman, but 50 percent is real.'[160]

But on top of this there is the remarkable degree of self-assurance that these people have typically displayed. Again and again they have left others with the strong impression that they really do believe in their own gifts. Geller has impressed almost all who have met him – I include myself among them – as a man with absolute faith in his own powers. He comes over as being, as it were, the chief of his own disciples. And it is hard to escape the conclusion that in the past and maybe still today he has had incontrovertible evidence, as he sees it, that he is genuinely psychic.

Let me give a small example: when Geller visited my house and offered to bend a spoon, I reached into the kitchen drawer and picked out a spoon that I had put there for the purpose – a spoon from the Israeli airline with EL AL stamped on it. Geller at once claimed credit for this coincidence: 'You pick a spoon at random, and it is an Israeli spoon! My country! These things happen all the time with me. I don't know how I influenced you.' I sensed, as I had done with Robert, that Geller was really not at all surprised to find that he had, as he thought, influenced me by ESP. It was as if he took it to be just one more of the strange things that typically happen in his presence and which he himself could not explain *except* as evidence of his paranormal powers – 'those oddly clownish forces', as he called them on another occasion.[161]

The suspicion grows that someone else has over the years been 'helping' Geller without his knowing it, by unilaterally arranging for a series of apparently genuine minor miracles to occur in his vicinity. A possible candidate for this supportive role might be his 'shadow', Shipi Shtrang. Shtrang, Geller's best friend from childhood, later his agent and producer, and whose sister he married, would have had every reason to encourage Geller in whatever ways he could; and Geller himself is on record as saying that his powers improve when Shtrang is around.[162] (Noting the family relationship between Shtrang and Geller, we might note too that John the Baptist and Jesus were related: their mothers, according to Luke, were first cousins.) There is, however, no real evidence that Shtrang has been involved.

Now, maybe this all seems too much and too Machiavellian. If you do not see how these examples have any relevance to that of Jesus, you do not see it, and I will not insist by spelling it out further.

But now I have a different and more positive suggestion to make about why a man as remarkable as Jesus (and maybe Geller too) might have become convinced he could work wonders – and all the more strongly as his career progressed. It is that, in some contexts, the very fact of being remarkable may be enough to achieve semi-miraculous results.

I have as yet said little of Jesus as a 'healer'. My reason for not attending to this aspect of his art so far is that so-called 'faith healing' is no longer regarded by most doctors, theologians or parapsychologists as being strictly paranormal. Although, until quite recently, the miracle cures that Jesus is reported to have effected were thought to be beyond the scope of natural explanation, they no longer are so.

It is now widely recognised by the medical community that the course of many kinds of illness, of the body as well as of the mind, can be influenced by the patient's hopes and expectations and thus by the suggestions given him by an authority figure whom he trusts.[163] Not only can the patient's own mental state, guided by another, profoundly affect the way he himself perceives his symptoms, but it can also help mobilise his body's immunological defences to help achieve more lasting recovery. It is unfortunately true that only certain sorts of illness benefit, and that in any case the effects are not always permanent – so that the pain or the stiffness or the depression tends to return. But, at least in the short term, the cure can be dramatic.

To say that these cures have a normal explanation, however, is not to deny that they may often rely on the *idea* of a paranormal explanation. In fact, it is often quite clear that they do rely on it. It is for most people, including the healer, extremely hard to imagine how the voice or the touch of another person could possibly bring about a cure unless this other person were to have paranormal powers. It follows that the more the patient believes in these powers, the more he will be inclined to take the suggestions seriously – and the better they will work. Equally, the more the healer himself believes in his powers, the more he can make his suggestions sound convincing – and again the better they will work.

The consequence is that a kind of virtuous circle can be established. Success in bringing about a cure feeds back to the healer, boosting both his image in the eyes of the world and his image of himself. And thereafter nothing succeeds like more success. The process must of course be launched in some way. There has to be some degree of faith present initially, or otherwise the process cannot be expected to get going. But all that this requires is that there should already be some small reason – however unsubstantiated – why people should consider the healer a special person.

In Jesus' case we can assume that, for some or all of the reasons given earlier, his reputation as a potential miracle worker would in fact have been established early in his career and have run ahead of him wherever he went. He would very likely have found therefore that he had surprisingly well developed capacities for healing almost as soon as he first attempted it. And thereafter, as word spread, he would have got better at it still.

Thus, even if I am right in suggesting that his own or others' subterfuges played some part in creating the general mystique with which he was surrounded, we may guess that in this area Jesus would soon have found himself being given all the proof he could have asked for that he was capable of the real thing.

A minor but instructive parallel can again be provided by the case of Uri Geller. As far as I know, Geller has never claimed to be able to heal sick human beings, but he has – as we saw earlier – certainly claimed to be able to heal broken watches. In fact this was one of the phenomena by which he made his name.

In a typical demonstration Geller would ask someone to provide him with a watch that had stopped working and then, merely by grasping it in his hands for a minute or so, he would set it going again. In his own words (as ever, disarmingly ingenuous): 'I put an energy into it. I don't know what kind of energy it is, but apparently it fixes the watch. I don't think it will ever stop again. Maybe it will, but it's working because I'm around now.'[164]

As with human healing, this kind of watch-cure may in fact be perfectly genuine. It works when it does because the commonest cause of a watch breaking down is that it has become jammed with dust and thickened oil; and, if such a watch is held in the hand for a few minutes, body heat can warm and thin the oil and free the mechanism. When the psychologists David Marks and Richard Kammann, investigating the phenomenon, collected an unbiased sample of sixty one broken watches and subjected them merely to holding and handling, they found that 57 per cent were successfully started.[165] As with human healing, the cure does not work if there are actually parts broken or missing, nor is it usually permanent. But the effect is unexpected and impressive all the same.

The cure can easily *seem* paranormal. So, it is not surprising that few if any people watching Geller realised they could in fact perfectly well do it on their own without Geller's encouragement. What probably occurred, therefore, was another example of positive feedback. The higher were people's expectations of Geller's powers – based, as with Jesus, on his preceding reputation as a psychic – the more likely they were to rely on him to give the lead with his suggestions, and hence the more successes and the more his reputation spread.

But the crucial question now is what Geller himself thought of it. Is it possible that he was as impressed by his own achievements as everybody else? Suppose he himself had no more understanding of how watches work (at least until it was forcibly brought to his notice by sceptics) than Jesus had of how the immune system works. In that case he could easily have deduced that he really did have some kind of remarkable power. Like Jesus, he would have been finding that in one area he could genuinely meet his own and others' expectations of him.

And yet . . . And yet 'about the ninth hour Jesus cried with a loud voice, saying, My God, my God, why hast thou forsaken me?' Many have speculated on what he meant. But if at the point of death Jesus really did speak these opening lines of the Twenty-second Psalm, the clue may lie, I suggest, in the way the psalm continues. 'Why art thou so far from helping me? . . . Thou art he that took me out of the womb; thou didst make me hope when I was upon my mother's breasts.'[166]

It was Jesus' tragedy – his glory too – to have been cast in a role that no one could live up to. He did not choose to be taken from the womb of a particular woman, at a particular place, under a particular star. It was not his fault that he was given quite unrealistic hopes upon his mother's breasts. He did his best to be someone nobody can be. He tried to fulfil the impossible mission. He played the game in the only way it could be played. And the game unexpectedly played back – and overtook him.

15

Into the Light

Our interest in the case of Jesus should go beyond mere curiosity about how he did it or what his complex motivation may have been. Many centuries later his life and works continue to provide not merely an explanatory challenge, but a magnificent, if enigmatic, example of the power of supernatural belief. However, in making the excursion of the last two chapters and giving such a particular interpretation, I have revealed more of my own attitudes – and biases – than is consistent with any continuing attempt to present a 'balanced' treatment of the wider issues.

To speak plainly now, my own view is that the problem does not lie only with Jesus or his imitators. Rather, I think the search for the paranormal is *all* a big mistake. Sad to say, there has never yet been an authentic example of soul-power worth the name. The phenomena never pass muster. Their promoters always emerge with egg on their faces, with their hands in the till, or whatever other cliché suits the case.

I should not expect many readers to accept this conclusion without some degree of spiritual and perhaps even scientific resistance. But I submit that it is the only result we can come to when we examine the record and judge what we find there by the standard I suggested: namely, the argument from unwarranted design.

Let me reiterate what this strategy of examination amounts to. What we have to do is to ask of any candidate phenomena whether, if they are what they are supposed to be, they conform to the right kind of pattern. If they do not, and in particular if they seem to be inexplicably constrained so far as any paranormal explanation of their origin goes, we must conclude that they have failed to pass this 'design test'.

My view is that there are really not any well-documented phenomena that do pass. The reasons for failure go far beyond the fact of the phenomena being, as we have already noted, typically so unreliable and coy. The truth is that in every case, or at least in every set of cases taken together, where there might seem to be primary evidence of telepathy, mediumship, haunting, reincarnation, or whatever, it turns out that there are further limitations, oddities and idiosyncrasies that make no sense in terms of the paranormal explanation that is being offered.

Admittedly, in many cases we may have no clear idea of how else to explain the phenomena in normal terms. We may have to confess that we are baffled. But it is one of the strengths of the argument from unwarranted design that it does not depend on providing any particular alternative explanation – let alone on proving specific fraud or illusion or stupidity. It depends simply on judging the phenomena by their own lights.

I would accept of course that it is only when we do have an idea of what we are 'supposed' to be dealing with that we can possibly be in a position to say what would and would not be appropriate limitations and constraints. In other words, only when we have a good idea of what the underlying design process is *meant* to be, can we say what counts as unwarranted design. We shall, therefore, be able to bring this argument to bear only on those phenomena that people do indeed take to be evidence of some kind of specific paranormal power. And we should not expect to be able to apply it, for example, with phenomena that are by everybody's reckoning completely unaccountable.

However, this is not, for our present purposes, a serious problem. Even if certain investigators have been interested in exploring anomaly for its own sake, it is clear that most have had a much more positive agenda. Their ultimate goal has been to discover a set of present facts that not merely confirm the existence of the human soul, but confirm it in a way that specifically holds promise for the future. Hence the phenomena that have chiefly interested the searchers have always been those that can be supposed to be – and ideally can *only* be supposed to be – products of an individual's *paranormal powers of mind*, in other words those that can be interpreted as 'psychic'.

My immediate plan is to tackle some of these psychic phenomena at rather closer quarters – moving in from the age-old general concerns with the soul and mankind's future to concentrate on the more particular issues that have arisen in the relatively newly defined area of parapsychology and psychical research. The focus of the book will therefore become narrower, before it broadens out again

'Psi phenomena' can conveniently (though not entirely unambiguously) be subdivided into either cases where a mind is apparently engaged in paranormal *action* – psychokinesis or PK – or those where a mind is engaged in paranormal *reaction* or *reception* – extrasensory perception or ESP. I shall try to show how once an investigator does in fact decide to treat a phenomenon as being a case of PK or ESP he is in effect adopting a particular theory of it and implicitly committing himself to a particular type of causal explanation. From the critics' point of view, therefore, the situation immediately becomes one where the argument as to what is warranted or unwarranted by this explanation can begin to bite.

I shall not make a detailed inventory of claim and counterclaim in relation to particular examples. The history of these has been well told elsewhere,[167] and it would be tedious, as well as somewhat presumptuous of me, to pick over the record in an effort to assess the credentials of every candidate phenomenon in turn. Rather, what I shall do is discuss the principles involved in putting this kind of evidence through the design test, with illustration as needs be.

16
P? K?

Psychokinetic phenomena can be broadly defined as cases where it appears that the mind or soul is inducing material changes at a remote location in the outside world, without the mediation of any force or process known to science. In general it can be assumed that the state of mind responsible is some kind of wish or request – a mental picture of a desired goal – and that the material change that occurs is in the direction of this goal.

It is perhaps an open question whether the effect is produced directly by the mind acting at a distance from its home base in the body, or whether it involves the mind leaving the body and visiting the remote location, or even whether it involves the mind relaying the request to an independent supernatural agency. The simplest assumption, and the one I think most people would adopt to start with, is that there is indeed a direct causal link. But, whatever the means, the effect involves a miraculous transfer of information and of energy and in many cases the creation or destruction of matter.

The cases of most practical concern and human interest are those where the mental state responsible belongs to a living person: as when someone is able – merely by wishing it – to bring about rain, to levitate a table, to remove a tumour, to influence the throw of a die, to encourage seeds to grow, to puncture the tyres of a car, to make someone turn round merely by staring at their back, etc. But there are also cases where the mental state can be assumed to belong to the spirit of a person who has died: as when a poltergeist or ghost is able to move the furniture, to clank chains, to direct the movements of a ouija board, to produce rapping sounds and answer questions (one rap for 'yes', two for 'no'), to appear as a luminescent spectral form, etc. And there are cases too where the mental state belongs neither to a dead nor to a living person but to some kind of deity: as when a god or angel or devil is able to cause a flood, to make a statue weep, to intercede in a battle, to project the image of the Virgin Mary on to a church wall, to make a woman pregnant, and so on.

Now, since we shall be looking for evidence of uncalled-for and unreasonable constraints, we need to know what kinds of limitations on PK – if any – we might actually expect. And, as a guide, we can start by considering the types of limitation that apply to people's normal psychomotor powers, their ability to get things done by ordinary bodily means.

Here there are of course *physical* constraints: certain tasks may be beyond a person's strength or his dexterity or may require accessory tools he has not got (e.g. he may be unable to tear a telephone directory in half, or to pick up a single grain of salt, or to sign his name without a pen). There are *cognitive* constraints: certain tasks may be beyond his skill or his intelligence (e.g. he may be unable to play the violin, or to juggle seven oranges at once, or to draw a perfect circle freehand). There are *volitional* or *emotional* constraints: certain tasks may be beyond what he is willing to engage in (e.g. he may be unable to bring himself to dive from the high board, or to handle a live snake, or to take his clothes off in public).

Should we expect similar sorts of limitations to apply to PK?

As far as physical and cognitive constraints go, we might expect PK to be completely unconstrained. Since *ex hypothesi* the person's mental state is producing the material change without any of the usual intermediate steps – without involving either any physical effector organ or any intellectual construction – then, provided only that he can picture in his mind what he wants the end result to be, it should be within his paranormal grasp. The fact that a person is, say, too weak or clumsy or insufficiently knowledgeable or skilled to do something normally would be no reason why he should not do it paranormally.

Volitional constraints, however, would be another matter. Any constraint that operates at the level of what a person is willing to do – in other words, at the level of the initiating mental state – is presumably going to be just as limiting on PK as on normal psychomotor power. So we should expect at least the usual emotional blocks, inhibitions and preferences – the affective, aesthetic and ethical constraints that govern normal behaviour. But more than that, since the lack of physical and cognitive constraints would mean that the use of paranormal power carries additional risks and responsibilities, we might expect there to be extra 'rules of paranormal conduct' (rather as a giant has to be extra careful not to cause harm, or a genius to be extra careful not to seem arrogant).

In relation to this need to show particular restraint with PK power, the philosopher Stephen Braude has observed that the great spirit mediums of the nineteenth century – who could, Braude believes, have done whatever they liked – 'considered opportunistic uses of the power of the spirit to be morally inconceivable or repugnant'; and that in general 'conspicuous manifestations of everyday psi might be contrary to our psychological welfare or interests'.[168] Thus we should not be surprised and certainly not suspicious if someone who did indeed have the power to win at roulette, or to unlock a safe or to afflict an enemy with boils, were in fact to resist the temptation to do so.

So far, then, the only constraints on PK that we would have reason to expect would seem to be those imposed by the subject's willingness to contemplate the end result. In principle almost anything imaginable – at least anything a person would let himself imagine – should be attainable by paranormal means. 'Ask, and it shall be given you; seek, and ye shall find; knock, and it shall be opened unto you.'[169]

In practice I think we can assume that almost nobody believes that this is how it really is. Or if they ever did believe so, they have presumably been quickly disillusioned. And yet perhaps their disillusionment has not been total. Indeed, anyone who looks back with a sympathetic eye over the plethora of PK phenomena that have been reported down the ages might be struck at first not by the limitations but by the freedom, not by the paucity of phenomena but by just how much has apparently been achieved. Name it, and there is probably a case on record of someone somewhere having pulled it off by paranormal means. Nothing, it seems, has been in practice too big (did not Joshua destroy the walls of Jericho?), nothing too small (have not the subjects of recent experiments been able to affect the radioactive decay of single atoms?), nothing too complicated (are not psychic surgeons able to accomplish the most tricky medical procedures?), nothing too presumptuous (did not Geller, in a casual moment, stop Big Ben?). True, no one has yet succeeded in turning lead permanently into gold or in living for ever – but maybe no one has yet tried hard enough to do so.

The only slight puzzle might seem to be why these powers should have been granted to certain special individuals and not others (and particularly not oneself) and why they should not work more reliably or when they are most needed. But then, as we have seen, this sort of semi-random selectivity coupled with a certain degree of anarchy has always been a trademark of the paranormal, going back to biblical times – and it may be less puzzling if we see it as part of the tradition.

But it is when we look more closely and ask about *who* precisely has done *what*, *when* and *where*, that these 'slight puzzles' begin to become serious worries. For then we are bound to note, not so much evidence of there being an excusable degree of randomness, as evidence of there being some highly peculiar *patterns* in the distribution of talent, the frequency of its deployment, the circumstantial details and the nature of the effects. Impressive as the record may look overall, when it is taken item by item and psychic by psychic it begins to look unaccountably queer.

Consider some representative examples of the kind of major phenomena that have been championed over time both by lay observers and by parapsychological investigators. What do we see laid out for our edification and instruction?

Here we have an Italian monk flying through the air, there an

English peasant woman giving birth to rabbits.[170] Here a Scottish gentleman making an accordion float in midair and play soulful tunes, there a French maiden producing 'full form materialisations' of the King of Bulgaria via her mouth. Here a Russian grandmother stopping a frog's heart from beating, there a twenty-stone matron teleporting across London. Here an Indian yogi creating fire out of nothing, and there a Polish journalist conjuring up fairy lights that dance on the keys of a piano. Here a Chicago bellhop taking fuzzy photographs of a toy aeroplane by merely staring at the camera, and there (I would not want to leave him out) a young Israeli former fashion model bending the Marquess of Bath's soup ladle.

Assuming that the phenomena reported *are* indeed examples of PK, that is to say of wishes being translated into external facts, the most telling feature would seem to be the utter arbitrariness of who can achieve what. To start with, nothing would have led us to expect that the wishes of *these* (otherwise unremarkable) people would be so much more effective than those of their relatively impotent peers. Even after these individuals have come to our notice, nothing about them – personal merit, mental capacities, genetic constitution, specialised training – provides obvious grounds for their being able to operate at such a different level from the rest of us. Maybe there are indeed unknown constitutional reasons which, if we only knew them, would explain why these individuals should be prodigies, even *idiots savants*, of the paranormal. But as things are, the only common factors that stand out are a tendency to self-advertisement and in many of the cases a known propensity to combine their 'genuinely' paranormal acts with 'supplementary' faking.

Suppose, however, we give them the benefit of the doubt and allow, nonetheless, that the members of this motley group are for some reason genuinely paranormally gifted. Even then, nothing would have led us to expect that their gifts would be so *specialised*, so kitschy, so preposterous – typically, so irrelevant to anyone's real needs or expressed desires. There can be no question about their ability to amaze and shock us with their unexpected phenomena – the ectoplasmic extrusions, breaking glasses, sounding trumpets, spinning compass needles, misbehaving recording apparatus, etc., etc. But no question either about how surprisingly lacking in human relevance or purpose it all is.

Is it conceivable that the failure of these paranormal specialists to perform as we might hope and expect is the result of volitional constraints, of the kind discussed above? Could it all be due to self-censorship or modesty, a need not to show off or to offend? Not likely. If shyness were an issue, we might expect, for example, that a good deal of what could be done by PK would be reserved for times when no one else was looking and the potentially embarrassing performance would never come to light. But – though it is of course difficult to gather evidence on this – the truth seems to be the precise opposite. PK demonstrations are reserved for public consumption, and the rest of the time the super-psychic goes about his or her life as if not in possession of *any* special power.

Furthermore, not only are many of the (few) things that these people *do* succeed in doing immodest in the extreme, but there would seem to be many things that they do *not* succeed in doing (or do not even try) that, if only they did, would gain them nothing but social credit and respect. So many ways that their powers might be made to serve the public good, if only they would arrange to use them in the right way. But, unfortunately, it seems to be a general characteristic of PK that the person responsible cannot 'arrange' to do anything much with them, even if he would like to. Nor can he do things on demand from others. There has never yet been a psychic who could, for example, take instructions from an audience about what *they* would like to see done. 'Simon says: turn the light off, levitate that pencil, ring the bell . . .' The psychic has his routine. The audience must take it or leave it. But if, as it should be, it is merely a matter of his *willingness* to act, this is, if you think about it, a bit odd.

No, it is perfectly obvious that there have in fact always been additional major constraints at work, limiting what can be achieved by PK. Just as with the earlier examples of unwarranted design – the taciturn 'talking parrot', the coy 'impossible triangle' or hat-bound 'clever Hans' – we are here dealing with phenomena that would seem to have far too many conditions attached to their expression: too many conditions, that is, for them to be regular examples of what they are theoretically supposed to be, namely the direct influence of mind on matter. Indeed, so obvious is it that, if we were to stick with the simple suppositions about how PK works, outlined above, we could say without more ado that *all* the candidate phenomena show signs of there being some *other* design process at work, *all* fail the test. We could conclude, in short, that this sort of generic PK must be a fantasy.

Might we then be able to modify the theory of PK, so as to give some of the phenomena that do occur at least a better chance of passing?

There are two possibilities, which I mentioned at the start, that could perhaps go some way towards this. Both would retain the idea that PK is producing the material change without involving any of the usual bodily effectors, but both would bring in an intermediary operator of another unusual kind.

The first possibility would be to suppose that, even though PK does not involve using the physical body as such, it does involve using some kind of phantom body or para-body working at a distance. In other words, we might suppose that, when someone wishes to achieve something at a remote location, the result of his *wishing* to be there, doing whatever it is, is to create a phantom of himself which then travels to the place and takes the job in hand. It would be like dreaming of visiting somewhere and making something happen there – and then, on waking, finding that one's dream body had really done so.

But a person's phantom body, apart from its ability to act at a distance from its home, might have no greater powers than his normal body. If, for example, someone could not play the piano under normal circumstances, then very likely his phantom would not be able to play the piano either. In which case we would have a reasonable explanation for why there should be a whole lot of otherwise unexpected physical and cognitive constraints on his ability to do things by PK. Indeed, in general, we would expect a person to be able to achieve by PK only what he could have achieved by direct contact if he had been there.

Furthermore, the ability to project one's phantom body

reliably to a target location might actually not be something everybody is good at. It might in fact be something of an art, requiring special training and/or native talent (as, for example, throwing one's voice does). Then, presumably, some people – and who knows in advance who they would be – would be considerably better at it than others. In that case we would have a reasonable explanation for why there should be such large individual differences in PK ability.

The other possible way around the problems would be still more radical. It would be to suppose that PK does not in reality work by direct action at all, even by a phantom body, but rather it works by engaging the assistance of an independent agency. In other words, we might suppose that, when someone wishes to achieve something, this wish gets drawn to the attention of a higher authority, which then makes its own decision about whether to grant it. This authority we should assume is all-powerful, but choosy. Man proposes, but God (for we may as well call him that) disposes.

It would follow presumably that a person could achieve by PK only such things as God approves of. There would therefore be in effect another layer of volitional constraints, involving not so much the person's own preferences and rules of conduct as God's: and no doubt God's decisions as to which wishes get fulfilled and which do not might seem by human standards arbitrary. His ways are not our ways, and our ways not his ways. In which case we would here have another possible explanation for why human PK abilities sometimes appear random. Moreover, if we assume that it would be God's prerogative to favour certain special individuals over others, then here too we would have grounds for expecting that some people – and again who knows who they would be – would have more PK ability than others.

Each of these suggestions would obviously bring with it several additional problems, and it is by no means clear that either of them amounts to a coherent theory. Nonetheless, each does have some intuitive appeal. On the one hand, the idea of a phantom body, acting as a paranormal surrogate for the real one, features strongly in folklore; and on the other hand, the idea of wishes being granted by God (or it might be one of his saints) is central to religious assumptions about why and how prayers work (when they do). Perhaps we should not be surprised to find thoughtful people coming round to these kinds of explanations – especially once they realise that the generic version of PK cannot cope.

Yet, if the advantage of these alternative theories of PK is supposed to be that each in its own way can resolve – or at least relieve – all the problems associated with the limitations on the expression of PK, we have to ask how they themselves would fare in practice with the factual evidence. Or rather – since this is the way round I have been arguing it – how the factual evidence would fare with these alternative theories.

The truth is that the evidence would remain, so far as I can see, a total mystery and a total mess.

The idea of a phantom body is, when it comes to it, really much less useful than we might have thought. It could, for sure, help to explain why so many of the things that are achieved by PK are of a kind that would be within a person's normal capacity if only he were bodily present to do them. And it could explain why, moreover, certain sorts of things never happen at all: why, for example, no one has ever been known to succeed by PK in stopping a charging bull or in creating a Leonardo painting. But it would go almost no way towards resolving the particular puzzles of who can do what, when. Even with the semi-normal limitations that the use of a phantom body would impose, we would still expect psychics to have a much wider repertoire than they actually do have. And even supposing that not everyone might have the faculty of projecting themselves in this way (though it is not at all clear why such a useful skill should not have evolved to be part of everyone's natural endowment), we should still expect it to be more widely shared than apparently it is.

The idea of an independent supernatural agency is perhaps potentially more helpful. It might make sense of why there is no simple relationship between wishing and achieving – though only because, in effect, it passes the explanatory buck over to God. But even so it would still leave us with a whole lot of explaining to do. For even granted that we might expect God to be relatively inscrutable, absolutely nothing would lead us to anticipate that he would have quite such a bizarre sense of priorities, such strange taste in the people whom he favours and such a gimcrack mind. Should we be considering the possibility that God himself does not have an entirely free hand in what he can do, that he is not in fact *all*-powerful?

Maybe it is significant that, even after people have 'passed over to the other side' and ought therefore to be closer to God literally as well as metaphorically, the quality of the PK phenomena they produce does not greatly improve. A cold vapour oozes through the bedroom, a candle is mysteriously snuffed out, a potted cactus falls to the floor, the words I AM FRED are written in lipstick on the bathroom mirror, the cat looks terrified, and so on. Such evidence certainly suggests that ghosts and poltergeists are as restricted in the range of their effects as living beings are – which does perhaps indicate that the problem is a general one, which goes right up to the top.

But more significant still is the fact that so many of the phenomena directly attributable to God himself or to his right-hand agents are in the same class too. A saint's blood liquefies, a concrete statue comes to life, a picture-book image of the Virgin Mary appears on the wall of an Irish church. In every case, there are the same unexpected conditions and petty restrictions – the blood in the vial requires the helping hand of a priest, the statue in the grotto only rocks its head when it is seen at night and the halo is lit up by electric light bulbs, the image on the church wall at Knock shows flat figures that neither move nor speak and happens to resemble closely a lantern-slide on sale in Dublin.

Maybe, as Dr Johnson remarked about a woman's preaching or a dog's walking on its hind legs, the noteworthy thing about these miracles is that, even though they are not done well, they are done at all. Maybe the truth is that God himself really is – how may we best put this? – 'psychokinetically challenged'. In that case it would certainly be very hard to say what PK phenomena achieved with God's assistance would be warranted by the explanatory model. But the better course for those who care for explanatory sanity must surely be to leave God out of it and somehow or other put human psychology back in.

17
E?S?P?

If we now turn our attention to extrasensory perception, we can apply much the same mix of arguments as we did with PK.

Extrasensory perception can be defined broadly as what happens when someone's mind comes under the influence of distant events without there being the opportunity for observation or communication by any channel known to science. In most cases ESP manifests itself as a change in what the person knows or believes or feels, and it can be assumed that this change is towards the person's becoming aware that the external event is happening. ESP is, therefore, in effect the reverse of PK. With PK, a mental state – a picture of what the subject wishes to happen – *creates* the distant event that corresponds to this picture. With ESP, a mental state – a picture of what is already happening – *gets created by* or *in response to* the distant event.

Cases of ESP are often divided for convenience into two categories, clairvoyance and telepathy. With clairvoyance, the event that the subject becomes aware of is a material fact about the world: as when someone is able to read what is inside a sealed envelope, to visualise that a child is in imminent danger, to describe to a stranger the layout of his sitting room, etc. With telepathy, the event that the subject becomes aware of is the content of another mind: as when someone is able to recognise which playing card another person is looking at, to anticipate that someone is about to call them on the telephone, to feel that an absent loved one is in trouble, etc. The other mind does not, however, have to be that of a living person. It could be the mind of a departed spirit or even a divinity: as, maybe, when someone is able to receive messages from the dead, to undergo regression to an earlier life, to meet his ancestors in a dream, or to hear God speaking to him.

Now, since we shall be looking, as before, for evidence of uncalled-for and unreasonable constraints, we need to know what kinds of limitations on ESP – if any – we might actually expect. And, as a guide, we can start by considering the types of limitation that apply to people's normal powers of sensory perception and communication.

We can note again the three categories of constraint. There are physical constraints: a person may be unable to receive certain kinds of message because the physical signal that carries it never reaches him, or because even if it does he is not equipped with appropriate sense organs to pick it up. There are cognitive constraints: a person may be unable to interpret the message once he has received it because he lacks the information-processing capacity or the interpretative skill required to work out what the signal means. There are volitional – though let's now call them attentional – and emotional constraints: a person may show 'perceptual sets' and 'perceptual defences' – preferentially tuning in to some kinds of message or blocking or tuning out others.

Should we expect similar types of limitation to apply to ESP?

If ESP really is a matter of the image of an external event being impressed directly on the subject's mind, then presumably there should be few if any of the normal physical or cognitive constraints. Provided only that the event in question is one that the receiver can in principle 'get his mind round' (and not something totally alien to his way of thinking or feeling), then the simple fact that the event is happening ought to be enough to make it extrasensorily perceivable, even if normal perception would not be practicable. It would follow for example that, since clairvoyance does not involve the use of eyes, lack of light should be no hindrance – and it should presumably be just as possible to picture what is happening at night as in the daytime. Or, since telepathic communication does not involve any intermediary spoken language, lack of a common vocabulary should not matter – and an

Englishman ought to have no special problem in reading the mind of, say, an Eskimo.

As with PK, however, the question of volitional or attentional constraints would be another matter. To start with, there must presumably be some way of limiting the quantity of information that comes in, some kind of filter: otherwise, there would be nothing to stop all the facts and thoughts in the world coming through at once and blowing the subject's mind. It would be reasonable to expect to find ESP showing clear evidence of selective attention to a particular region of space or a particular person, just as normally occurs when someone chooses to look in a particular direction or to listen out for a particular voice. And we might also expect there to be the typical emotional biases and preferences: emotionally loaded signals ought to have a better chance of being picked up than neutral ones – although certain particularly disturbing signals might be selectively blocked off.

Again, as we noted in relation to PK, the lack of the usual physical and cognitive constraints would mean that the use of ESP to pick up information carries additional risks and responsibilities. ESP could, for example, be used to gain secret information and to intrude on other people's privacy. Hence we might expect there to be certain extra self-imposed restrictions in the interests of decency (rather as there are special rules governing telephone tapping by the police, or the use of long lenses by investigative journalists). We should not be surprised, and certainly not suspicious, if someone who did have the extrasensory capacity to spy on a couple making love, or to cheat in an exam, or to pry into another person's private thoughts, were in fact to turn down the opportunity.

These things considered, we should expect that, even if ESP is not completely unrestricted, it should in theory provide a communication channel of enormous potential. Once people have mastered the skill – if that is what is required – they ought to be able to exploit it in a huge number of ways. (Rather as, when a child knows how to read, a whole world of books is opened up to her.)

But what of the reality? At first examination, the reality does indeed look promising. Putting everything together, the evidence that has accumulated over the ages is undeniably impressive. Most things that could in principle become known to a human mind have, it seems, sometime, somewhere become known to someone by clairvoyance or telepathy. From detailed visions of sinking ships to vague impressions of a loved one needing help, from accurate descriptions of where a treasure is hidden to a general sense that the card in question is a spade – the amount of information that has been exchanged over the psychic airwaves has arguably been truly phenomenal.

Certain people are, admittedly, for some not very obvious reason much more 'sensitive' than others. And even with the best of them ESP still seems to be something of a hit-and-miss affair. But again, as with PK, it can at least be said that this variableness has always been part of an honourable tradition.

Indeed, it would seem that even the great artists of classical times had their bad days. When King Croesus of Lydia in 550 BC conducted one of the first experimental tests of ESP, he found that out of the seven best oracles in the country only one was on form. Croesus sent messengers out with instructions to approach each of the oracles on the same date and ask, 'What is the King of Lydia doing today?' And then in a move designed to eliminate mere guesswork, he proceeded on that date to do something most unlikely: he stewed up a lamb along with a tortoise in a bronze cauldron. Five of the oracles failed outright to get it, one came close, but only the Delphic oracle described the scene spot on.[171] (You win some, you lose some – and when Croesus followed up his exercise in consumer research by taking the Delphic oracle's ambiguous advice about his battle plans, he famously lost the lot.)

Nothing is perfect. But it can fairly be said that the overall picture is really not too bad. And we should note in particular that even if some people evidently have more ESP ability than others, the ability is by no means restricted to a tiny group of specialists. While PK, by contrast, is relatively rarely encountered in everyday life, ESP – at least on a small scale – seems actually to be quite commonplace. Most people know of examples in their personal experience, and everyone has been told of amazing cases by their friends. What is more, there is, we are reliably informed, a good deal of confirmatory evidence from laboratory studies: evidence that shows that otherwise unremarkable people, brought in off the street, can in fact demonstrate a little bit of ESP more or less to order.

So far, then, it would seem that the believers can take heart. There is no reason to suppose that the evidence for ESP is going the same way as PK.

Yet, as with PK, it is when we look more closely at the pattern of the hits and misses, at who is able to gain what kind of information in what circumstances, that we cannot but notice unaccountable peculiarities emerging. The problem is not merely that the evidence for ESP appears, in close-up, to be more and more patchy, it is that it begins to look quite dotty. Little islands of it here and there, and nothing in between. No rhyme or reason for what gets through and what does not.

My point is not that someone who genuinely possesses the ability for ESP – or any other form of psychic power – must be assumed to be capable of doing *absolutely everything*. It is, rather, that if a person has indeed been using this power when he performs a particular task, he should at the very least be able to use it to perform other *comparable* tasks – comparable, that is, according to our understanding of what the power involves.

In short, we should expect to find that a person's psychic abilities – like other more normal abilities – will *transfer* across situations. But this is precisely what we never do find.

Suppose we examine the performance of those individuals whose reputation has run highest – the soothsayers, mediums, clairvoyants, and others, who in the tradition of the oracles have made a public show of their specially developed powers of second sight.

No doubt their performances have sometimes been strikingly successful and convincing to many who have witnessed them. They have regularly done certain things which *without a faculty of ESP* they ought not to have been able to do. Yet almost never can it be said that they have done even a tiny portion of the things which *with a faculty of ESP* they ought to have been able to do. Grant someone a genuine faculty of 'mind reading' or 'remote viewing' and you would hardly expect them to expend it on the miserly demonstrations that have always been typical – the paranormal equivalent of parlour-game tricks, hunt the thimble, blind man's buff, charades.

Instead of proving their powers in an open and straightforward way, it seems to delight these gifted psychics to play and tease. Instead of communicating or perceiving in any ordinary sense of the words, they prefer to filch and purloin information. And even then they pass on only smatterings, hedged with caveats and couched in riddles.

Here we have someone divining the contents of a locked casket; there reading a fortune in the tea-leaves (or the tarot cards or the sparrow's entrails . . .). Here describing the owner of a pocket-watch by the vibrations he picks up; there reading the Bible with her fingers (and there again, to cap this, reading it with the skin of her backside).

Seldom if ever will these paranormal scryers respond to specific requests of which they have had no warning – and then only if they can have face-to-face or, better still, palm-to-palm contact with whoever knows the secret. When allowed to run free without feedback from the sitter, instead of divining information of real human interest they blather, duck and weave – in the manner of 'if you go to war a mighty nation will fall', or, less portentously, 'I'm picking up a scar on your left knee', 'I think you know who I mean when I say "John" ', 'the number you are thinking of contains either a 3 or a 7'.

Well might T. H. Huxley remark (in relation to communications from the dead, but it might have been about 'thought transfer' in general): 'The only good that I can see in the demonstration of the truth of "spiritualism" is to furnish an additional argument against suicide. Better live a crossing-sweeper than die and be made to talk twaddle by a medium hired at a guinea a séance!'[172]

Moreover, as with PK, these powers – which, in view of the soul's reputation for shyness, might be expected to work best of all when out of the limelight – appear paradoxically to be reserved almost entirely for public consumption. A clairvoyant may regularly demonstrate to an amazed audience his ability to tell what is written on any page of any book taken at random; but never, so far as I know, has it been heard of for this same clairvoyant to sit reading a novel with its covers closed (or – why not? – while the book remains on the shelf in the next room, or in the bookshop).

Strangely enough, instead of conferring the countless benefits we might expect, these powers seem good for only one thing: namely, to take part in stage-shows to prove that they exist.

And the experimental evidence? If there are such obvious problems with 'naturally occurring' cases of ESP, is there anything better to be found in laboratory-based studies?

Although they have been surrounded with more scientific mystique than the studies of spontaneous phenomena, the laboratory tests of ESP have basically come out of the same stable. And it is all of a piece with this tradition that, just as there have been specially gifted performers on the stage or in the drawing room, so there have turned out to be specially gifted experimenters in the parapsychological laboratory: individuals who, either by their own virtues or with the assistance of good subjects, have obtained results that other experimenters cannot match.

Many things could be said about the unexpected constraints that apply to ESP in the laboratory – that is, about when, where and in whose hands these experiments have 'worked' to give positive results. But they can, I think, all be summarised by one depressing rule (perhaps it should be called Sod's Law of Parapsychological Research): this is that the only experiments that have ever worked fall either (a) into the class of those for which there is no independent confirmation that things happened as reported, or (b) into the class of those where it has turned out later that – either by bad luck or bad design – the positive results might possibly have been due to something other than ESP.

The former class I shall leave on one side for the moment. But I can illustrate the latter by considering one recent and widely publicised example of an experimental study. This is the major study of telepathy that was undertaken by the American researcher Charles Honorton and his colleagues between 1986 and 1989.[173]

I shall break with the convention of this book and describe this study with a certain amount of experimental detail.

Honorton used a variation of what is called the Ganzfeld technique. In essence the set-up was this. One person, the Receiver, sat in an isolated room of the laboratory wearing ping-pong balls over his eyes and with white noise playing into his ears through headphones (the idea being that in this state of blankness – the ganzfeld – he would be in an especially receptive state for ESP). Another person, the Sender, sat in another room down the corridor and watched a film clip on a TV screen, which could be one of four possibilities, randomly selected. The Receiver was asked to report the images that entered his mind. At the end of the experiment the Receiver was shown the four possible clips and, with the help of a written transcript of his imagery (and in some cases with active encouragement from the experimenter), he was asked to say which of the clips he thought he had been picking up.

Overall, using 241 different Receivers in 355 sessions, Honorton got strikingly positive results – with the correct target being chosen 35 per cent of the time rather than 25 per cent as would have been expected if the choice was random. Although 35 per cent is not of course anywhere near a perfect score, this figure – with such a large number of trials – is hugely significant statistically, and it provides very strong grounds for saying that there must have been some kind of information transfer between Sender and Receiver.

Honorton's conclusion – widely accepted not only among professional parapsychologists but much farther afield – was that this information transfer must indeed have been genuinely paranormal. But was it? Further investigation has shown that all was not well with these experiments.

At least two problems stand out. First, as Honorton acknowledged at the back of his published paper, during the first four-fifths of the trials there was unfortunately a flaw in the apparatus, such that the sound from the film clip was leaking ever so slightly into the Receiver's headphones. Second, inadequate precautions were taken to isolate the experimenter from the Sender, so that the experimenter by hearing the Sender's reactions to the film clips might have received hints about what the Sender was seeing (and remember that during some, but not all, of the trials, the experimenter himself helped the Receiver with making his final judgement).

Richard Wiseman, a friend and former colleague of Honorton, has subsequently reanalysed the raw data trial by trial and shown that *all* the positive results can be attributed to those trials in which one or other of these sources of 'sensory leakage' was at least a possibility. In fact, in the relatively few trials (100 in all) where such leakage of information would *not* have been possible the Receivers did no better than chance (26 per cent correct).[174]

Now, the fact that the only trials that 'worked' were those where there could have been an explanation other than ESP, does not of course prove that the positive results on these trials were definitely not due to ESP. Indeed, I would not be surprised to hear a defender of the experiments arguing not only that these results actually still were due to ESP, but that it just happens to be true that for some unknown reason ESP works best when it is not the only means of information transfer available. (I am not joking – this is just the kind of argument that gets put about among committed psychical researchers.) But it hardly needs stressing that nothing in our theory of ESP would have led us in advance to expect this. When a pattern emerges 'for some unknown reason', this is precisely when we should say, 'Whoa, I smell a rat.'

The conclusion has to be that with ESP in general it *is* the same story as PK. One way and another, the phenomena never live up to what might be expected. Excuses have to be found, special factors mentioned, appeals made to unanticipated quirks and conditions. But in the end the constraints on the kinds of information a person can apparently acquire by paranormal means are too numerous, too peculiar, and too suggestive of normal human agency to be worth even trying to accommodate within the framework I outlined at the start of the chapter.

As with PK it might of course be possible to suggest *ad hoc* ways of modifying the framework so as to be able to explain more of what is actually observed. Thus, perhaps we should be thinking in terms of each human being having a phantom body that can roam abroad and relay information back to its owner – so that when someone wishes to see what is happening at a remote location he sends his phantom out on a mission to have a look and report back? In which case perhaps we would have a perfectly good explanation for why a person should be able to discover by ESP only what he could, with a little subterfuge, have discovered by normal perception?

Or perhaps we should be thinking in terms of some kind of celestial information service, so that when someone wishes to find out something he calls up God and humbly asks *him* to take a look and report back? In which case perhaps we would have an explanation for why a person should have so little control over when and where ESP will work for him – as if indeed it depends on the co-operation of an awkward third party who very likely has his own agenda?

But no. The arguments against taking such baroque suggestions seriously were given at the end of the last chapter and do not need rehearsing.

18

Need You Ask

I want to return briefly to the question of experiments. If this had been a different kind of book, I might well have wanted to discuss some others of the hundreds of experimental studies that over the last century have made strong claims to demonstrate the reality of PK or ESP. My excuse for not doing so here is simple. It is that, as most of the experimenters themselves would grudgingly agree, not one of these studies has ever demonstrated that the paranormal phenomena occur *other than* when a particular experimenter tests for them with particular subjects under particular conditions.[175] These constraints are as clear a sign as need be of unwarranted design. Unless and until there is evidence of phenomena that behave more in line with our advance expectations, I see no reason to take these studies seriously (at least not as demonstrations of the paranormal – though maybe we should take them very seriously as demonstrations of something else).

There is, however, a further observation I would make that bears indirectly on every study in the field. It is simply this. Quite apart from any other unexpected limitations, it seems to be the case that experiments to test for ESP or PK have 'worked', if they have done, only if they were *intended* to be experiments to test for ESP or PK. That is to say, evidence of a paranormal ability to pick up information has regularly been found in studies that have been deliberately designed to look for it; but, strangely enough, when similar tests of people's ability to pick up information have been carried out in the course of inquiring into something else unrelated to the paranormal, there has never, so far as I know, been any such evidence at all.

Compare the following two hypothetical situations. In the first, a parapsychologist holds up a card with some letters written on the back of it, and asks you to try to say what they are. This is a test of ESP. In the second, an optometrist holds up a card with some letters written on the front of it, getting smaller and smaller, and likewise asks you to try to say what they are. This is merely an eye test. The two tests are obviously quite similar. But they have been undertaken with different ends in view, and have been given different names.

What difference would this labelling make? All the difference in the world, apparently. For in the first situation, even though the letters are completely invisible, you would, if the parapsychologists' story is to be believed, have a fair chance of being able to read them by ESP; but in the second, once the size of the letters is too small you would, if the optometrists are to be believed, have no chance of reading them at all.

Now it is true that this eye test is a relatively informal procedure, and it might be argued that a small amount of ESP would actually go undetected by the optometrist. But the fact is that just such tests of the limits of people's normal powers of perception have been run again and again in conventional psychological laboratories, using methods that would be exquisitely sensitive to any kind of information transfer. This is precisely how psychologists measure such things as visual acuity, hearing thresholds, discriminative ability, and so on. And in literally thousands of experiments they have established that there really are sensory stimuli that people *cannot* see, cannot hear, cannot feel, cannot smell, cannot discriminate, cannot recognise, even when these stimuli are physically distinct and known to another person. In these thousands of experiments they have therefore incidentally, but nonetheless conclusively, shown that ESP does not occur.

Is it possible that the stimuli that are used for testing in the conventional psychology laboratory are just too trivial or insignificant to register in the paranormal lens? In case anyone should want to argue this, let me mention a study of a rather different kind that involved a very big stimulus indeed.

A few years ago, in the course of an experiment that had nothing whatever to do with anything paranormal, I and a colleague conducted a survey in which 300 Cambridge students were asked in the middle of the day to say what phase they thought the moon was in.[176] To our considerable surprise we found that their answers bore no relation whatever to the real phase of the moon (and it made no difference how confident they said they were).

Such ignorance of a major fact of nature would seem remarkable by any standards. But if ESP is a reality, it ought surely to be considered doubly remarkable. First, because, with an object the size and status of the moon, direct clairvoyance should presumably have been relatively easy. Second, because at the time of asking there must have been tens of millions of people on the dark side of the globe who were in sight of the moon at that very moment and so could have communicated the information telepathically.

All this has a bearing on a problem I have heard raised from both sides. It has been said that there is a sort of Catch-22 about research in parapsychology: on the one hand no respectable scientist will take the experimental results seriously until they have been replicated by other respectable scientists, but on the other hand no respectable scientist will take the trouble to try to replicate the results until he considers them worth taking seriously.

Yet in truth it is not much of a problem at all. For the fact is that respectable scientists have all along been unwittingly attempting to replicate – or often to anticipate – the research in parapsychology. Every time they have conducted an experiment which implicitly relies on there being *no* secret communication with the subject of the experiment, *no* physical effect of their own wishes on the experimental outcome, *no* cheating and *no* fiddling of results, they have *de facto* been running a test for ESP and/or PK. Only they have not called it that: they have called it psychology, or biology or physics.

Parapsychologists frequently complain that their subject is underfunded. Perhaps they would feel better if they realised that nearly every dollar spent on conventional research could be seen as a dollar spent on parapsychology if only the scientists would call it by the right name. Whether the results of these conventional experiments would then be different – whether, for example, if I had *meant* the moon survey to be a definitive test of ESP, I would have found many more people giving the right answer – I do not know.[177] I am sure there are parapsychologists who would suggest so. Somehow my better judgement suggests not.

19
Keeping the Faith

It could have worked. But it has not. The extraordinary facts that people hoped would force a revision of the materialist world-view could have been discovered; and once discovered they could have stood up to critical examination. But in reality, after several centuries of active searching, all there is to show for it is a museum full of well-I-never curiosities and disputed laboratory data.

What Hume wrote about miracles two hundred years ago applies more than ever to the current situation. 'There is not to be found any miracle attested by a sufficient number of men, of such unquestioned good-sense, education and learning, as to secure us against all delusion in themselves; of such undoubted integrity, as to place them beyond all suspicion of any design to deceive others; of such credit and reputation in the eyes of mankind, as to have a great deal to lose in case of their being detected in any falsehood; and at the same time, attesting facts performed in such a public manner and in so celebrated a part of the world, as to render detection unavoidable.'[178]

I cannot emphasise too strongly what a disaster all this has been for parapsychology – and indirectly for the whole anti-materialist campaign. While other sciences have clothed themselves in glory, parapsychology has lost even the undergarments that it started with. Not only have the researchers failed to discover significant new facts, but by nagging away at the few facts that they thought were already in the bag they have slowly but surely taken away the credibility even from those.

The irony is that it is the parapsychologists themselves who, by doggedly following up every herring in their path, have provided the best reasons for not taking the phenomena at their face value: they who have diligently catalogued the antics of the mediums, they who have patiently conducted the tedious tests of card guessing, they who have revealed the ludicrous constraints that apply across the board. And they who have thereby done most to close down one of the last theatres of the soul. I am reminded of what the Russian philosopher Shestov wrote about one of his country's most genuinely insightful playwrights: 'Stubbornly, despondently, monotonously, during his entire period of literary activity . . . Chekhov did one thing only: in one way or another he killed human hopes.'[179]

It is all very well for John Beloff, gentleman and scholar that he is, to write: 'Too often critics of parapsychology are content to use mockery and ridicule in their efforts to bring the field into disrepute. And, since the literature of psychical research is full of fraudulent and farcical incidents, they are assured of an easy time. But in the interests of truth this temptation should be resisted.'[180] Why should it be resisted? The recurrence of farcical incidents *is* the truth. And laughter, it has been said, is the best detergent for nonsense.

This is, I think, a fair reading of the situation. But it is not the way the parapsychologists choose to read it. Nor is it the message the general public has been getting from them. On the contrary, the surprising thing is that most parapsychologists are still in remarkably good heart. Far from admitting defeat, they talk as if they had been winning all along. A few years ago, members of the Parapsychological Association were asked in an opinion poll whether or not they agreed with the following statement: 'ESP is so well established that new research which asks only "Does ESP occur?" is uninteresting.' Such was the confidence of these professionals, that 90 per cent agreed.[181]

In other areas of scholarly investigation it would certainly be rare to find so many people holding to a hypothesis long after the weight of evidence has come down firmly against it. As the philosopher Jerry Fodor gently put it: 'When you keep putting questions to Nature and Nature keeps saying "no", it is not unreasonable to suppose that somewhere among the things you believe there is something that isn't true.'[182] But in the case of the searchers for the paranormal, it is clear that they do *not* take Nature's 'no' for an answer. Indeed, some at least seem quite capable of hearing it as 'yes'.

The question why so many people are so unwilling to accept defeat deserves close examination.

To begin with let me underline the fact that not many people approach the problem of choosing between paranormal and normal explanations in the particular way that I have been recommending. Instead most tend to rely on what they regard as a more obvious and straightforward method: which is to argue that a phenomenon has to be considered paranormal unless and until it can be proved normal. Thus, when they observe or are told of something that seems suitably extraordinary, the question they ask is not whether there is any way of making sense of the *constraints* on the phenomenon if it has a paranormal explanation, but rather whether there is any way of making sense of the phenomenon *as such* if it has a normal explanation.

John Beloff, for example, in a paper called 'What is your counter-explanation?', adopts just this seemingly reasonable line. 'If asked what it is that makes me side with believers rather than the sceptics, I would have to say, I suppose, that it is . . . the global impression I derive from my survey of the literature that something real is going on that defies conventional explanations.'[183]

It should be noted that, by asking for a *counter*-explanation here, Beloff is inviting us to take it for granted that the believers for their part do have a paranormal explanation that is worth countering. Nonetheless, if we leave this potential difficulty aside, it is easy to see why Beloff's way of reasoning often has such immediate appeal. For there does at first seem to be a certain logic to it. 'If a phenomenon is paranormal, the sceptics will be unable to supply a normal explanation for it. In this case it seems they have indeed been unable to supply a normal explanation. Therefore the phenomenon must be paranormal.'

Perhaps it sounds all right if said rather fast. But as a logical argument it is of course fundamentally misguided. As misguided as, say, the following: 'If my car has been abducted by aliens, I shall not be able to find it. As a matter of fact I cannot find it. Therefore it must have been abducted by aliens.'

What those who would argue this way have failed to take on board is that our inability to explain away a phenomenon in normal terms is not, repeat *not*, strong evidence for its being paranormal. It is equally likely – no, much more likely – that there is a normal explanation which, as it happens, has eluded us.

As I stressed when I first introduced the argument from unwarranted design, one of the great advantages of *my* way of approaching the material is precisely that it allows us to conclude that the paranormal explanation does not work without being obliged to replace it with a normal one. It allows us therefore, if we wish, to stay above the fraught and often unresolvable arguments about what *really* happened in particular cases – arguments which are, it should be said, the meat and drink of the paranormal literature.

The feuding that has gone on between sceptics and believers has, of course, been huge sport for the protagonists. (Indeed, it has involved challenges of a kind rarely encountered by more conventional scientists. A report by Baron von Schrenck-Notzing, who investigated the source of the ectoplasmic materialisations produced by the medium Eva C, exemplifies the kind of sacrifice that has had to be made in the line of scientific duty: 'A finger was introduced into the vagina of the medium . . . but with negative result.'[184]) But the real danger for the critic is that once he takes part in these debates he may be thought to have tacitly agreed to play by the believers' rules.

I do not mean to suggest that critics should stay *hors de combat* altogether. I think they ought to make it perfectly clear, if challenged, that they do not consider the provision of a counter-explanation the *sine qua non* of an adequate refutation. But this by no means debars them from tentatively suggesting a counter-explanation when they believe they have one. Indeed, I recognise that, if they are frank about it, it may be very difficult *not* to suggest one. For in many cases it will be perfectly clear to everyone – believers and sceptics alike – that there is the possibility of a depressingly obvious explanation: namely, that in reality the reported phenomena did not occur at all – at least not as reported. From which it follows, as night day, that whoever so reported them must have been guilty, if not of outright dishonesty, then, to say the least, of gross misprision.

It seems quite clear that one of the reasons for the parapsychologists' stubborn persistence is that this is a conclusion that many of them are unable to take.

True, few if any thoughtful people can be unaware of the human *potential* for giving false reports: of succumbing, as Hume would have put it, either to 'delusion in themselves' or to 'design to deceive others'.

Whatever anyone's particular views about the paranormal, we all know that almost everybody – ourselves included – will on occasion exaggerate, dissemble, embroider the truth, be 'economical with the *actualité*' as an ex-Defence-Minister so nicely put it. We know that most people will cheat if they can get away with it – at least on a small scale. (In the USA 95 per cent of students admit to engaging in one form or another of dishonesty in their academic studies;[185] in the UK 50 per cent say they have cheated in their course-work, and 13 per cent admit to doing so in their final exams.[186])

We know of famous frauds and hoaxes, in art, in letters and in science: the Piltdown skull, the Loch Ness monster photographs, the Turin Shroud, the Hitler diaries, and so on. We accept – even expect – that respected figures in business and politics will withhold vital information or make misleading statements without turning a hair. We are not shocked to hear the definition of a diplomat as 'a man sent abroad to lie for his country'. And even at the level of the American presidency we cannot say we are surprised when we hear it said of Richard Nixon that 'lying was so habitual to him that, if he ever found himself telling the truth, he would be obliged to tell a lie to set the record straight'.

We know too, probably from our own experience, some of the temptations that may lead to such semi-casual deception. The desire to please, to show off, to draw attention, to win favours. But especially, perhaps, in the context of the paranormal, the desire to gain what I have elsewhere called 'witness power': 'One of the basic principles of social life is that society accords a special place to the person who has *something to say*. To have been present at, or even intimately linked to a newsworthy event makes one a valuable resource to the community. One becomes the person who *was there*, who has information to impart ... No wonder that we are sometimes tempted to assert that we have been present at events where we were not.'[187]

We all know that men and women were deceivers ever. And some of us may even have come across theoretical justifications for it as an optimal strategy in life. I remember myself being struck by the novelty and yet intuitive obviousness of the following comment by the sociobiologist Robert Trivers: 'The most important thing to realize about systems of animal communication is that they are not expected to be systems for the dissemination of truth. Instead, they are expected to be systems by which individual organisms attempt to maximize their fitness by communicating to others things that may be true or false.'[188] But Trivers was merely expressing for the individual what H. G. Wells said about the group: 'The Social Contract is nothing more or less than a vast conspiracy of human beings to lie to and humbug themselves and one another for the general Good.'[189]

We know all this. Nonetheless it will still come as something of a shock if and when we are forced to recognise that some particular person has actually been deceiving *us* about a matter *we* care about. Even if we *can* argue that it is being done in a good cause, we shall be reluctant to acknowledge it.

In fact when it is done in a good cause, we shall be all the more reluctant. For then it will come as a double blow. We shall not only be having our faith in our informant shaken, but also be losing the support for the good cause. If a friend tells us that we have won a million pounds because she reckons, quite correctly, that the news will make us happy (and, by the way, make us think well of her too), then, when the truth comes out, we are going to be upset not only about the money but about the betrayal of trust.

In all, while it is certainly not news in general that people cheat, it can be very bad news in particular. And if and when it becomes clear that someone has been cheating us about the reality of miraculous phenomena, we are sure to feel a deep sense of disappointment. Maybe there will be some who, on reflection, choose to class it as a forgivable exaggeration, a white lie, even as compensation for all the materialist propaganda that we have to live with. Even so there will be no escaping that the same evidence that had first been seen as evidence for a remarkable and desirable human characteristic, paranormal soul-power, has become instead further evidence for an unremarkable and undesirable one, normal human untrustworthiness.

Laugh as they may, even the sceptics must see this as a kind of tragedy in the old sense. In the very attempt to establish a more hopeful picture of 'what we are', so as to permit a more promising vision of 'where we are going', the search for the soul will only have led to an even worse diagnosis and prognosis than we had to start with. Fortunately (since I suppose the avoidance of tragedy is always fortunate) it seldom seems to come to this – because, as the survey data show, almost all of those most deeply involved in the research have found the strength to ignore the tell-tale signs.

There is a further factor that is very likely helping to protect believers. This is their propensity for rewriting history, or at least selectively editing it, in ways that have tended to leave a much rosier glow around the 'classic cases' than is right. There lies behind it some classically crooked thinking.

We have already seen, in discussing the legacy of Jesus, how the memory of a hallowed precedent, assumed authentic, can dull people's critical response to examples that come later. More insidious still, however, is the way this memory can help to shield the original example itself.

Consider, as a start, the following not wholly convincing argument. 'If Jesus performed all those miracles by the use of psychic power, he must have been the son of God. If he was the son of God he would have had no need or reason to have cheated. If he had no need or reason to cheat he would not have done so. If he did not cheat then he *must* have performed all those miracles by the use of psychic power. Therefore he *must* have been the son of God . . .' and so on in circles, until all reservation ceases.

Something obviously wrong somewhere (though where exactly does the logic fail?). But, while the circularity may be obvious when set out like this, it would not be anything like so obvious if the steps were separated. Imagine that in childhood, before you thought of questioning it, you were told as a fact that Jesus performed miracles and therefore was the son of God, and not till later in life did it occur to you that the miracles might not be genuine. By that time, you might well find that your critical faculties had already been hijacked. For how could you possibly entertain such doubts about the works of a man whose works had already proved he was never to be doubted! (The importance of the first step taken in childhood was not lost on the Jesuits: 'If I have the teaching of children up to seven years of age or thereabouts, I care not who has them afterwards, they are mine for life.'[190])

This style of reasoning is often to be seen in the way professional parapsychologists look back – nostalgically – on the famous cases from the past and then let these cases influence their judgement of what comes later. Thus, for example, 'If person X was able to do all those wonderful things without practising any sort of deception, it proves that psychic powers exist. If psychic powers exist, X would not have needed to use deception, and nor would his successors, Y, Z, etc. . . .' Even if later analysis makes it pretty obvious that X probably did use deception, the damage – if that is the word – has been done. The idea that psychic powers exist, once planted, will not be easily shifted.

It is the old story that mud sticks – except that here rather than mud it is more like untarnishable gold leaf. Just as the Princess of Wales continues to be revered as a princess long after the break-up of her marriage, or the Turin shroud to be worshipped as a cult object after its exposure as a fake, or Nixon to be admired as a great American after his impeachment, so psychic phenomena can, it seems, survive almost any amount of subsequent disgrace.

Stage conjurors have often had occasion to notice a similar effect: that members of their audience will insist that they must have been using paranormal powers, even if they have in fact openly announced that they have been fooling everybody (and even sometimes after they have shown *how* they have been fooling them).

Harry Houdini found it almost impossible to persuade his admirer Sir Arthur Conan Doyle, that he, Houdini, was really not capable of dematerialising and rematerialising. Doyle rationalised Houdini's denials of his own powers by arguing that, if Houdini were to let on that he used paranormal powers rather than trickery, his 'brother magicians' would consider he was using 'illicit' means.[191] In other words, according to Doyle, Houdini had to cheat about the fact that he did not cheat, since other conjurors would see it as cheating not to cheat (if you see what I mean).

But it is not only the case that the beliefs, once established, become remarkably immune to refutation; it may even be that attempts at refutation have the opposite effect. In 1991, James Randi hosted six television programmes, 'James Randi: Psychic Investigator', in which, by working through and exposing a series of fraudulent cases, he set out to 'disabuse us all of any belief in the occult, in necromancy, astrology, divination, secondsight – anything that comes under the heading of the paranormal or the psychic'.[192] A large-scale study was undertaken by the Independent Broadcasting Authority's Research Department, which assessed people's beliefs before and after the series had been screened.[193] It turned out that those who viewed the programmes showed no decrement whatsoever in the level of their paranormal beliefs (and the number of people reporting personal experience of paranormal phenomena actually went up slightly).

Evidently there is no such thing as bad publicity. Perhaps Randi, by attempting to expose particular examples of psychic phenomena as fakes, in effect merely drew people's attention to the possibility that other examples could be genuine. After all, we generally take it for granted that the existence of a 'fake' implies the existence of an original of which the fake is an imitation. How can you have a fake Titian unless there are genuine Titians to imitate? How can you have someone feigning a headache unless there is such a thing as a real headache?

When a child in a toyshop at Christmas-time asks her mother about the old man in the red suit, 'Mummy, is he the real Santa Claus?', what message does the child get if she is told that 'No, he is only pretending'? Or for that matter what message from the episode that I heard reported on the radio last year, that 'in a shopping centre in Milton Keynes this afternoon a fake Santa Claus was arrested and led away by police; mothers put their hands over their children's eyes'?[194]

Can you fake what is already fake? As we saw, when we discussed the *folie à deux* between the child spoon-bender and his father, what was happening there was that each was in fact faking a phenomenon faked by the other. But of course neither knew, and the whole point of what they were doing was that each assumed he was indeed faking the real thing.

Language, as has often been noted in other contexts, may easily develop a life of its own.[195] To talk of faking a psychic phenomenon can have the effect of dignifying the genuine phenomenon that is supposedly being faked. But, more insidious still, merely to talk about the possibility of any phenomenon *being* psychic can be enough to give the concept undeserved status – a warrant, if not of its real existence, at least of its theoretical respectability.

This power of words to reify the things that they refer to may partly explain why, from the beginning, parapsychologists have been so eager and shameless in introducing their own new terminology. The *Handbook of Parapsychology*[196] contains a Glossary in which are listed more than three hundred specialist terms. They range from 'apport' (an object that has paranormally travelled from somewhere else and passed through intervening walls), through 'psychoboly' (the use of PK for malevolent purposes), to 'responsive xenoglossy' (the ability of someone to converse in a foreign language they have never learned). But especially revealing are concepts such as the 'decline effect' (the tendency for positive results in parapsychological experiments to get weaker as time goes on), the 'sheep–goat effect' (the tendency for people who believe in psi to get better scores in experimental tests than sceptics do), the 'error phenomenon' (the fact that a procedural error by an experimenter seems to 'activate psi' and is therefore often associated with a better result), and so on.

As just one example of the influence of this kind of language, let us remark the way in which Beloff can, by labelling himself a 'psi-inhibitor', explain away the fact that he himself has never been able to obtain first-hand evidence of psi. In his autobiographical essay he describes how, because of his own poor record as an experimenter, his mentor, J. B. Rhine, suggested he might be better employed on theoretical matters. 'I was', he writes, 'already acquiring the reputation, which has clung to me ever since, of being a negative or psi-inhibitory experimenter and Rhine, of course, had no use for anyone who could not deliver positive results.'[197] (We might remark, too, that there seems to be a correlation – which someone should do some research on sometime – between psi-inhibitoriness and scholarly integrity: besides Beloff, the distinguished philosopher Charles Broad, the criminologist Donald West, and the psychologist Susan Blackmore – each well disposed towards psychic phenomena but each, to their own chagrin, annoyingly psi-inhibitory.)

But this is only the beginning of what can follow from the trappings of scholarship. If merely attaching a name to something confers a kind of respectability, then attaching a name and address will do so even better. When a phenomenon can not only be given a name but located in a historical context with a string of references attached, it will be accorded more attention still. Such an effect is indeed obvious within the somewhat pedantic and self-conscious culture of academic parapsychology. And it goes some way to explaining how it is that undertakings that would otherwise seem grossly eccentric become accepted without embarrassment as legitimate scholarly pursuits.

Imagine that in a tour of a university you were to walk in on an experiment in progress. There she is, wearing ping-pong balls over her eyes, white noise playing into her ears, telling her thoughts into a tape-recorder; while there is her best friend in another room, watching a video of a car chase, and doing his level best to beam the image through to her. Here is the Professor who seems to be in charge. 'Whatever are you up to?' 'It's a *Ganzfeld Experiment* – testing for *telepathy* – there are over twenty papers on it in the *Journal of Parapsychology*.' 'Oh, that's what it is, now it makes sense . . . But hang on a minute, haven't just about all the earlier studies been shown to have methodological problems with them – apparatus failure, faulty statistical analysis, evidence of experimenter fraud, or whatever?' 'Well, yes. But that's why it's all the more important to have another go. You see, the point is to confirm what these earlier studies *would have proved* if there had not been those unfortunate errors that were only discovered later.'

With all these factors taking their toll on the researchers' critical abilities, the chances of common sense prevailing are slim. There is, however, one further and probably decisive factor.

I have been discussing the search for psychic phenomena as if it were a genuinely open-minded inquiry whose findings could in principle go either way. But, looking back over the record of parapsychological research and observing the refusal of its leading figures ever to take 'No' for an answer from Nature, I suspect that few have been ready to accept that the findings *could* go either way. Brian Josephson (the distinguished physicist and paranormal advocate) probably spoke for most of his fellow parapsychologists when he recently remarked: 'It's inevitable that there will be an acceptance [of the reality of psychic phenomena]. I'm not exactly sure what will cause it, basically it's just a case of making everyone wake up.'[198]

Such an attitude amounts to a kind of paranormal fundamentalism. Those who think like this know in their bones that psychic phenomena *have to be* genuine. Though they may grudgingly admit that the public proof which they themselves have so long been seeking has not yet come to light, they have absolute faith that the phenomena *must* be lurking somewhere.

✳

It is time that we raised some more general questions about the mind-set of these committed believers in the paranormal. If something other than public proof has got to them and turned them, what is this something else? If they are already *partis pris,* what took them?

What took *them,* and we should also be asking what has taken most of *us*? For we should open up the discussion again to include all ordinary believers as well as the advance guard. It is true that the parapsychologists, as a group, have become the most obvious and vocal heirs of the tradition of philosophical and scientific inquiry that I have been sketching. It is they who have made themselves particularly responsible for the task of beating science at its own game, valiantly playing St George to the dragon of materialism. But whatever their additional expertise and enthusiasm, these professional researchers obviously belong within the much wider community of those who continually demonstrate their unshakeable faith that there must be *something* out there, *something* in it.

We saw in earlier chapters how far ordinary people's beliefs are driven by general anxiety about their future happiness. Everyone's wish to hold on to their dreams and hide even from themselves the truth about the world they live in is no doubt a constant source of inspiration for continuing the search. It was well said by Francis Bacon that 'What a man would like to be true, he preferentially believes ... Numberless and sometimes imperceptible are the ways in which the affections colour and infect the understanding.'[199] But while, in the present context, we should recognise what a powerful source of mystification this can be, I would suggest there are several rather more specific influences at work as well.

20

Three Givens

I referred to 'paranormal fundamentalism'. But this choice of words should not be taken to imply that such prior confidence in the existence of the paranormal is necessarily mistaken or irrational. It could be that, in fact, this confidence is perfectly well justified.

There are certainly plenty of less controversial examples of research projects where it would be entirely sensible for the researcher to refuse to accept defeat, because he reckons he has independent grounds for knowing that the phenomena he is looking for *must* be lurking somewhere.

If, say, you were an explorer on an expedition to discover the source of the Nile, you would presumably insist that, since there has never yet been a river without a source, then somebody – and why not you – can be sure of discovering the Nile's source someday. If you were a fossil hunter searching for the missing link between man and ape, you might be confident, on the basis of your absolute trust in the theory of evolution, that if you go on looking long enough you have a real chance of success. If a cryptographer, trying to crack the code of a message passed between enemy agents, you would know that since the message must be decipherable eventually by somebody, the code must exist. If a sea-captain, searching for an island you marked on your map on an earlier voyage, you could be pretty sure that this island that you yourself had previously visited must still be there.

In all these cases your trust in the eventual outcome would be nothing if not reasonable. Seek and ye *shall* find, knock and it *shall* be opened unto you. Likewise (but like exactly *which* of these examples, if any?), it might perhaps be true that if you were seeking for evidence of soul-power you could also have reasonable advance grounds for your presumption of success.

The existence of paranormal phenomena -- all would probably agree – has yet to be finally confirmed by some kind of clinching public proof. But there are and have always been many who nonetheless feel privately that they have lesser proofs that are already *quite good enough for them.*

Suppose someone were to set out on a search to prove the existence of rainbows. (Yes, rainbows.) And moreover that he found himself having to prove it in the face of the raillery of sceptics who have been firmly maintaining that the whole idea of rainbows is riddled with paradox (you can just hear them: 'Why has no one ever brought a rainbow home, why do rainbows always recede as you approach them, why is a rainbow visible from one side but not the other?' and so on).

There are, I suggest, three main lines of argument that he would be likely to offer in defence of his continuing commitment to the search. Three reasons for supposing that his advance belief in the phenomenon was and is justified. I shall call them, respectively, (i) 'the argument from seminal personal experience', (ii) 'the argument from external authority', and (iii) 'the argument from *a priori* reasoning'.

First, of course, the argument from seminal personal experience, where the argument is based on what was been experienced by the believer at first hand: 'I saw a rainbow myself last June. I watched it for a full two minutes while it arched radiantly over the wheatfield. It was a key moment in my life. I felt as if Nature were reaching out to me to reveal the perfect laws that underlie the seeming chaos of existence. Having personally witnessed it, I can never doubt again . . .'

Next, the argument from external authority, where the argument is based on what other people, whose opinion the believer has reason to respect, insist is true for them: 'Even though I myself have never been privileged to see a rainbow, my professor, whom I absolutely trust, tells me he saw one last year and so did my wife's father. What's more I have seen pictures of them in books and read descriptions of them by some of our best poets. The weight of other people's testimony is overwhelmingly convincing . . .'

Last (but in many cases, if not this one, crucially important), the argument from *a priori* reasoning, where the argument is based on what can be worked out from first principles: 'What I already know about the nature of light and the shape of raindrops allows me to reconstruct how rainbows are produced and why they behave the way they do. Ever since I first wondered what would happen *if* the sun shone through rain in a certain way, I have been anticipating that rainbows must occur. I believe, in short, that rainbows are a logical and practical outcome of the way the world is made . . .'

The goal of the next few chapters will be to examine the part that each of these very different lines of reasoning does in fact play in the creation of fundamentalist attitudes towards the paranormal.

21

Being There

Why did I say 'first of course' the argument from personal experience? I did so because it is widely taken for granted that personal experience, where it is available, is bound to be by far the most persuasive influence in establishing belief.

Thus, you will find it confidently stated in just about every commentary on the origins of the paranormal mind-set that, for example, as James Alcock writes, 'most people who believe in the paranormal cite personal experience as their primary reason for doing so'.[200] Or again, as Ayeroff and Abelson write, that ' "true believers" in the paranormal almost always report having had a "confirmatory incident" at some point in their lives.'[201]

It was, as we noted earlier, recognised – if somewhat reluctantly – by Jesus himself that first-hand exposure to miraculous phenomena can be effective in changing people's minds where nothing else is. 'Except ye see signs and wonders,' he chided his followers, 'ye will not believe.' And the story of his disciple Thomas has long stood as the paradigmatic example of how a doubter will not be satisfied by anything less than seeing or touching for himself. 'The other disciples therefore said unto him, We have seen the Lord. But he said unto them, Except I shall see in his hands the print of the nails, and put my finger into the print of the nails, and thrust my hand into his side, I will not believe . . . Jesus saith unto him, Thomas, because thou hast seen me, thou hast believed: blessed are they that have not seen, and yet have believed.'[202]

Philosophers, moreover, have generally accorded direct sensory experience a unique role in acquiring 'true' knowledge. Plato in the *Theaetetus* argued that a jury in a trial, when they pass judgement on a crime they did not witness, can never be sure their verdict is the right one: 'only an eye-witness could know'. Descartes made it a cornerstone of his philosophy that the only way of acquiring knowledge of the world is to do it entirely by oneself. Locke wrote that 'we may as rationally hope to see with other men's eyes as to know by other men's understandings' (which is to say not at all).[203] In general they have insisted that the only facts about the world we can ever know absolutely and for sure are those that we have observed with our own bodily senses. Those who believe without seeing may be blessed, but they are probably being foolish.

True, this argument as to the superiority of first-hand knowledge must not be pushed too far. Some more modern analysts would say that it is fundamentally question-begging, since it is by no means clear that a hard and fast line can be drawn between first-hand and second-hand experience.[204] Even when we engage in so-called direct observation, it is surely the case that we still see and think and remember through the conceptual filters we have acquired from our language and our culture: so that every scrap of our experience, however seemingly immediate, is ultimately experienced the way it is thanks to the experiences of other people (many of them long since dead). Nonetheless, it would be silly to deny that there is a rough and ready distinction to be made between witnessing an event ourselves and being informed about it. Some experiences are obviously less second-hand than others. And, in general, we presumably ought to place greatest faith in our own observations.

In modern times people's insistence on the superiority of direct sensory knowledge has if anything grown stronger, and they have correspondingly become more and more demanding of it. Few these days would let themselves agree with the remark of Pascal I quoted earlier, that 'Miracles are no longer necessary because we have already had them.' Rather, they would line up with Tom Paine in asserting, 'I am contending for the rights of the living and against their being willed away by the manuscript-assumed authority of the dead.'[205] In fact, as ever more subjectivist ideologies – existentialism, feminism, post-modernism – have taken hold in Western culture, the cult of personal experience has come to seem ever more natural and reasonable, even virtuous.

Carl Jung said: 'Our age wishes to have actual experiences in psychic life. It wants to experience for itself, and not to make assumptions based on the experience of other ages.'[206]

Now, as we shall see later, whatever people may say they wish to experience, and whatever the theoreticians recommend, it is not actually true in real life that *except* people see signs and wonders they *will not* believe. Nor is it true that they *do not* make assumptions based on the experience of other ages. It is, however, undoubtedly true that if *and when* people do see signs and wonders they *very often will* believe – especially if they themselves are the subject of the sign or wonder. Even if in reality seeing is not a necessary condition for believing, it is certainly sometimes a sufficient one.

Down the ages people have repeatedly testified that it was indeed a particular event, of which they themselves were either the subject or a first-hand witness, that converted them to a belief in the reality of paranormal powers: a voice from the clouds, a visitation by a ghost, a remarkable example of precognition, an oceanic feeling of unity with all of nature, a demonstration 'before my very eyes' of a physically impossible feat, a coincidence so meaningful yet so outrageous as to defy chance explanation.

Writing of what he sees as the paradox of the 'bright believers' – intelligent and critical people who have nonetheless sold out, as he sees it, to irrational beliefs – Tony Pasquarello has commented: 'Let us note the frequency with which extraordinary, miraculous, mystical, or "born again" type experiences have played a pivotal role in their beliefs. Everyone pays homage to the psychological persuasiveness and epistemic priority of first-person experience.'[207]

John Taylor, for example, a professor of physics at London University, described the remarkable change he himself underwent when he watched at close hand while Geller, during a BBC television programme in 1973, first duplicated a drawing in a sealed envelope and then went on to break a fork by stroking it: 'I felt as if the whole framework with which I viewed the world had suddenly been destroyed. I seemed very naked and vulnerable, surrounded by a hostile and incomprehensible universe. It was many days before I was able to come to terms with this sensation.'[208] When he did come to terms with it, he emerged as an evangelical believer in ESP and psychic metal-bending. Even such an arch-pragmatist and sceptic as the philosopher A. J. Ayer found it impossible to resist the blandishments of his own personal near-death experience. During a severe bout of pneumonia, having lost consciousness, he found himself entering the presence of a red light which was 'responsible for the government of the universe' and with which he could debate the laws of time and space. In a newspaper article, following his recovery, he wrote: 'On the face of it these experiences are rather strong evidence that death does not put an end to consciousness.'[209]

Some converts have insisted that for them their personal experience does and should rank above *any* other evidence, even objective scientific evidence – and have gone on to demand that it should be granted equivalent respect by others. Carl Sargent, the first parapsychologist to get a Cambridge doctorate, made the following reply when he was challenged to explain some suspicious anomalies in his telepathy experiments: 'I stand by all the data reported; it is a matter of utter indifference to me whether Blackmore [his accuser] or anyone else in parapsychology believes me or not. I know the results were real because I was there and *my experience* tells me so. If I learned one thing in parapsychology, it is that results and statistics and data never changed anyone's mind about anything; experience is the only arbiter.'[210]

On the basis of such seminal experiences, several have founded shrines, some complete religions.

Obviously there is great need to be careful. Friedrich Nietzsche, himself no slouch in the cause of subjectivity, roundly condemned those who have *uncritically* placed their own experiences upon a pedestal: 'One kind of honesty has been unknown to all founders of religions and their likes – they have never made of their experiences a matter of conscience and knowledge. "What did I really experience? What happened in me and around me then?

Was my mind sufficiently alert? Was my will bent against fantasy?" – none of them has asked such questions, none of our dear religious people asks such questions even now: they feel, rather, a thirst for things which are *contrary to reason* and do not put too many difficulties in the way of satisfying it – thus they experience "miracles" and "rebirths" and hear the voices of angels!'[211]

I need not reiterate the arguments of the earlier chapters as to why these sporadic phenomena cannot possibly bear the weight that has been put on them. Pasquarello neatly summarised it: 'It is boring to have to repeat that we cannot infer from the fact that there are "pink elephant experiences" that there exist pink elephants.'[212] And perhaps it is also boring to have to repeat that if pink elephant were actually to exist, the elephantologists would still have to come up with an explanation for why the PEEs should occur only in such restricted times and places, in such peculiar forms, to such a limited range of people.

Still, it certainly does seem that the experiences can and do turn the minds of those who have them. Michael Argyle has pointed out, that we may be getting a somewhat exaggerated picture if we focus on 'grand conversions' and especially if we use mainly literary examples for illustration.[213] It might be that the members of the religious, philosophical and scientific élites who have so eloquently testified to the role of personal experience in their own cases are not representative of the wider community. But in fact the story is probably not so different for humbler sections of the population. In the survey to which I referred in Chapter 1, conducted in the town of Reading, ordinary people were asked about the influences that had chiefly shaped their views about the paranormal: 60 per cent of those who said that they had themselves had a psychic experience went on to say that this personal experience was indeed the most important factor behind their belief in paranormal powers.[214]

It should be said that when the people of Reading were invited to describe a particular example of a psychic event they had experienced, the kinds of thing they actually came up with were surprisingly modest. The following are typical:

'I dreamt of a woman – I'd never seen her before. Then two or three days later she walked into the hairdressers where I worked. I recognised her from the dream and she recognised me.'

'I feel that my wife is still with me. She died last year. She was sick and when she wanted me she'd call "George! George! George!" non-stop until I came. I still hear her sometimes.'

'I got up one morning about six o'clock to make the baby's bottle and all of a sudden this awful feeling of fire came over me. I felt as if I wanted to run away from a fire but couldn't. I went back to bed and didn't think any more about it. Later at nine I switched on the news and heard that an old man had died in a fire in his living room in Sheffield at six twenty.'

'I call someone on the telephone and they say they were just about to call me.'

'My neighbour's dog died, but next morning early I saw it in the garden but she'd died the previous night. I'd seen it in the garden and said "Hello Trixie, what are you doing out at this time?" '

'I went to a medium, she said I would meet someone, where we would meet and gave me the initials. It was incredible because it turned out to be my husband.'

But, even if these examples seem somewhat run-of-the-mill, the survey suggests that they were impressive enough to the people who reported them. When asked if a psychic experience had 'changed their life', 35 per cent of those who had had an experience said 'yes'. And when asked to elaborate, they cited such explanations as that 'it's made me realise there's more to life than I thought before', or that 'there has to be something else other than just life; I no longer believe that we live all this time and just finish', or that 'we don't use the power of our mind to its full extent and there are greater forces than we know of, a superior power we can tap and utilise'.

✳

All this fits with what I said is the conventional assumption about the primacy of first-hand experience. But I must now come to what does not fit at all.

I have been playing along with the usual story for the sake of argument. But the truth is that statistics of the kind I have just quoted, though technically correct, are potentially misleading. Although it does indeed appear to be true that personal experience of psychic phenomena is highly influential *with those who have had it*, this need not mean that personal experience is the chief factor in generating belief across the population as a whole. The fact that such experiences may be sufficient, does not entail that they are in any way essential.

The question must be: has everyone who believes in the reality of paranormal phenomena had some kind of direct experience of them? And the clear answer from the surveys is that as a matter of fact, no: most of those who believe *have never had any relevant seminal personal experiences at all.* Thus in the Reading survey it was found that, while 68 per cent of the general population definitely believed in at least three categories of paranormal phenomena, only 26 per cent said they had had *any* psychic experience themselves.

This is the typical finding of other surveys too. The numbers vary according to exactly how the questions have been phrased, but it has been found, for example, that while about 70 per cent of people in Britain believe in ESP, only about 30 per cent say they have had it happen to them personally; or, while 45 per cent believe in ghosts, only 15 per cent have themselves seen or heard one.[215] In general it seems that only a third or so of those who believe in any particular category of phenomenon have had first-hand experience of it – leaving about two thirds of believers without any personal grounding.

The picture is, as might be expected, a little different in the case of the professional parapsychologists.[216] Among members of the American Parapsychological Association, where 90 per cent said they had complete or strong belief in ESP, 59 per cent said they had at least some experience of it themselves (though in most cases they thought it rather unimpressive). But this still leaves more than a third of them completely out in the cold. John Beloff is an important case in point. He himself has had, he says, *no* experiential grounds for what he calls 'my basic conviction that psi is real': 'Never at any time, alas, have I been favoured with one of those inexplicable incidents which so many people I have met can recall from their past and which have played their part in the lives of so many of my fellow parapsychologists.'[217]

We are faced then with a clash between what is commonly assumed about the factors that sustain belief and what the evidence actually suggests. It is simply not the case that, as asserted by those psychologists at the head of this chapter, 'most people who believe in the paranormal cite personal experience as their primary reason for doing so', or that ' "true believers" in the paranormal almost always report having had a "confirmatory incident" at some point in their lives'.

But if is this not the case, what is? What factors do people themselves cite as the primary source of their beliefs?

In the Reading survey further information was gathered by asking the respondents to indicate, by selecting just one factor from a check-list, which influences they themselves considered to have been most important in their own case. Of those who were definite believers in the paranormal, just 21 per cent selected 'personal experience', while 17 per cent selected the fact that 'someone I know has had a psychic experience' and, remarkably enough, 33 per cent selected the fact that 'I have seen or heard about psychic phenomena on TV or radio' and a further 20 per cent that 'I have read about them in books or newspapers' (although less than 1 per cent selected 'scientific evidence').

In the survey of Parapsychological Association members, a statistic was used to assess 'the degree of belief acquired from different sources'. The findings were similar – except that, as might be expected, these experts put more weight on their own in-house publications than on the popular media. The figures (for what they are worth) were that 17 per cent of belief was attributed to personal experience, 15 per cent to events described by close acquaintances, and 61 per cent to experimental data and published reports.

The proper conclusion would therefore seem to be that, while there can be no question that personal experience may be influential with those fortunate enough to have had it, in the larger picture such experience counts for comparatively little. Far more important in shaping people's beliefs about the paranormal is the evidence they are being offered directly or indirectly about events that have been happening to others than themselves.

22

Inside Stories

The evidence seems to be showing that even though most people are believers in the paranormal, most have never had what they would call a psychic experience of their own. This is unexpected from the point of view of conventional wisdom about what supports belief. But it is, I would say, even more unexpected from the point of view of elementary cognitive psychology.

Psychologists who study how the human mind works are no longer greatly surprised by the occurrence of psychic-like experiences. Indeed, it has become almost a cliché of experimental psychology that, whether or not there are any genuinely psychic phenomena, it is more or less inevitable that most individuals will think they are experiencing them every so often – simply because of the vagaries of perception and memory and the mind's capacity for imaginative recreation.

Long ago, the great Elizabethan physician Sir Thomas Browne remarked on how exotic – and quixotic – our internally generated world may be. 'We carry within us the wonders we seek without us,' he wrote, 'there is all Africa and her prodigies in us.'[218] And a wealth of more recent work has confirmed just how far our picture of the 'external reality' surrounding us is in fact a creation of our own theories and fancies – a hypothetical construct raised from ambiguous data.

Graham Reed has written, for example: 'All our commerce with the world is *constructive, interpretative and tentative* . . . Once this view is accepted, many of our "anomalous" experiences seem much less sinister and inexplicable . . . We need not invoke reincarnation to explain why we "recognize" something we have not previously encountered. We need not rely upon spiritualism to explain why we occasionally "see" somebody who is not there or "hear" our name called when no living person has called it. Our cognitions are dynamic, and each of us is continually constructing his own models and arriving at decisions according to his experiential history and his personal schemata.'[219] And in a similar vein, James Alcock has stated: 'An understanding of the psychology of human perception, cognition and behaviour suggests that, even if psi phenomena were not to exist, the kinds of *experiences* that people report under the rubric of "psychic" should be *expected* to occur from time to time.'[220]

Indeed, far from being abnormal or crazy, the powerful urge to see paranormal causes everywhere is, according to William Grey, 'actually an expression of the very same capacities that enable us to develop some of our most important and profound insights about the world... Psychics and other "credulists" are typically engaged seriously (but misguidedly) in that most characteristic of human enterprises: the attempt to capture our chaotic and fragmentary experiences in a network of meanings and to discover the hidden connectedness that (we hope) underlies all the disorderly and recalcitrant happenings in the world.'[221] 'Why do so many people believe in psychic phenomena?' asks psychologist Susan Blackmore. 'Because they have psychic experiences. And why do they have psychic experiences? Because such experiences are an inevitable consequence of the way we think ... like visual illusions, they are the price we pay for a generally very effective relationship with a massively complex world.'[222]

Thus, even if ghosts, telepathy, precognition, second sight, and so on do not actually exist, nevertheless – according to what all these psychologists are saying – the human mind would seem certain to invent them. Maybe not all Africa in all of us, but surely more than a few psychic-like experiences in more than a few of us (and certainly more than 26 per cent).

And yet, in reality it seems *it is not so*. The actual figures that the surveys show for the number of people reporting any such experiences are so remarkably low that I think I should quote some of the data in more detail.

In the massive survey carried out by the Independent Broad-casting Authority in Britain in 1991, respondents were asked 'Have you ever . . .' about the following experiences: 'Felt you knew the thoughts or actions of a person in a different place which later turned out to be true?' – 79 per cent said 'No', and only 21 per cent 'Yes'. 'Heard or seen "supernatural" objects or beings?' – 90 per cent said 'No', 10 per cent 'Yes'. 'Heard or seen objects moving absolutely of their own accord?' – 94 per cent said 'No', 6 per cent 'Yes'.[223]

In a Gallup poll in the USA in 1990, they were asked, 'Have you ever . . .': 'Felt that you were in touch with or getting a message from someone who was far away without using the traditional five senses?' – 74 per cent said 'No', 25 per cent 'Yes'. 'Seen or been in the presence of a ghost?' – 90 per cent said 'No', 9 per cent 'Yes'. 'Personally seen someone moving or bending an object using just mental energy?' – 92 per cent said 'No', 7 per cent 'Yes'.[224]

As you can see, the concordance between the British and American data is striking.

But now let's take, for instance, the question relating to telepathy. 'Have you ever felt you were in touch with . . . , felt you knew the thoughts of . . . ?' I have to say that, in advance of seeing these data, I would have guessed that almost everybody would have said 'Yes'. After all, to say 'Yes' would not necessarily imply any commitment to actually believing in the paranormal, it would just be to acknowledge having had a valid feeling of a paranormal kind about what is passing in another person's mind. And, given that almost all of us spend such a large part of our lives speculating about what other people are thinking and doing, and that we are mostly rather good at normal mind-reading, the chances are very high that we do sometimes score seemingly paranormal 'hits'. It is therefore remarkable that three out of four people in fact said 'No' to the question – especially when the majority of those who said 'No' were, as the same surveys showed, firm believers in ESP.

The explanation – somewhat galling, I suppose, to psycholo-gists who positively relish evidence of human fallibility – must be that ordinary people, rather than being easy dupes of their own mental constructions, tend if anything to be over-cautious. They are, it would seem, less than eager to acknowledge that something strange and psychic-like is happening (even when and if apparently it is). And the reason, presumably, can only be that in general *people know themselves too well to take it seriously*. That is to say, most people most of the time are all too well aware of how their senses can trick them, their emotions get the better of them, their wishes distort, their judgements let them down.

With hindsight, I think we should not be so surprised that this should be the case. After all, the world gives people plenty of practice, in areas other than the paranormal, for getting the measure of themselves. So much so, that it could be argued that they would have to be highly unobservant if they were *not* to discover how unreliable and subject to illusion their own minds can be.

To take obvious examples, every child must soon grasp, for instance, that sticks do not really bend when they enter the water, that an image in the mirror is not the solid object that it seems to be, that the room does not move when you press on an eyeball, that you do not become invisible to others when your eyes are closed, that pins and needles in your limbs are not pins and needles, that an imagined monster is nothing to be afraid of, that time continues on its course while you are asleep, that dreams are only dreams, and so on . . . not to mention all the new illusions which late-twentieth-century children must quickly come to terms with such as television images, holograms, and interactive computer games.

In fact the distinction between appearance and reality, shadow and substance, mental and physical, must surely be one of the *first* things anybody learns. The contrary idea, popularised especially by Jean Piaget, that human beings are slow to become 'realists', and that for at least several years a child 'does not distinguish the psychical world from the physical world',[225] has never been more than a psychologist's myth. More recent research has comprehensively refuted it.[226] And the related notion, that so-called savages are stuck permanently in this supposedly childish state, is worse than a myth, it is a calumny. 'The primitive [person]', Piaget wrote in 1929, 'does not distinguish mind from matter,'[227] and you might still read in 1993, from a philosopher of science, Alan Cromer, that 'most of humankind, for most of its history, never learned to distinguish the internal world of thoughts and feelings from the external world of objects and events'.[228] But this is, of course, patronising nonsense (just imagine how 'most of humankind' would have fared if it were true!).

No. The truth surely is that almost everyone, at least by the time they get to adulthood, has become relatively familiar with, wise to and even cynical about the gulf between how things *seem* to them and how they *are*. They have become, in short, much more down to earth, sensible, and sensitive to their own failings than they are customarily given credit for.

Perhaps they are even *too* down to earth and sensible at times – too ready to dismiss a strange experience as 'just one of those things' or to explain it away by some mundane hypothesis. Walter Scott, for example, recorded in his diary in 1828: 'At dinner-time, I was strangely haunted by what I would call the sense of pre-existence – a confused idea that nothing that passed was said for the first time, that the same topics had been discussed, and the same persons had stated the same opinions on the same subjects ... I think the stomach has something to do with it.'[229] It has probably been the fate of a good many genuinely anomalous and psychically suggestive experiences to have such rather too sensible interpretations put on them. The ploughman in Brueghel's painting, if he had looked up when Icarus fell from the sky, would quite likely have thought it had something to do with his lunch.

But now we seem to have a paradox – or perhaps I should say still more of a paradox than we already had left over from the previous chapter.

It was already a problem to explain why, if people have a general philosophical prejudice in favour of getting all their information at first hand, nonetheless when they are asked about the main source of their paranormal beliefs they mostly refer to evidence of paranormal happenings in the lives *of others*. But now we have the added problem of explaining why, if people are in fact

so dismissive of these experiences when they happen to themselves, they should be so much *less dismissive* of them when they
happen to others. If they do not usually trust in the paranormality
of their own experiences, why should they ever be prepared to
place such weight on the reported experiences of comparative
strangers?

I would suggest that the answer lies, in part at least, in the very
immunity of strangers to the critical examination that individuals
can direct upon themselves. While each of us may be thoroughly
acquainted with our own weaknesses and foibles, we simply do
not have the same access to the inner world of others.

In our own case we can, as Nietzsche recommended, 'make of
our experiences a matter of conscience and knowledge'. Even if
not all of us actually do, we *can* ask and usually answer: 'What did
I really experience? What happened in me and around me then?
Was my mind sufficiently alert? Was my will bent against
fantasy?' But, while we can answer these queries in relation to our
own experiences, it is for obvious reasons much more difficult to
do so in relation to the experiences of others. In their case we
simply cannot run the quick veracity checks we can run on
ourselves. We do not have the background information that might
lead us to reassess the situation and find a more normal
explanation. We have no way of telling how many times this has
happened before, or what was subsequently learned about it. We
can never be sure whether the other person genuinely believes
what he is saying or is merely speaking for effect. We do not know
whether he has perhaps got his fingers crossed even as he speaks.
In general we lack the sobering insight that might help us, if it were
our own case, to restrain belief.

The paradox is therefore not so much of a paradox. It actually
makes considerable sense that our severest – and certainly best
informed – criticism should be reserved for ourselves or our very
close acquaintances. It is not so much that familiarity breeds
contempt, as that familiarity – and the inside knowledge that it
brings – often provides just enough ancillary information to make
the seemingly extraordinary more ordinary, the out-of-this-
world more part of it again.

There is nothing like local knowledge to cut a person down to size. 'A prophet is not without honour,' it was said, 'save in his own country, and in his own house.'[230] And, when Jesus returned home to Nazareth, he was indeed treated by his friends and neighbours with suspicion rather than with honour, precisely because they already knew too much about him. 'Is this not the carpenter's son?' they murmured, 'is not his mother called Mary? and his brethren, James, and Joses and Simon, and Judas? And his sisters, are they not all with us? Whence then hath this man all these things?'[231]

But the point is that by the same token there is nothing like distance-generated ignorance to raise a person up.

This distance effect, this honouring of strangers, is not of course in any way unique to the area of the magical or paranormal. It is characteristic of how we react to other people's experiences across the spectrum. And in some contexts it even serves us well.

When, for example, we look at an actor weeping with joy, or a ballet dancer standing on her points, or a politician kissing a baby, or a photographic model showing off his body, we seldom, if ever, *then* ask Nietzsche's questions: 'what are they really experiencing? what is happening in and around them then?' Instead we actually take advantage of the lack of insight, occasioned and permitted by our distance from them, to invent just so much or little as we please.

We *need* not acknowledge that the actor has no real engagement in the plot. We need not be aware of the dancer's pain, or the politician's duplicity, or the model's indifference. We are free, as we would never be if we ourselves were centre stage, to ignore all qualifications, riders, and complications and to think the best. It is precisely because we do *not* know all there is to know about these strangers that we can readily go in for the 'willing suspension of disbelief' that Coleridge said constitutes 'poetic faith'.[232]

Then, equally, when it comes to assessing the stories we are told about the paranormal, we *need* not think of all the reservations we would make if it were us. We may be quite well aware that if it were in fact ourselves telling the tale, all would not necessarily be what it seems. And yet, though we might guess that other people are not very different from ourselves in this respect – 'If you prick us, do we not bleed? if you tickle us, do we not laugh?' . . . *If we are tempted to cheat or exaggerate, do we not succumb?* . . . 'if we are like you in the rest, we will resemble you in that'[233] – nevertheless we often choose to take them at their word.

We do so because, of course, we *like* to hear these stories, especially when they supply us with the evidence of soul-power that we cannot in good conscience obtain first-hand. And so – be it a report of the Virgin appearing to a child in a Yugoslavian village, or of a young woman being abducted by a UFO, or of the name of the winner of the Derby appearing in the tea-leaves, or of an experiment on PK yielding wildly significant results – we are only too ready to receive the news as 'gospel'.

We are therefore highly impressionable, not to say vulnerable. We may become positively eager to give the benefit of the doubt to reports of experiences that we would never consider seriously if they were ours. And all it may take, then, to finally convince us, is that these stories should be attractively and authoritatively packaged.

23
On Good Authority

To remind you of the figures from the surveys, it seems that more than half of all believers are relying for their evidence about the paranormal entirely on what other people tell them. Even granted that people's standards of criticism are likely to be laxer with respect to others' experiences than they would be with their own, these figures suggest more than mere willingness to listen with an open mind – they suggest positive pressure coming from outside.

Let us turn to what I said was likely to be the second major influence in generating the paranormal mind-set, namely cultural authority. For, as soon as we look at which reports of psychic phenomena go down well and which do not, it seems pretty clear that the chance of a story being attended to depends at least as much on its provenance as on its content: indeed, that there are some stories which in their own right would never be taken seriously at all by anybody, yet which are being treated with respect and even awe because of who in particular is telling them in what cultural context.

When William James remarked that 'our faith is faith in someone else's faith',[234] he did not mean it as a compliment. The fact that an idea was good enough for Moses, is not and presumably never has been a good enough reason for considering it good enough for me. Among rationalists at least, it has been customary to scoff at those poor people who believe something merely because they are told by a respected authority that it is so.

Yet, while it is easy to disparage the human tendency to 'believe what one is told', it would be a mistake to underestimate the crucial and often highly adaptive role that this tendency to put our

faith in others has played and still does in all our lives. We can well
begin this discussion, therefore, by considering how it operates in
other areas than the paranormal.

Even the most cynical commentators could not dispute that there
must be at least some contexts and occasions when faith in
authority pays off: contexts where, if we are offered information
by another person, we can and should gratefully accept it and
believe in it. In fact this is obviously the primary route by which
people acquire most of their basic beliefs during the first part of
their lives and also many of their more interesting beliefs later on –
especially, inevitably, the more outlandish ones.

Thus it is presumably only as a result of what we ourselves have
been told by 'usually reliable sources' that most of us believe (if we
do) that, for example, human beings are descended from monkeys, that meteorites fall from the sky, that a bomb the size of a
football destroyed the city of Hiroshima, that a single individual
wrote Shakespeare's plays, that on 20 July 1969 a man walked on
the moon. Since we were not and could not have been there to
witness these strange happenings and we do not have the means to
infer them from first principles, there is in fact nothing else we
could rely on for the information. Sometimes – and certainly in
cases such as these – we have either to take someone else's word
for it or else we remain ignorant.

This does not mean, however, that we should let all words from all
people count equally with us. For sometimes it will happen that
we get to hear different messages from different sources, and then
we may need to decide *whose* word to trust (and maybe, too,
whose not).

What kind of people ought we to consider most reliable? It is
clear where our original ideas of what constitutes a 'good
authority' will probably have come from. At the beginning of our
lives it will have been our parents who provided us with the model
of trustworthiness. It will have been they who, of all people in the
world, could be assumed to have the most immediate interest in

setting us on the right road, and the least interest in cheating us. Just as we could rely on them to feed us before we could feed ourselves, so we could rely on them to teach us before we could teach ourselves – and we could take it for granted that *they* would not poison either our bodies or our minds.

Maybe nobody subsequently has ever deserved quite the same degree of trust from us. But, in the longer run, our horizons would have been far too limited if we had accepted instruction only from our real mothers and fathers. Hence it was bound to happen that, usually with our real parents' blessing, we generalised from their example to others who equally might be thought to have our interests at heart. Inevitably the mantle of authority therefore got extended: from parents to teachers, doctors, policemen, priests . . . and so, in time, to statesmen, newspaper leader-writers, television presenters, and so on.

But note that the faith that most of us have eventually come to put in these high status people need never have been 'blind'. It may be that as children we had no choice but to believe our parents, and even now that as adults we have little choice but to believe the newscaster or the weatherman: but even so, we have never had simply to take their authority for granted. Whenever we have been able to check up on it, we have soon discovered that putting faith in the superior knowledge of these people really works. What they say is true has generally turned out in practice to be true.

These highly placed individuals are, however, not the only sources we are likely to consider we have good grounds for treating as authoritative. For it is widely assumed that what others lack in personal stature they can make up for in numbers. 'Fifty million Frenchmen can't be wrong', or at any rate, other things being equal, they probably are not wrong. And, as experiments in social psychology have shown, it may actually take only a handful of other people, insisting in our presence on the truth of something, to make us believe it must be so – or at least assent to it in public.

Solomon Asch, in a celebrated series of studies in the 1950s, showed how peer group pressure can lead someone to change his mind, even about such a seemingly unarguable matter as the perceived length of a line.[235] Asch found that when, for example, a group of six people (under instructions from the experimenter) all said that two identical lines looked unequal in length, there was a strong tendency for a seventh (uninstructed) group member to say the same.

Richard Crutchfield, in similar experiments, found that when four people all indicated by pressing a switch that they agreed with a surprising (even outrageous) statement, a fifth member of the group would tend to follow them.[236] He found that bright college students could be persuaded for example that most Americans are over sixty-five years old, that the average American has a life expectancy of twenty-five years, and that the same average American eats six meals a day – perhaps accounting for the fact that he only sleeps four hours a night. Most striking of all was the reaction to the statement 'Free speech being a privilege rather than a right, it is proper for a society to suspend free speech whenever it feels itself threatened.' In a control group free of group pressure, only 19 per cent of subjects agreed with this statement; in Crutchfield's situation, 58 per cent agreed.

Now, as such experiments illustrate, and as hardly bears repeating, we should not *always* rely on the good faith of those who invite us to believe them – however high in status or however numerous.

History has many cautionary tales. There have been times when entire societies have taken leave of their senses – and not only popular opinion but the whole panoply of art, science and politics have come together to put pressure in a false direction. Soviet Communism is a dreadful modern example. 'How a doctrine so illogical and so dull can have exercised so powerful and enduring an influence over the minds of men, and through them, the events of history,' must, said J. M. Keynes, 'always remain a portent to historians of opinion'[237] (and he said that in 1926).

Charles MacKay, in his wonderfully sobering book *Extraordinary Popular Delusions and the Madness of Crowds*, written 150 years ago, instanced many other examples of people blindly following the lead of others, whether in matters of gambling their money in the South Sea Bubble or launching moral crusades against long hair.

Of MacKay's lesser cases, I like this one: 'A panic terror of the end of the world seized the good people of Leeds and its neighbourhood in the year 1806. A hen, in a village close by, laid eggs, on which were inscribed the words, *Christ is coming*. Great numbers visited the spot, and examined these wondrous eggs, convinced that the day of judgment was near at hand.'[238]

Presumably, if these good people had been encouraged to make up their own minds on this freak event, few would have taken it at face or bottom value – because it would likely have occurred to them that an egg which comes out might be an egg which has been put in. But when great numbers around were acclaiming the miracle, it was apparently much harder to resist.

Misplaced trust in the reliability of the group consensus has undoubtedly played a part in many scams. It is why conjurors find it easier to perform their tricks before a crowd than before a single individual – a hundred pairs of eyes working together being paradoxically less observant than one pair that is free to roam. It is why spiritualist mediums try to make sure of having a majority of regular attenders and confirmed supporters in their seances before introducing a new member. It is why television comedy shows lay on canned laughter from the audience, why gurus have an entourage of yes-men, and why publishers cover the backs of their books with puffs from friendly VIPs.

Even so, the dangers of listening to other people should not be exaggerated, and for the most part will almost certainly be outweighed by the rewards. Human social arrangements are such that the risk of being the target of deliberate disinformation is relatively small. In ordinary life there really are often solid reasons for allowing experts who because of their expertise know *better*, or groups who because of their numbers know *more*, to do the research and thinking for us. Those who have been to previous sittings with the spirit medium have had (you might well assume) more chance than yourself to detect fraud, those who provide the puffs for the book have (you might well assume) actually read the book and thought about it.

Life is too short to go round doubting all the time. If we are to get on in the world, our default assumption has to be that expert opinion is on the whole true and that majority opinion is also on the whole true. To insist on remaining chastely uninfluenced by other people might be the acme of prudence, but it would be a denial of one of the greatest benefits of culture.

There is in any case a further safeguard that often applies, and that is particularly relevant to the discussion of the paranormal.

Even though we may have to acknowledge that other people do not tell the truth all of the time, there are a variety of signs we can look for as to how likely it is that they are telling the truth on this particular occasion. That is to say there are 'metalinguistic conventions', recognised throughout the culture, that can indicate whether what is said within a particular 'frame' is meant to be believed – or maybe not.[239]

To take the standard example, a so-called 'play face' is used by both humans and many non-human animals as a sign to a partner that what is about to happen is not to be taken too seriously, while a 'mean face' may be used to do the opposite. Correspondingly there are a whole lot of cultural frames – the theatre, a joke, an after-dinner speech, April Fool's day, even (as Dr Johnson said) a funeral oration – where we would know better than to expect a high degree of truthfulness; and there are other frames – a university lecture room, a pulpit, a witness box, a marriage ceremony, a scientific journal – where we would expect it.

But leaving aside these formal public contexts, there are also more private person-to-person ways of indicating the level of veracity that can be assumed. In particular, when someone is genuinely telling the truth but thinks he may be doubted, he can resort to one or another kind of prefatory declaration. Thus (depending on the degree of fervency appropriate): 'I promise what I say is true,' 'I swear to God it is,' 'Scout's honour . . . cross my heart . . . cross my heart and hope to die . . . swear on my mother's grave . . . ,' etc. Of course none of these provides the listener with a cast-iron guarantee of truthfulness, but they do at least raise the stakes and reduce the likelihood of casual cheating.

✳

Now, taking all of this together, we can say that our attitude to the stories we hear from other people will be strongly influenced by three 'credulity-inducing' factors. Information that otherwise might not be taken seriously will become increasingly credible when it is told either by a person of high status, and/or by several people at a time, and/or in the context of one of these truth frames.

The combination of all three factors might indeed be all but irresistible. Imagine (if you dare) a group of surrogate parent-figures swearing to the truth of some event and crossing their hearts in chorus as they do so. Whether or not you let yourself imagine it, it will not escape your notice that the image bears a strong resemblance to some of the rituals of Christianity (and of Islam, and of Judaism, and just about every other creed, including Communism).

But let us now consider what bearing all this has on the maintenance of paranormal beliefs more generally in Western culture. Admittedly, outside the arenas of the churches, our own culture does not make such a show of these beliefs as did the cultures of the ancients or as do some contemporary cultures in other parts of the world, nor does it so actively lay down the law from the pulpit or the palace. Most people in modern Western societies are, or so we like to think, largely left to make up their own minds. Nonetheless the word – if not to say the Word – about the paranormal still gets very effectively spread.

As I have remarked before, beliefs in paranormal powers – or echoes of them – remain central to our own cultural institutions at every level. They are there as an élite opinion, there *en masse*. They continue to run right through our art and entertainment, our music, painting, literature, architecture, theatre, and cinema. They still dominate our calendars. They are invoked in all our rites of passage – at weddings, births and funerals. They follow us to school, on to the sports field, on to the battle ground, in and out of love and sex. They creep into our beds and keep us wide eyed in the night.

Many, probably the majority, of the public figures whom we look up to – the princes, presidents, popes, pop stars, parliamentarians, press barons, prime-time presenters, prima donnas, premier league players, etc. who act as society's opinion formers –

acknowledge by words or actions their own acceptance of the paranormal ethos.

It may manifest as the born-again religiosity of a Cliff Richard, the star-gazing of a Nancy Reagan, the spirit-channelling of a Shirley MacLaine, the eco-mysticism of a Prince Charles. But more insidious, because so much more reserved and sensible, it may appear as the liberal-minded 'openness to possibilities' of a Jonathan Miller: 'I suppose that my interest in the supernatural is again part of this interest that I have in there being two domains – that beyond the world of what is visible lies the possibility that there might be something else, if only one could get the right entrance.'[240] (If *only!*)

What is rare indeed is to find any public figure disavowing paranormality entirely. And if any do privately have doubts about it, they are probably well advised to keep these to themselves and play along: for, as every public relations consultant would tell you, no one ever did his image any good by openly declaring his preference for common sense. Bertrand Russell, much as he may have wanted to be loved, cannot have thought his *Sceptical Essays* were going to go down well with Mr Averageman: 'I wish to propose for the reader's favourable consideration a doctrine which may, I fear, appear wildly paradoxical and subversive. The doctrine in question is this: that it is undesirable to believe in a proposition when there is no ground whatever for supposing it true.'[241]

At the level of more everyday interactions with our peers, the weight of popular opinion is heavily pro-paranormal. Indeed, with at least two-thirds of ordinary people being confirmed believers in psychic powers, the likelihood that a person will come under pressure from his friends and family is very high. On the basis of the figures from the opinion polls,[242] we can estimate that in Britain the chance, for example, of a man marrying a woman who is a believer is 79 per cent, the chance of his having at least one parent who believes is over 90 per cent, and the chance of his finding himself sitting with a believer when he joins two other couples at a café table is 99 per cent. Admittedly in the latter situation the chance of all four being believers, so that – as in the Crutchfield experiment – they all exert pressure the same way, is considerably smaller. But since those who believe are more likely to speak up than those who do not (it is the believers, after all, who have all the best tunes) the probability that a lunchtime conversation will be biased in the paranormal direction remains overwhelming.

However, the greatest influence of all – because it can invoke both prestige and weight of numbers – is likely to be the championing of the paranormal cause by the mass media. A rough and ready survey of American popular papers has suggested that credulous articles describing ghosts, telepathy, astrology, etc., tend to outnumber sceptical articles by about two to one.[243] But probably just as important as the stance that is taken is the huge amount of coverage that the phenomena are given – putting them in terms of newsworthiness right on a par with the unquestionably genuine issues of crime, sex and politics (and implying too that they rank well ahead of conventional science).

'I read it in the paper.' 'I heard it on the news.' 'I saw it on TV.' Newspapers, radio and television stations, which so confidently claim to speak *to* the people *for* the people by appointment *of* the people, should have a particular responsibility – so the people themselves might well assume – to get it right. And, as the surveys discussed earlier showed, most people do in fact have remarkable faith in them: 60 per cent say the published media have been their chief source of information.

Yet in reality, of course, the media serve other masters than they claim to. James Lett, an anthropologist, has made a special study of the media in North America and the way they treat the paranormal. He writes: 'Book and magazine publishers, television and movie producers, and newspaper and broadcast journalists are all sure about one thing when it comes to the paranormal: it sells. There is a huge market for stories (true or not) about ghosts, reincarnation, ESP, psychics, UFOs, ancient astronauts, Bigfoot, the Bermuda Triangle, and every other imaginable variety of the paranormal, and the media reap huge profits by producing a large quantity of uncritical material to supply that demand ... There are two reasons for the paranormal receiving such a prominent play in the news media. In the first place, journalists know that the public is greatly interested in stories about the paranormal, and there are major incentives – they are called ratings and circulation – to give the public what it wants. In the second place (and this is the more disturbing and more dangerous of the two factors), most journalists lack the knowledge, training, and experience to critically evaluate paranormal claims. Journalism professor Philip Meyer admits that many journalists don't even care about the objective truth of the matter: "It doesn't make any difference what the facts are – if somebody with an impressive-sounding degree or title says something interesting, then it's a story".[244]

Even though the more serious newspapers and broadcasting channels sometimes mix their pro-paranormal stories with sceptical commentaries, nonetheless they too know better than to make a habit of appearing to be rationalist killjoys. If, for example, a reporter can in a single story both flatter people's sense of their own specialness and insult materialist science at the same time, then this is pretty sure to be the way the story will be angled. So, as Lett continues, 'on balance, the message of both the entertainment and the news media with regard to the paranormal is the same: namely, [to put it at its mildest] that there is, or at least very well may be, another dimension to ordinary reality that is well known to the average citizen but obscure to established scientists, who tend to be cloistered, conservative, and closed-minded.'

Since many conventional scientists themselves are sensitive to this latter criticism and are anxious not to fit the caricature, they too sometimes lean over backwards to present 'the other side'. The result is that even such a responsible magazine as *New Scientist* regularly draws its readers' attention to supposedly novel findings in parapsychology. Thus, for example, under the headline 'Martial arts students influence the past', you might have read recently of how some experiments by Helmut Schmidt have demonstrated retroactive psycho-kinesis of the most remarkable kind.[245] Schmidt is said to have found that if martial arts students focused their mental energy on the numbers coming from a random number generator they could not only influence the sequence of numbers, but could do so retrospectively several months after the numbers had already been recorded. What is more, the article explains, there is a new development of quantum theory which might possibly account for such backward causation.

Now, maybe the author of the article simply did not know of the devastating methodological criticisms that have been made time and again of Schmidt's studies, as for example this by James Alcock: 'None of the studies as they stand would be accepted for publication in a good psychology research journal . . . They are all flawed, some terribly so.'[246] But it is quite likely that even if the author did know he would not have felt obliged to 'censor' the story – since he and the editor might have considered it too good to lose.

This brings me to the question of truth frames. When a report of a strange finding appears, say, on the science page of *The Times* or in the 'Horizon' slot on BBC television, then the very fact that it has been placed in this respected setting is some sort of guarantee that the report can be taken at face value. In such a context the writer or presenter rarely if ever feels it necessary to preface the report with a claim that what follows is being reported in good faith and that reasonable care has been taken to check its truth (although he may find it politic to cover himself by, for example, referring to the findings as 'unorthodox').

Most paranormal stories in the media do not, however, have the advantage of appearing in quite such august settings. And in fact it is not unusual to find the stories preceded by editorial statements which do indeed make some sort of promise as to truth-telling. Thus, for example, several recent television drama-documentaries in the United States (e.g. 'Unsolved Mysteries', 'Haunted Houses: Real Stories', 'Beyond Reality') have been fronted by statements to the effect that 'The following story is true to life and is based on events that were reported and documented by the people involved.'[247] This does not quite amount to the television station's staking its reputation on the truth of the paranormal claim. But many viewers presumably take it to be an implicit endorsement.

Similar conventions operate in everyday exchanges. Unless the person telling the paranormal story is in fact one of those better-than-life people who can be assumed never to tell lies (David Attenborough, say, or the Dalai Lama) the story's credibility may always benefit from a rider to the effect that 'I wouldn't be telling you this if it weren't true'. Such pledges are frequently offered – even between friends. And there can be no question about how well they often work. For a listener to maintain scepticism in the face of assurances like this is, as I know to my cost, not merely regarded as unfriendly, it can come close to social suicide.

But there is a larger and still more interesting point to be made about truth frames and the paranormal. It is that almost *all* paranormal stories, whether or not preceded by any special claim, tend to have a somewhat self-righteous aura to them – a tag of holiness, a certain touch-me-not feel. It is almost as if, just because they concern the paranormal, they get to be intrinsically truth-framed.

The explanation is partly, but only partly, the nature of the subject matter. Many of the stories do of course concern emotionally sensitive areas of people's lives, such as death, love, money, and illness. And this alone may be enough to ensure that even a sceptic will not dig too deeply into what really happened – for fear of opening sores or destroying cherished illusions.

I suspect there is, however, often another explanation. And it originates with what is, arguably, one of the most remarkable confidence tricks our culture has played on us. This has been to persuade people that there is a deep connection between believing in the possibility of psychic forces and being a gracious, honest, upright, trustworthy member of society.

The connection very likely gets established through a process of reasoning as follows. Whether or not people have had any explicit religious education, they have all been exposed to the idea that some kind of supernatural parent figure watches them and cares for them. It may easily follow therefore that people's sense of justice and propriety persuades them that, if such a figure does exist, then *not to believe in him* would be ungrateful in the extreme – and only wicked children could possibly be so ungrateful. But, if unbelievers are generally wicked, it is natural (although hardly logical) to assume that believers are generally good. So whether or not a person believes in this supernatural parent becomes in itself a measure of his moral virtue.

Admittedly, for a person to be a believer in this supernatural parent does not entail that he should also be a believer in all manner of other paranormal influences (though he may well be so). But there has been in practice sufficient overlap between religious and other forms of paranormal belief for the effect to have been that the halo that surrounds 'God-fearing people' has spread to just about every other category of believer.

The absurd, but quite widely accepted result has been that every paranormal story that we hear is supposed to be automatically worthy of attention and respect.

Taking all these things together – the clamour of voices asking to be believed, their pedigree, their number, and their framing – it is hardly surprising that the majority of people end up believing at least some part of what they are being told about the paranormal. With so much smoke, even a dispassionate observer could hardly fail to assume that somewhere there is a roaring fire.

24

It Stands to Reason

When discussing why someone might believe in rainbows, I suggested that, as an alternative to having personally seen one or having heard of them from others, he might possibly have got there by *a priori* reasoning: that is to say, by working out in advance that when sunlight falls on raindrops in a certain way it will create a coloured bow when seen from a particular direction.

In the case of rainbows this suggestion may have seemed a bit implausible. I did, however, hint at other cases where such reasoning might more plausibly be assumed to play a role. There was the evolutionist, for example, who believes purely on theoretical grounds in the existence of the missing link between man and the apes, even though neither he nor anyone else has yet found any fossil evidence of it. Or, still more obviously, there was the explorer who is quite convinced that there has to be a source of the Nile, even though he has neither been there himself nor knows of anybody else who has.

In the latter case, the belief stands firm for the simple reason that to deny it would lead to a *reductio ad absurdum*. We may not think of this as a form of reasoning much used in ordinary life (though consider how often we do in fact adopt a particular idea because we can see the falseness of its opposite). But we should note that it is regularly put to more formal use. Thus mathematicians would argue, for example, that there have to be infinitely many prime numbers, on the grounds that if there were not infinitely many some particular number would have to be the largest prime – and it is easy to show that the idea of any number being the largest prime is self contradictory. More pertinently, perhaps, there have been philosopher-theologians who have argued that we must believe in the existence of God because it can be demonstrated that his non-existence would be logically impossible. There are various versions of this latter argument, the neatest (the so-called 'ontological argument') being that, if God is defined as the one being who is perfect in every respect, then he has to exist since if he did not exist he would obviously be lacking something and hence be less than perfect.

The question is whether ordinary people apply any such *a priori* reasoning to the case of their own souls and their potential for exerting psychic powers.

Given how much weight I have been putting up till now on what has been revealed by public surveys, I should acknowledge that this is actually *not* one of the reasons for believing in the paranormal that has emerged from the surveys. Nor, I might add, is it something that gets regularly brought up in conversation – as, say, the empirical evidence does.

However, this lack of explicit citation does not mean much. In none of the surveys were people actually invited to mention *a priori* reasoning as such. In the Reading survey, for example, where people were asked to nominate from a checklist the most important influence on their beliefs, *a priori* reasoning was simply not included on the checklist; nor was it in the survey of members of the Parapsychological Association (although in their case a few of these relatively sophisticated respondents did raise the issue for themselves – making reference, for example, to 'intuitive reasons for believing' or 'deduction from other facts').

Besides, it could well be that, even though nearly everybody realises that their beliefs about the paranormal are in fact being affected by some form of *a priori* reasoning, it does not come up as an issue because it seems like something to be taken for granted: something everybody else can be assumed to be aware of and therefore, paradoxically, not worth discussing. Sometimes the more obvious something is, the less it will be commented on. If people are asked what they are standing upon, few would bother to make mention of their feet.

*

It was the renowned cultural historian Edward Tylor who was, I think, the first explicitly to draw attention to the possibility that the human penchant for thinking things through from first principles could be the key factor in turning people towards belief in paranormal powers. Recognising that similar beliefs have been characteristic of all known human societies throughout history, he suggested that their origin lay not in anybody's direct observation of paranormal phenomena as such but rather in what inevitably happens when 'thinking people' start reflecting on the meaning of certain relatively familiar facts of life.

He pointed to two sets of human experiences which in combination would, he thought, have led people on. 'It seems as though thinking men, as yet in a low level of culture, were deeply impressed by two groups of biological problems. In the first place, what is it that makes the difference between a living body and a dead one; what causes working, sleep, trance, disease, death? In the second place, what are these human shapes which appear in dreams and visions? Looking at these two groups of phenomena, the ancient savage philosophers probably made their first step by the obvious inference that every man has two things belonging to him, namely a life and a phantom.'[248]

People would have recognised, Tylor said, first that 'life' or 'the animating principle' can leave a person's body, as it does in death or dreamless sleep, so that although the body persists the conscious self is gone; and second that a ghostly version of this conscious self can wander and go visiting, as may happen when it turns up in another person's dream or vision. From which they might well have drawn the reasonable conclusion that the ghostly self that sometimes turns up elsewhere is one and the same entity as the animating self that sometimes leaves the body. If the self returns to the body the man wakes or escapes from his trance; if it stays away, he dies and his body corrupts, although as a ghost it may continue to haunt other people's lives.

From this it would surely have been but a short step to believing in the possible occurrence of a variety of more exotic paranormal phenomena. For, as Leonard Zusne has written, 'Once the premise of immortality, immateriality and transcendence is granted, every magic act on the part of the transcending self becomes possible: after all, it belongs to a different world, one that is not bound by the limitations of gravity, density, and time and space in general.'[249] Psychic action at a distance, telepathic communication, reincarnation, messages from the dead, and so on – all would become not merely real possibilities but, with just a little imagination, real probabilities. So much so that if these phenomena were not in fact to be encountered in real life, it might seem quite reasonable to invent them: which is, arguably, what in culture after culture actually transpired.

Admittedly, these conjectures of Tylor have generally cut little ice with modern anthropologists – who have criticised him for what they see as armchair theorising and Just-So story telling. I would say, however, that such criticism is less than fair.

As stories go, Tylor's account has considerable appeal, even if as an historical hypothesis about the origins of paranormal beliefs it is of course impossible to verify. But then part of the reason it appeals is precisely that it strikes us not as an historical hypothesis at all but as a current one – we can all imagine ourselves and our neighbours reasoning in very much this way. But in any case the accusation of armchair theorising plays straight into Tylor's hands. For his theory is a theory *about* armchair theorising – about the widespread human tendency to indulge in idle (or maybe not so idle) speculation about life and death. Rather than Tylor assuming, as many of his contemporaries would have done, that primitive peoples were uninterested in or even incapable of abstract reasoning, he took it for granted that some at least among them would have been bound to sit back and speculate about what it all means. Although his 'thinking men, as yet in a low level of culture' may have been less comfortably seated than he himself was, he properly credited them with philosophical flights of fancy comparable to those we value in ourselves.

I think that Tylor's fault if anything was that he was actually too cautious. Rather than supposing that there were only a relatively few 'savage philosophers' who thought this way, he should have recognised that the kind of arguments he attributed to this group of savants were – and of course still are – likely to arise in the minds of all ordinary people, and not only adults but children too.

Whether or not Tylor was right in the detail of his views need not be our concern. What matters is the general line he took: the idea that ratiocination in and of itself can be a major cultural force, and in particular that human beings might be expected to have found their way to believing in the paranormal by what starts out as a non-paranormal route.

But there has always been, I think, a still more obvious route to take than Tylor's. For, if people can reason their way towards the paranormal on the basis of the experiences of weird phenomena like dreams and visions, all the more should they be able to do so on the basis of the experiences of ordinary, waking, mental life. In fact if there were ever a good reason for believing in an immaterial soul with potential paranormal powers, it is arguably the incontestable, universally experienced, continuing miracle of human consciousness.

How comes it that we have such astonishing powers of perception, intelligence, language, imagination, will-power, strength of purpose, skill in action? How can the mental and the physical worlds interact in such coherent and purposeful ways? How can we be so lucky as to be blessed with self-awareness? Why ever should it feel as it does feel to be each of us?

Look into a human mind from the inside and all you find is thoughts and feelings, look into a human body from the outside and all you find is flesh and blood. How can two such entirely different kinds of things keep such consistent company? What possible explanation can there be for these minds belonging to these bodies? Can anyone deny – unless they resort to some very special pleading – that human mental life seems to be simply too good to be true?

It was precisely the contemplation of such matters that famously led René Descartes (sitting on a stove to do *his* armchair theorising) to embrace the hypothesis of 'dualism'. It was from these few deeply perplexing but incontrovertible facts that he thought he could argue that the conscious mind and the physical body really must be independent entities, belonging to different qualitative realms – the former made of what he called, in Latin, *res cogitans* or 'thinking stuff', the latter of *res extensa* or 'extended stuff'.

Neither entity, he concluded, absolutely requires the existence of the other: bodies without minds are possible in principle, and minds without bodies are possible in principle. In human beings, however, God has so arranged it that the two do in fact coexist in a wonderfully intimate relationship. This relationship is made possible because – but only because – there is a special channel in the human brain (located, Descartes surmised, in the pineal gland) that is capable of carrying causal influences in both directions. These influences involve the direct effect of mind on matter and of matter on mind. These normal psychophysical interactions are therefore, strictly speaking, paranormal. In so far as they operate only within the brain, they may be a unique and exceptional case. Nonetheless the possibility in principle of paranormal interaction has to be conceded.

Now, the dualist solution may of course bring with it some problems of its own. But it does at least seem to overcome the even bigger problems that attach to the only obvious alternative: namely, some form of monism – which means in effect some form of 'physicalism'.

The physicalist view would be that, instead of our minds being an immaterial adjunct to our bodies, they are some kind of *product* of our physical bodies. And the very idea of this, it has frequently been argued, is on the face of it preposterous. 'Isn't it perfectly evident to you', the philosopher-novelist Colin McGinn asks in a dialogue with himself, 'that consciousness simply *could not* be produced by mere combinations of particles, however subtle the combination? Matter is just the wrong *kind* of thing to give birth to consciousness ... You might as well assert that numbers emerge from biscuits or ethics from rhubarb.'[250]

If McGinn's line in this dialogue is right – and the only alternative to dualism turns out to be so plainly untenable, when you come to think of it – it follows presumably that dualism *has* to be the answer. Indeed, we can employ the form of *a priori* argument we encountered earlier: the soul exists because its non-existence would lead to an absurdity.

It would be wrong to pretend that this is something absolutely everybody does stop to think about – or that the 'mind–body problem', as modern philosophers conceive of it, is a burning issue for all human beings. Still, I doubt if there is anybody who has not at least noticed that there really is a puzzle here, hardly a person who has not observed that their own mental life *is* on the face of it too good to be true, and therefore, I would guess, hardly anyone who has not been drawn to dualism as at least some sort of a solution. For one really does not have to be a great philosopher (indeed one must not be *too* great a philosopher) to arrive at this solution. If Descartes and McGinn can get there by arguing that dualism has to be true because the alternative of physicalism simply cannot be true, then so too can lesser thinkers.

Besides, ordinary people are likely to get not a little outside cultural help. Descartes, so he claimed, ploughed the furrow for himself, clearing his mind of every external influence before proving from first principles that his answer to the puzzle was necessarily correct. Yet the fact that the reasoning that leads to dualism could in principle be carried through in a cultural vacuum does not mean it has to be. In real life much of the work has been done by thinkers up ahead, and the dualist solution is already there for the taking – being promulgated in all the ways described in the last chapter. In particular much of our everyday *language* is well and truly dualist, riding on the firm assumption that mind and body are – as the very words imply they are – categorically distinct.

This is not to say that there are not also more recent cultural influences working *against* dualism. As I am sure you realise, the whole trend of modern psychology and neuroscience is in fact totally antithetical to dualism and will not admit to there being even a hint of paranormal interaction between mind and brain. Yet the impact of these new ideas on ordinary people is probably minimal.

To start with, the various explanations that are currently on offer for how the conscious mind could achieve what it does entirely by normal physical means are hard for most laymen to understand. But they are hard too, it should be said, for many of the scientists themselves, and there is still very little agreement even among the *cognoscenti* about which explanations work and which do not.

All but a few contemporary psychologists agree that there will eventually prove to be some sort of satisfactory monist theory of mind–brain relationships: a theory, that is, which does succeed in showing how mental activity and brain activity can be one and the same thing. But at present there really is very little consensus about the form, let alone the substance, of this theory-to-come. Some go for computer analogies, others seek the answer in complexity theory or neural Darwinism, others think it all hinges on quantum theory . . . and perhaps the one and only thing that every theorist agrees on (and, being one of them, I can say this without fear of contradiction[251]) is that there is something wrong with everyone's theories other than their own! The result is that the 'problem of consciousness' continues to be referred to in the literature – even the scientific literature – as the one great unsolved problem of our times.

In these circumstances, it is hardly surprising that dualism still dominates popular thinking. While the problem of consciousness remains a problem even for the experts, ordinary people can be forgiven for supposing that they have (and always have had) the essence of the answer already in their pockets: the simple, easily graspable, patently obvious, and metaphysically comforting idea that mind and body belong to different spheres and may in principle lead relatively independent lives, even while the mind has effects *on* the body and the body effects *on* the mind.

My point is this. Once a person has arrived at this dualist model of what it is to be a human being, it is certain to be a powerful enabler of paranormal belief across the board. Once he has arrived at this model of what goes on quite naturally inside himself when he wills, acts, perceives, and so on, the way is open to legitimising paranormal action in the world beyond.

I said above that the case of mind-over-matter interactions occurring within the brain ought perhaps to be regarded as exceptional. This is certainly what Descartes and other relatively conservative dualists have assumed (in Descartes' model, for example, the pineal gland constituted a one-off bridge between thinking substance and extended substance, whose like did not occur elsewhere). I suspect, however, that the more natural and usual way to read the dualist message – and extrapolate from it – is much more radical.

If it can happen inside the brain, why not outside? In fact could it not be argued that, compared to what happens every day inside our heads, when our minds lead our bodies the amazing dances that they do, such public phenomena as spoon-bending or card-guessing should be considered very small beer? Once we admit that mind-over-matter effects can and do occur in a single case, the absolute taboo on non-physical causation has been broken. The world is then the paranormal's oyster.

Perhaps most people would not draw out this argument quite so explicitly. Professional parapsychologists, however, have been eager to do so. Several have openly acknowledged that it is their faith in mind–body dualism that justifies and motivates their search for paranormal phenomena in general. So says M. A. Thalbourne: 'Whether we like it or not, and despite the best efforts of an Eccles or a Popper . . . the dominant mode of thinking among present-day scientists is that of Central-State Materialism. Parapsychologists alone constitute a professional group where Dualism is still the most popular assumption.'[252]

John Beloff has been even more plain-spoken: 'The dominant tradition in psychical research has always regarded psi as making sense only within a dualist ontology. Might it not be that psi arises from the fact that mind can directly influence matter and matter mind? Normally these interactions would be confined to the mind–brain system where they would be going on all the time.

Once in a while, however, they may spill over into the environment and it is only then that they would count as "paranormal" within the terms of the accepted definition.'[253]

But these statements only make explicit what I think the vast majority of people take for granted: that if – and maybe only if – mind and body are what almost everybody thinks they are, would paranormal phenomena make sense.

You may feel that the argument of this book is beginning to come full circle. I started by arguing that we need evidence of paranormal phenomena in order to justify our belief in the existence of the soul. Now I am saying that it is because as natural dualists we already believe in the soul that we hope and expect to find evidence of paranormal phenomena.

There is, however, no reason why both should not be true. It is entirely typical of human belief systems that there should be this sliding relationship between evidence and theory, with the push coming now from one side, now the other. The balance differs from person to person, and very likely within each individual from time to time. But most of us make progress by throwing our weight alternately from foot to foot.

Beloff, who has always been highly respectful of facts, pointedly insists in his many writings on the subject that for him it really is the phenomena which have persuaded him of the truth of dualism, and *not* the other way around. Here in a letter to me for example he typically makes the evidence come first: 'If psi phenomena occur we must adopt some other conception of the way the mind works, for example that the mind generates ideas and that these ideas somehow fulfil themselves in the real world. This may smack uncomfortably of magic but only observation can tell us whether or not such magic is a fact.'[254] Probably everyone will half agree with this 'only observation can tell'. But I strongly suspect that for many people it is nonetheless their basic belief that the mind *must be magic to be a mind at all* that encourages them, to begin with, to go out and look.

25
Beyond the Limits

My question, three chapters back, was: what creates the mind-set which encourages people to go on searching for the paranormal? Why – after all the disappointments, after the false dawns and fast eclipses – do so many still think there must be something there?

The answer, as we have seen, may lie partly in personal experience, partly in faith in the opinions and experiences of other people, and partly – perhaps mainly? – in philosophical reflections about consciousness and the relation of mind to body. To these three powerful influences, add the comfort and joy of being allowed to have one's soul back from science. No wonder, then, that the majority of people are so well disposed towards the field of parapsychology in general and so eager to listen to particular stories.

Let me turn to my own final reasons for remaining sceptical: reasons why I myself am in the end so certain that the parapsychological quest is a wild goose chase and all claims to have actually captured particular paranormal phenomena are false. I have reserved these arguments till now partly so as not to shoot my fox and bring the whole discussion to a premature conclusion; but partly, also, so as not to seem to rest my case on arguments that may strike some readers as too picky – I might almost say too bureaucratic – to be an adequate response to the challenge of the paranormal.

What I shall do in the next chapter is to provide an argument as to why neither ESP nor PK, at least as popularly conceived, could possibly occur even in theory, let alone in practice. But first I shall try to put into perspective the idea that there may be *logical* objections – and not just scientific and empirical ones – to the existence of psychic phenomena.

It is important that the nature of this argument should not be misunderstood. When I argue – as I shall – that most if not all psychic phenomena are indeed 'logically impossible', I must not be thought to be saying that there are logical objections to the occurrence of the surface phenomena that people interpret as being psychic. Rather I shall be saying that, if and when these surface phenomena do occur, there are logical objections to this being the correct interpretation of them.

Logical analysis, we should be clear, should never be taken to be a way of regulating what is true or untrue at the level of raw facts. Rather it is a way of regulating what can be said about the underlying relations between such facts. To take a trivial example, logic could have nothing to say about a report that one woman, Mary, was born in 1964 and another woman, Kate, was born in 1947; but it could say quite categorically that if these were their birth-years it would be impossible for Mary to be the mother of Kate. Or to take a more pertinent one, logic could not comment on the claim that someone has dreamt of a certain number, and that this same number has been selected by the lottery computer the next day; but it might well be able to comment on whether it could possibly make sense to claim that the dream was causally responsible for the computer's selection.

I should agree with the defenders of the paranormal – I already said as much when discussing the Humean argument in Chapter 11 – that it would be unwise for a critic to try to legislate on any grounds at all as to whether it is *empirically* possible for strange phenomena to happen. Predictions made in advance may be and frequently are wrong-footed by reality, events occur even though nothing like them has ever been observed to happen in the past, unimagined contingencies do arise, seemingly absurd eventualities do come to pass.

Pascal, writing a century before Hume, sought to pre-empt Hume's argument against the reality of highly improbable events (and indeed Hume's favourite illustrative example) by pointing out that it is no more impossible *in principle* that a dead man should come back to life than that an unborn man should achieve life in the first place. 'Which is harder, to be born or to rise again? That what has never been should be, or that what has been should be once more?'[255] And he explicitly scorned any argument based simply on previous precedents. 'Habit makes us find the one easy, while lack of habit makes us find the other impossible. Popular way to judge!' Next, as if warming to his theme, he proceeded to argue for the possibility in principle of virgin birth: 'Why should not a virgin bear a child? Does not a hen produce eggs without a cock? ... And how do we know that a hen cannot form the germ just as well as a cock?'

In the same vein we might well ask, for example (if it were not that we already know the answer in these cases): why should not a man be struck by lightning six times, why should not corn-circles appear overnight in the fields, why should not Houdini escape from a water-filled milk churn, why should not life emerge on Earth, why should not England win the World Cup ... or why should not Shakespeare's birthday be encoded in the Book of Psalms? Provided we stay strictly at the level of raw facts, the answer evidently is that there is no reason why not – either in principle or, it seems, in practice either.

But now suppose we go beyond the purely factual level and start asking questions not only about whether something could possibly occur but *what could possibly explain it* if and when it did occur. Suppose, that is, we move from fact to interpretation. Granted that it would be unwise to rule out the empirical possibility of certain facts, would it be equally unwise to rule out the logical possibility of certain explanations? We enter here a different game.

Consider the case of resurrection. If Pascal is right and we cannot absolutely disallow the possibility that a man might in fact rise up from the dead, can we nonetheless absolutely disallow certain potential explanations of what casual process could lie behind it? The undertaker suggests to us, for example, that the explanation for his client's rising from the dead is that 'once the man was removed from the ice box, the warmth of the radiators made his bodily functions return to normal'. While there might be much else that we would like to know about what went on here, there would be nothing obviously incoherent or self-contradictory about this explanation – and it would not be one we could rule out in advance on purely logical grounds. However suppose the undertaker suggests instead that the explanation for the man's rising from the dead is that 'at five past two his biological clock started to run backwards and caused his body to revert to its pre-death state'. Here, although the explanation might sound at first quite reasonable, we would discover after a moment's thought that the idea of a biological clock going into reverse could not possibly make sense – and therefore this explanation is one we absolutely could and should rule out.

Or consider some of the other examples that I mentioned. In every case there would be some explanations which, however improbable, would not be impossible in principle, but others which we could logically reject from the start. We might allow, for example, that a possible explanation of a man being struck by lightning six times is that he has made a habit of carrying an umbrella in thunderstorms, but we could reject out of hand the explanation that his name was Bernard. We might allow that the explanation of Houdini's not drowning in the milk churn is that he held his breath, but we could reject the explanation that he drank the water. And so on.

But now, partly so as to clear up some unfinished business from the earlier chapter but more so as to steer the discussion towards a particular kind of logical impossibility, let me close in on the particular case of Shakespeare and the Book of Psalms.

The bare facts, as I gave them, were as follows. William Shakespeare, whose name is an anagram of 'Here was I like a psalm', was 46 years old when the King James translation of the Bible was completed; and in the 46th Psalm, the 46th word from the beginning is 'shake' and the 46th from the end is 'spear'.

We should assume, I think, that the existence of this set of facts does represent a genuine explanatory challenge. Although there is no obvious way of calculating just how improbable it is that such a neat pattern could have arisen merely by chance, the odds against it must certainly be long. Such patterns do not turn up every day, even if you go looking for them. If you check through the other 149 psalms, for example, looking at the *n*th word from the beginning and the *n*th word from the end of the *n*th psalm, you will find no hint in any other case of a similarly interesting name or phrase.

However, if there *is* to be an explanation, whatever could it be? Are we to suppose that Shakespeare's birth could somehow have been causally responsible for those particular words appearing in those positions in that psalm? Or, vice versa, are we to suppose that the words of the psalm could somehow have been responsible for the birth of a boy called William Shakespeare? Perhaps neither sounds in any way like a real possibility, logical or otherwise. But before we rush to judgement on this, let's consider what might have been going on at the ground level.

Shakespeare was already a famous figure on the literary scene in the early 1600s when the English translation of the Bible from the Hebrew was being made by the team of scholars in London. He would quite likely have been a friend of one or more of the translators; and indeed it is not impossible that he himself might have been asked to advise on the translation – especially when it came to the richly poetic language of the psalms.[256] We know that Shakespeare and his fellow poets loved wordplay and riddles, and frequently teased their readers with cryptic references and signatures. Thus, it is by no means inconceivable that someone involved in the translation might have deliberately planted the two key words in the 46th Psalm. They could have done it precisely to celebrate the great man's birthday.

Thus the first explanation, that Shakespeare's birth was in some way responsible for the words of the psalm, is actually not only logically possible but even rather plausible. (Indeed, the very fact that the existence of this pattern of words is known to us today is, I would say, good grounds for saying it *must* have been planted there deliberately – for how else, unless someone at some time knew what to look for, would the existence of the riddle have come to light?)

By contrast, however, the alternative explanation, that the words in the psalm were somehow responsible for Shakespeare's birth, runs straight up against a series of deep theoretical objections. To begin with there is the small point that, since Shakespeare's birth occurred earlier in time than the biblical translation, this explanation would have to involve some kind of backward causation – which, if not strictly impossible in principle, nonetheless quickly leads to all sorts of logical absurdities. But, over and above this, and arguably still more decisive, there is the point that this explanation promises, at an *informational* level, much more than it can possibly deliver – the problem of what we might call 'inadequate prescriptive power'.

The nature of this problem will become much clearer when we come to discuss it in relation to more standard psychic phenomena. But to put it in a nutshell now, the problem arises when *too little a cause* is made responsible for *too large an effect* – when, as here with Shakespeare, a relatively simple event (the text of a psalm) is suggested as the cause of a relatively rich and complex event (the birth of a baby called William to the wife of Master Shakespeare in 1564). And the reason this presents so great a difficulty is that, while it is indeed logically possible for a simple event to trigger a complex one, it is not possible for a simple event to *prescribe the content* of a complex one. While you can, for example, use a single toss of a coin to set a major train of events in motion, you clearly cannot use a single toss to specify which of a thousand different outcomes will result (or which of ten or even which of three). You cannot – cannot logically – get an informationally richer message out than you put in.

It is precisely on this test of 'prescriptive sufficiency' that the interpretation of psi phenomena *as* psychic falls apart.

Before I get to this, however, and before the discussion turns more technical, let me return to an exchange between Pascal and one of his religious mentors, that touched on matters closely related to this one of logical impossibility – and that can give us one more take on the issue as a whole.

In 1656 Pascal sent a letter to the Jesuit Abbot of Saint-Cyran, asking his opinion of various problems concerning miracles.[257] Pascal's own position (as we have already had occasion to note) was that 'my view is that any effect is miraculous when it exceeds the natural powers of the means employed. Thus I call it miraculous when illness is cured by touching a sacred relic, when a man possessed is healed by invoking the name of Jesus, etc., because the effects exceed the natural powers of the words used to invoke God or the natural powers of a relic, neither of which can heal the sick nor drive out devils.'

The learned Abbot replied that theologians distinguish two sorts of miracles. On the one hand there may be miracles that are 'supernatural in the manner in which they are produced', *quoad modum*, where phenomena which are not in themselves beyond natural limits are being produced by means that are not naturally capable of producing them, so that the *process* that leads to them is miraculous. The Abbot's example was 'when Jesus Christ healed the eyes of a blind man with mud' – the point being that, while recovery from blindness as such is not unnatural, recovery as the result of the laying on of mud is. On the other hand there may be miracles that are 'supernatural in substance', *quoad substantiam*, where the phenomena in themselves are indeed beyond the limits of nature, so that their very *existence* is miraculous. His example was 'when a single body is in two places at the same time' – the point being that in this case the phenomenon as such could never come to pass in the natural course of things.

Now, Pascal's definition of a miracle as 'any effect which exceeds the natural powers of the means employed' covers only the former kind of miracle. This is, however, not a serious limitation, since, as the Abbot observed, the former kind is much more common in practice than the latter. In particular 'most of the miracles performed for us in the Gospels are of this [former] kind'. And the same goes, we can be safe in saying, for just about all the miracles of modern parapsychology. Psychic phenomena in general are clearly examples of *quoad modum* miracles: phenomena which in themselves are nothing unusual – a die falling so as to show a six, a secret letter being read, a thought becoming known – but which are apparently being produced in highly unusual ways – the die falling that way as the result of a spoken invocation, the letter being read by staring into a crystal ball, the thought being communicated by telepathic projection.

There is, however, a major case of begging-the-question occurring here. Are we to take it for granted that the 'means employed' to produce an effect – in other words the factors intended by the agent to create it or interpreted by others as doing so – are indeed the factors truly responsible for causing the effect? Are we to assume, for example, that if someone prays for something to happen and it happens, then the prayer was responsible, or if someone tries to transmit a thought to another person and the person has this same thought, then the attempt to transmit was responsible?

Pascal never so much as questions this assumption of responsibility, and proceeds to wonder at *how* the means employed could be responsible for the effect. Such is also the usual line taken by contemporary parapsychologists (and probably most of the lay population too). But it is quite wrong, surely, to be asking *how in practice* the means could be responsible before we have established *whether in principle* the means could be responsible. Are we dealing here, as everybody assumes, merely with a case of an effect exceeding the natural powers of the means employed, or is it in another league: namely, a case of *an explanation of an effect* – namely, the explanation which labels the means employed as the means responsible – exceeding *the logical powers* of the argument employed?

To home in on the crucial issue: my view is that any interpretation of the relationship between two events X and Y as one in which *X prescribes the content of Y* has to be incorrect if and when this requires from X *more discriminative power* than it actually has. If such is the case, we had better conclude either that what we took to be a *quoad modum* miracle is actually a *quoad substantiam* one – or, much more likely, that we are dealing not with a miracle but with a mirage.

26

Nothing for Free

Logical objections, like those that came to the surface in the foregoing discussion, are of some theoretical interest. But there are surely people who would argue that in practice they could be of relevance only to the more far-out psychic phenomena – those that are already recognised by parapsychologists to be theoretically embarrassing.

So let me make the testing ground for the objections the relatively 'reasonable' phenomena of PK and ESP. There are, no doubt, softer targets such as life after death, psychic thoughtography, ectoplasmic materialisations and so on. But if I am to make a strong case against anything ever being genuinely psychic, I had better go after the basic phenomena that constitute what can be called the 'acceptable face of parapsychology' – those phenomena that are supposed to be reproducible in the laboratory, the kind of thing that could be taken seriously by a Turing or a Freud.

Earlier in the book I gave some summary definitions, to which it may be helpful to return. Cases of PK, I said, can be broadly defined as cases 'where it appears that the mind is inducing material changes at a remote location in the outside world, without the mediation of any force or process known to science. In general it can be assumed that the state of mind responsible is some form of wish or request – a mental picture of a desired goal – and the material change that occurs is in the direction of this goal.' And cases of ESP can be defined as cases 'where someone's mind comes under the influence of distant events without there being the opportunity for observation or communication by any channel known to science. In most cases ESP manifests itself as a change in what the person knows or believes or feels, and it can be assumed that this change is towards the person's becoming aware that the external event is happening.'

To give an insider's perspective on this, we can supplement my words with those of Robert Morris, Professor of Parapsychology at the University of Edinburgh, who approaches psi phenomena with the language of 'communications theory'. 'Each of the forms of psi can be seen as involving an apparent source of influence, an apparent receiver, and an apparent message or pattern of influence. For PK, the organism is the source and appears to influence the behaviour of a target aspect of the environment which serves as a receiver . . . For ESP, some target aspect of the environment serves as a source, seeming to influence the experience or behaviour of a receiver organism, generally a human . . . By construing psi in communication terms, we can tie it to models of communication drawn from other disciplines, and attempt to study it as we would other forms of communication.'[258]

Under these definitions, therefore, certain events occurring in one place, namely at the receiver, are to be explained as having been paranormally caused by certain other events occurring in another place, namely at the source. Just how this explanation is supposed to work in detail is usually left vague. But, if we take seriously the communications model, we have to suppose that some sort of causal chain is involved as follows: the source events are encoded as a signal (of unknown type) which is then transmitted (via an unknown medium) until it is picked up at the receiver where (by unknown means) it is decoded and produces some further events related to the first. Let's call what happens at the source the 'input' and what happens at the receiver the 'output'. The theory is that the input is instrumental, via this chain, in 'informing' – that is to say, literally providing the information for – the output.

The parapsychologists' question is how in practice this causal sequence works. Our own question, now that we have come so far, must be whether in principle any such sequence possibly *could* work even in theory.

*

The discussion has now to become slightly more intricate. However, it will at least make it easier to manage if, rather than trying to consider every possible permutation of different sorts of source and receiver, we limit ourselves to thinking about just two paradigm examples: of (a) someone trying to influence a remote physical event, and (b) someone trying to gain information from a remote mind. And we may as well place them, in imagination, in a relatively simple situation.

Let's suppose, then, that in the lobby of the Plaza Hotel in New York a die is being thrown in the air and falling on the ground, watched by the doorman. And in Cambridge, England, a student is being tested for her psychic powers. First, with PK under test, we should count it a convincing example of the student's powers if her *wishing* the die to fall with a particular number on top were to be reliably associated with its actually falling that way. Her wish would be the input, the fall of the die the output, and the correspondence of one to the other would be evidence of paranormal information transfer. Next, with telepathic ESP under test, we should count it a convincing example of her powers if her *guessing* that the die has fallen a particular way were reliably associated with its having been seen to fall that way by the doorman. Here the doorman's perception of it would be the input, the student's guess the output, and again the correspondence would be evidence of paranormal information transfer.

We should note a crucial – if obvious – feature of both these communicative interactions, which can be assumed to be characteristic of psi in general. It is that the information transfer between source and receiver does not result merely in there being a significant correlation between input and output, it results in there being a significant *resemblance:* the output is some kind of *copy* of the input, as regards both the subject and the content. Thus PK is all about wishes coming *literally true.* When a person wishes that a particular object shall be affected in a particular way, the result is not just that the wish has some kind of effect somewhere or other, it is that it has the wished-for effect at the targeted location. Likewise, ESP is all about learning *what is really going on.* When a person comes to believe that some particular thing is happening to some particular object, this belief is not just the result of some kind of thing happening to some object or other, it is the result of the believed-in thing happening to the identified object. In both cases, therefore, there is not merely a one-to-one mapping between input and output, there is a semantically transparent or meaning-preserving mapping.[259]

Now this kind of transparent mapping is of course part and parcel of what is implied by calling the interaction 'communicative'. Indeed, it is basic to the very idea of normal communication that the input at the source is causally responsible for bringing about a semantically equivalent output at the receiver. You might think therefore that any decent theory of 'paranormal communication' should be able to take this feature in its stride – which is why I said this feature is crucial. For the reality is, I believe, that *no* theory can possibly deal with it. What creates the insuperable difficulty in all realistic cases of supposed psi-communication is, as we shall see, the fact that the receiver has too many degrees of freedom, too much scope for not responding to an incoming stimulus in any standard way.

But there is, you may think, something rather tendentious about this. If in other spheres of communication meaning-preserving mappings are actually the norm – conversation over the telephone, for instance, would seem to do the trick quite nicely – why should it be so different with psi?

The telephone was in fact precisely the model that Freud himself chose for ESP. 'The telepathic process', he wrote, 'is supposed to consist in a mental act of one person giving rise to the same mental act in another. What lies between the two mental acts may very well be a physical process, into which the mental process transforms itself at one end and which is transformed back into the same mental process at the other. The analogy with other transformations, such as speaking and hearing across the telephone, is an obvious one.'[260] Freud was writing in the days when telephones required a fixed physical link. But now that we are familiar with go-anywhere cellular phones, the analogy would seem to be an even better one. And we have only to think of other wonders of modern communications technology – fax machines,

TV cameras, the internet, remotely controlled robots, and so on – to find seemingly obvious analogies not only for telepathy but for clairvoyance and psychokinesis too.

Then what if anything makes these analogies inappropriate? Why should psi be in a different class? We can easily imagine, for example, how in practice someone's verbal statement 'Fall so as to show a four' could be transmitted by normal means from Cambridge to the hotel lobby in New York and be transformed into a written instruction on a sheet of paper or a picture on a TV screen showing the desired outcome. So why should we not imagine someone's wish being transmitted by paranormal means and transformed into whatever kind of force-field would be required actually to make the die fall this way?

The answer is simple. You can only communicate in this sort of structured way when and if you – or whoever designed the communication line – know exactly what the characteristics of the channel are and what kind of receiver is on the other end. Otherwise, although it may be perfectly possible to have an effect of *some kind* at the receiver's end, the chances of its being the *intended* effect are virtually zero.

With telephones, faxes, TVs and so on, the receiver is a standardised device and all the relevant parameters of the transmission channel are fixed and known. The telephone ear-piece, for example, has been specifically designed so that its behaviour in response to any particular set of imposed electrical signals is entirely predictable. Hence all the transformation rules that are needed to ensure that the output resembles the input can be and have been established in advance. And in fact all that is required in practice is that appropriate transducers and translators be built in at either end.

With all realistic examples of PK or ESP, however, the truth is that the receiver – the die, say, or the student's brain – is usually far from being a standardised device and the parameters of the transmission channel cannot be fixed. Indeed, it is typical for the receiver to be in many ways an unknown quantity, of uncertain physical structure and qualities, of no fixed address, beginning in an unascertained initial state, in an uncertain environment, and subject to who knows what incidental constraints. The inevitable consequence is that there can be no telling whether, as a general rule, any particular set of influences applied to the receiver will have any particular effect. Hence there can be no question of relying on built-in transducers and translators.

To see just how bad the problem is likely to become, let us follow up on our imagined example of PK. Here the student's task, supposedly, is to bring her wish to bear on the die in order to make it fall so as to show a four. The die will, we can assume, only change its course and fall one particular way rather than any other if certain precisely determined forces act on it. So, if the student's wish is to have the right effect, she will have somehow to communicate exactly these forces and none other. Let's leave aside the $64,000 questions of just how the communication will take place or how the forces will actually come into being (these being ultimately factual questions not logical ones). Let's simply assume that the student can, through making exactly the right wish, magically direct that whatever patterned force field she specifies will materialise at whatever precise location she pleases.

Now, if the die were in fact to be a standard die which is being tossed in the air in an absolutely predictable way in a precisely known location, then any and every applied force field would have its own predictable outcome. It would be possible in that case to work out transformation rules such that each particular wish would indeed have the desired effect. In principle we might even imagine such rules being built into the student's head so that she has merely to wish and the result will follow automatically.

Unfortunately, however, the reality cannot be this at all. There are bound to be literally hundreds of unknowns about the exact nature and circumstances of the die. To begin with, there must be doubt about where exactly it is situated ('the lobby of the Plaza Hotel, New York' will hardly serve to pinpoint the location!). But, worse still, there will be question marks about its starting orientation, its height above the floor, its elasticity, the style of toss being applied to it, etc., etc. Perhaps all these things could in principle be known to someone. Yet we can be quite sure that they are not in practice going to be known or even knowable *to the student.* The problem is, of course, that what she does not know cannot be a determinant of the content of her wish. Her wish cannot therefore take account of what it would have to take account of to achieve its goal.

But, in any case, what would happen even if by some kind of remarkable providence all the requisite incidental information *could* be made available to her? Would it really make sense to imagine her wish taking account of it and containing all the detailed local instructions for how exactly to achieve the outcome in these circumstances? No, this is not part of the deal. No one is ever put to this much work in the making of a wish. When a person wishes for something, she expects merely to specify the final outcome without more ado. She expects, that is, *merely* to pray for rain, or merely to urge a spoon to bend, bend, bend, or merely to encourage seeds to germinate, or merely to will a random-number generator to stop being random, or merely to curse her enemy with boils, or whatever else people may (and do) merely try.

But, if all this is true with PK, do the same objections necessarily extend to ESP? Is it possible that the problems might be less intractable when there is another *person* rather than an inanimate object on the receiving end?

Let us consider our example of telepathy. Here the student's task, supposedly, is to guess what is in the doorman's mind when he is, say, looking at a die showing a four. Much as in the previous case, we can assume that, other things being equal, the student's brain will be moved to make such a guess only if certain very particular influences reach it. Thus, if the doorman's thoughts are to have the right effect, they must be capable of exerting just these influences. Let's again leave aside the question of exactly what kind of paranormal communication channel is going to be involved or how the influences will actually come into being, and let's simply assume that the doorman's thoughts are transformed into some kind of patterned energy field which is broadcast round the world and to which the student's brain, perhaps acting as some kind of resonator, can tune in.

Now, maybe the student's brain, unlike the die, *can* be

considered to be a standardised receiver. Maybe all human brains are so much alike in their construction and their stand-by state that every individual can be counted on to respond to the same input in the same way – so that, when the patterned energy field emanating from the doorman arrives in Cambridge and is picked up by the student, it will have an effect that in principle could have been predicted. In which case, the transformation rules necessary to ensure the resemblance between the doorman's thoughts and the student's guesses, could have been set up in advance. And in principle again we can imagine such rules being built into their respective heads, so that he has merely to think a particular thought and she will guess it automatically. The problems of designing the appropriate transducers and translators would of course still be considerable, but perhaps they would not be totally insuperable.

Unfortunately, however, again reality gets in the way. Although human brains do of course resemble each other at a gross level, their micro-architectures and the patterns of internal connections between nerve cells are such as to make every individual's brain a unique object – no more standardised or predictable in its fine structure than is a human fingerprint. Indeed no two people's brains – not even those of identical twins – are sufficiently similar in detail for exactly the same brain activity to underlie the same mental state. And it follows that no two are sufficiently similar for them to respond to any particular imposed energy field by having the same thought or feeling. In reality, therefore, the case with the student's brain is no better than that with the die (in fact it may be worse, since there are almost certainly vastly more ways for two brains to be different than for two dice to be). Here, just as before, the individual characteristics of the receiver cannot be known to the source, and so there is no way that the input can be tailored as it would have to be to achieve the right effect.

There might conceivably be one way around this. Even though the brains of different individuals are all structurally different, it is still possible they might all come to respond in the same and predictable way to the same input if they were to be *trained* to do so: trained, that is, to assign the same particular meanings to whatever particular thoughts are in the air – rather as, in the case of normal perception, different brains come to assign the same meanings to the same fields of light or sound.

The problem, however, with this suggestion is that in order for such training to occur there would have to be some way for the brain to obtain independent confirmation of where the input is coming from and what it signifies. Yet, in all but trivial cases, such independent confirmation will be precluded by the very fact that *ex hypothesi* there is no normal sensory contact between the source and the receiver. In the student's case, for example, there is no way she can learn to recognise the telepathic input as, say, 'the input that goes with the doorman seeing a four', since there is no way she is going to have this meaning confirmed – except by telepathy!

'Any interpretation of the relationship between two events X and Y as one in which X prescribes the content of Y has to be incorrect,' I concluded in the previous chapter, 'if and when this requires from X more discriminative power than it actually has.' The interpretation of PK as a case where the wish prescribes the wished-for outcome, or of ESP as one where one person's thoughts prescribe similar thoughts in someone else, both run flat up against this objection. The general conclusion about psi communication has to be that it does not happen.

John Beloff, who has worked through several of these issues for himself (and who has arrived – before me, I should say – at similar conclusions), accepts that these considerations do indeed provide a knock-down argument against any imaginable 'physicalist theory' of how psi works.[261] Beloff, however, thinks they would not count nearly so strongly against a purely 'mentalist theory' where the mind can interact with the world directly without recourse to any physical channels or forces whatsoever. Recall his remark I quoted in Chapter 24: 'If psi phenomena occur we must adopt some other conception of the way the mind works, for example that the mind generates ideas and that these ideas somehow fulfil themselves in the real world.'

But although I have been illustrating my case with physicalist analogies, the strength of the argument is that it does not have to do with physical processes as such but rather with *information*, and it really does not matter what the vehicle for the information is. Let the communication take place by p-waves or pigeon-post or pie-throwing, and the principle remains the same: namely, that by no means can there be more information being received than is being sent. Yet, as we have seen, in order for the mind's ideas somehow to fulfil themselves in the real world, there always *would* have to be more information arriving at the end point than could conceivably have been contained in the original ideas as such. There is no way round this. If we do not like the implications of it, we cannot breezily 'adopt some other conception of the way the mind works', any more than, if we do not like the fact that two plus two equals four, we can adopt some other conception of the way arithmetic works.

On the back of this, I can but raise a further question. Where does it come from, this strange yet familiar notion about 'ideas fulfilling themselves'?

It is certainly not Beloff alone who has been prepared to talk this way. The thirteenth-century scholar, Albertus Magnus, for example, wrote: 'a certain power to alter things indwells in the human soul and subordinates the other things to her, particularly when she is swept into a great excess of love or hate or the like. When therefore the soul of a man falls into a great excess of any passion, it can be proved by experiment that it binds things and alters them in the way it wants.'[262] And in recent years Helmut Schmidt, who has himself sought experimental proofs of the mind's being able to 'alter things in the way it wants', has made himself a leading advocate of the idea that a wish can directly create the wished-for state of affairs in the outside world merely by setting this up as its *goal*.

No need, Schmidt suggests, to worry as we did above about how the wish comes to contain all the requisite detailed information, since 'it may be more appropriate to see PK as a goal-oriented principle in the sense that it aims successfully at a final outcome, no matter how intricate the intermediate steps are'.[263]

What is more, Schmidt himself has claimed to show in his own (much criticised) experiments with Random Number Generators that a person's success at influencing the output really is quite independent of how, at the electro-mechanical level, the RNG actually works – and is unaffected even when, unknown to the subject, the nature of the mechanism is changed in the middle of an experimental session.

There is, I think, a fairly obvious answer to why this notion of 'goal-orientation' may seem so familiar. For – to return to one of the themes we touched on earlier – all of us do in fact have a familiar exemplar of such goal-oriented action of mind over matter *in the everyday control we voluntarily exercise over our own bodies.* Any of us in good health can, say, by merely wishing it, wiggle the fourth finger of our right hands, or stick out our tongue or bat our eyelids. If there are intricate intermediate steps and complex calculations involved in bringing off these bodily movements – as presumably there must be – we the authors of the actions are certainly not aware of them.

Given that people have this example of *normal* goal-oriented action before them all the time, it is probably only to be expected that they are tempted to take it as the model for other *paranormal* cases where they earnestly hope that something of the same kind may happen. What they are failing to acknowledge, however, is not only how special is the relationship we have with our own bodies, but *why* it is so.

The reason why goes straight back to the issues raised above. It is that in the case of our own bodies we are dealing with a *dedicated* communication channel where the transformation rules from input to output can be and evidently have been laid down in advance: a channel based as it happens on a set of fixed physical pathways, permanently in place, whose parameters are pre-established, and for which there has been ample time (both over the course of evolution and within each individual's life) to devise the protocols and install the requisite transducers.

Both nature and nurture have made a huge investment in designing and testing this mind–body relationship. Our lives depend on it. The crucial point is, however, that, of all the things in the world, our bodies are the *only ones* with which our minds can count on having a relationship anything like this.[264]

It is true that advance arrangements can sometimes be made for previously unrelated objects to become 'as-if' extensions of our bodies – prosthetic limbs are an obvious example – so that they do genuinely become part of our sphere of voluntary control. But to suggest that this sphere can be or ought to be extendable at will to encompass whatever previously unrelated bits of the universe we (or an experimenter) arbitrarily choose, is to fail to recognise the necessary pre-conditions for control to operate.

The truth is that there is not, and we can safely say there never will be, this quasi-bodily relationship established between a human being and a die, or for that matter between a human being and the rain, or a human being and a spoon, or a human being and the seeds of a plant, or a human being and a random number generator . . . or even, sadly, a human being and another human being.

27

On the Wings of a Dove

What it comes down to is the fact of our inescapable embodiedness. ' "I am body and soul" – so speaks the child,' Nietzsche wrote. 'And why should one not speak like children. But the awakened, the enlightened man says: I am body entirely, and nothing beside; and soul is only a word for something in the body .... You say "I" and you are proud of this word. But greater than this – although you will not believe in it – is your body and its great intelligence, which does not say "I" but performs "I" ... Behind your thoughts and feelings, my brother, stands a mighty commander, an unknown sage – he is called Self. He lives in your body, he is your body.'[265]

Early in this book, I outlined what I imagined to be people's greatest misgivings about materialism – especially the 'materialism of the strictest order', the idea of which reduced Elizabeth Barrett to a state of 'resistless melancholy'. 'It would mean subscribing to the thesis', I suggested, 'that every influence we have upon the outside world has to begin with physical changes occurring at our body surfaces ... That any further impression we make on our surroundings can only be a secondary effect of these poor causes. That when and if our bodily activity is inadequate to have the secondary effects we may desire, there is precious little we can do about it. That we can achieve nothing at all external to us by means of purely inner unexpressed mentation. That thoughts without causally sufficient action by the body must inevitably fail in their ambitions. That we have no magic powers. That prayer and spells are ineffective ...' And so on.

Does it matter if, as the analysis of the last chapters seems to show, this nightmare characterisation turns out to be in all essentials true? That Nietzsche was right? That we really are body entirely and nothing beside? And that the soul, being only a word for something in the body, is in effect a word for no soul worth the name?

Whichever way we look at it, it seems it does matter. The least that people have needed to keep them from despair has been, I argued, the assurance that 'where we are going' will not necessarily be so bad as we might fear, because 'what we are' is not so deficient as we might otherwise have thought. But now we have no grounds for even this modest optimism. *Now* we may have to accept that 'where we are going' is almost certain to be quite as bad as we might fear, because 'what we are' has turned out to be quite as deficient as we thought – if not still worse.

We heard Bertrand Russell earlier: 'Only within the scaffolding of these truths, only on the firm foundation of unyielding despair, can the soul's habitation henceforth be built.' For those who have always hoped for better, this is bound to take – at least – some getting used to.

If, at last, we are to rebel against this conclusion, it is clear we shall have to adopt a more assertive, less pessimistic and less apologetic attitude to the truths we have uncovered.

Perhaps, instead of meekly assuming that the world we live in is so much poorer a place than we would have liked, our lives so much less meaningful and our prospects so much less promising, we shall have to try to show that the real world – a world without soul-power – is after all *unsurpassably* rich, and that the alternative world – the world *with* soul-power – would have been nothing more than a snare and a delusion. Perhaps, instead of pining for our lost souls and absent psychic powers, we shall have to begin to take pride and pleasure in the facts of our embodiedness, our mortality and individuality.

To do so will of course mean undergoing a revolution in our typically obsequious attitude towards the paranormal: the attitude of 'even if it isn't true, I wish it were'. We shall have to stop conceding, as many sceptics – myself, as you saw earlier, included – have been prone to do, that people require the promise of the paranormal to make sense of their lives. We shall need to distance ourselves from all those beautiful lamentations about humanity's sad plight: the elegiac cries for mercy of Pascal, the existential cynicism of Camus or Monod, the puritanical asceticism of Russell. We shall have to banish the very idea that 'it would be pretty to think otherwise'. Our purpose, instead, must be to show not only that in the last analysis it is the normal world and not the paranormal one that has all the best tunes, but that the paranormal world would in reality not be pretty in the least – certainly the end of life as we know it, and very possibly unable to support life from the beginning.

Can a position like this – one which so firmly rejects not only the reality but the dream of the paranormal – be taken seriously? I think this is the position to which all our best understanding of nature tends. And though it would take another book to spell out the full reasons, I can here at least give some pointers to them. Pointers, that is, as to why our material bodiliness and limited longevity provide not so much a constraint on what we can achieve and experience, as the essential condition for our being able to achieve or experience anything at all.

To follow me in this, you will have to grant one basic premise. This is that the evolution of life on Earth – and all that we hold dear about ourselves as living beings – has depended primarily on the free play of a simple creative principle: namely, the process of natural selection described by Darwin. Even though there are still some who find it hard to accept that natural selection can have been the whole story behind all the variety and organised complexity of the living world, you must agree that it has at least played an essential role.[266]

The crucial question then becomes: what are the necessary conditions for natural selection to occur? And the answer to which I would now draw attention is that one of these conditions has always been that living organisms should be highly *discrete* in the way they go about things. Discrete, that is, in all the meanings of the word. Spatially discrete, with each organism occupying its own physically distinct body; temporally discrete, with each

*

having a limited lifespan with a clear beginning and end; informationally and intentionally discrete – and even discreet – with each following a more or less independent life-path in pursuit of its own private goals.

The reason is simply that natural selection depends on *competition* between *individuals*, and such competition has always required a large degree of independence and separate development. In the struggle for survival that takes place between the members of an evolving population every one is ultimately a rival to most if not all others, and progress results from the victory of certain individuals over others. Each of the myriads of variant organisms, that are continually being invented by mutation and recombination of genes, and then pitted against its peers in the struggle for survival, constitutes a new experiment. And for selection to work its magic, each has to be given the chance to prove itself independently, by what it is able to make of its own brief life by its own efforts. There must be no blurring of the spatio-temporal boundaries, no confusion as to where individual bodies or individual lives begin and end.

Indeed, similar principles apply to social and cultural evolution. In the world of competing ideas no less than in the world of bodies and genes separate development is essential to success: independence and solitude are the schools of genius, privacy is needed to shelter the tender shoots of innovation, virgin minds are the seedbeds of originality. 'Let a hundred flowers bloom and a hundred schools of thought contend' was never merely a Maoist slogan. Mao's point, like Darwin's, was that selection can only be effective provided that each of the hundred flowers is allowed the opportunity to bloom in its own fashion, each of the hundred schools of thought is given space to mature in its own way. Provided too that, when each flower or school has undergone its test of fitness and proved itself more or less successful, there is the opportunity for new generations to take the field and start over again. Although some sharing may be compatible with ongoing selection, there must be no merging of flowers or of schools into one common blossom or common ideology (however perfect at the time it seems to be).

*

In general, separateness, mortality and renewal have always been the friends of evolutionary progress. The corollary is that universality, immortality and persistency can only have been its enemies.

The strong implication has to be that it is only in a world where it has been practicable for living things to maintain and defend the physical, temporal and spiritual boundaries of their minds and bodies, that all the beauty and variety of life and culture could have come into existence. Which means in effect that it could only have happened in a world of normal laws. For it is precisely these defences that paranormal forces – if they existed – would undo.

Such a conclusion is no doubt somewhat daunting. It is not always easy to be an individual. There are probably times when every one of us finds it an absurdity that we do in fact have the boundaries that we do: that we have been fated to live here rather than there, now rather than then, in this body rather than another.

There are times, perhaps, when we would prefer to have no individuality at all, wishing, like Hamlet, that 'this too too solid flesh would melt, / Thaw, and resolve itself into a dew'.[267] Or other times when, better still, we would aspire to include all other individualities within our own, enlarging our interests until, as Thomas Traherne envisioned it, 'the sea itself floweth in our veins, till we are clothed with the heavens, and crowned with the stars: and perceive ourselves to be the sole heir of the whole world, and more than so, because men are in it who are every one sole heirs as well as we.'[268] Even Bertrand Russell came to the view in his old age that 'the best way to overcome [the fear of death] is to make your interests gradually wider and more impersonal, until bit by bit the walls of the ego recede, and your life becomes increasingly merged in the universal life.'[269]

The prospect of this kind of psychic redintegration is undeniably seductive – warm, humane, open, ecologically correct. It conjures up the idea of a return to the enveloping womb, to the human and physical environment where it once seemed we were placentally connected to the universe at large. Yet we should, I think, be thankful that it never was and never will be so. For the consequences would not at all be those for which we fondly hope.

The very word 'life' comes from the Old German *Leib* meaning body. Universal life, bodiless life, would be no life at all. And by the same token universal mind would be no mind. If our thoughts and actions were to wash around the universe in some great psychic field, there would be nothing left for us to be.

What we make of the world as it really exists, depends on how we look at it. We can be the optimist who brightly says, 'This is the best of all possible worlds,' or the pessimist who gloomily nods his head and says, 'How true!'

Elizabeth Barrett's friend Miss Bayley was 'calm and resigned' in the face of her conclusions about the truth of materialism. But resignation, sad resignation, is too passive (I almost want to say too ungrateful) an attitude to have towards the laws of nature which have permitted the creation of our world.

We can choose instead to see these laws not as imprisoning but liberating and empowering. For Lenin, 'Freedom is the recognition of necessity.' For Igor Stravinsky, writing about musical composition but no less about life in general, 'My freedom will be so much the greater and more meaningful the more narrowly I limit my field of action and the more I surround myself with obstacles. Whatever diminishes constraint diminishes strength.'[270] But it was Immanuel Kant who found the perfect image for the empowering effect of the bodily and mental limitations that nature has imposed on us, and the futility of trying to escape them: 'The light dove, cleaving the air in her free flight, and feeling its resistance, might imagine that its flight would be still easier in empty space.'[271]

There is a celebrated painting by Joseph Wright in London's National Gallery, titled *Experiment with an Airpump*, that shows precisely the plight of a light dove in empty space. The bewildered bird is gasping for breath in an evacuated glass jar, its wings useless by its side, while the experimenter and his family – in varying degrees of disbelief and shock – look on.[272]

The painting is generally regarded as having been intended as a commentary on the scientific Enlightenment. But I suggest we might more pointedly take it to be a picture of the vanity of the paradise promised by religion and the paranormal. For it is they, not science, which if they had their way would pump from the world the elements on which life has taken wing. They, not science, which by blurring the distinction between life and death, destroying the grounding of one mind in one body, confusing issues of personal responsibility, and undermining privacy, would rob the world of the oxygen of individuality on which all things bright and beautiful – natural and cultural – have relied for their creative energy.

It is not just that we have no need of the hypothesis. It is that we would probably not be here if it were true.

Notes

1 Pierre Simon de Laplace (1814), *Essai Philosophique sur les Probabilités*, Paris: Courcier.
2 Julien Offray de La Mettrie (1747/1992), *L'Homme-machine*, in *A Dictionary of Philosophical Quotations*, ed. A. J. Ayer and Jane O'Grady, p. 244, Oxford: Blackwell.
3 Cited in S. Harding and D. Phillips (1986), *Contrasting Values in Western Europe*, London: Macmillan.
4 See, for example, George H. Gallup and Frank Newport (1991), 'Belief in paranormal phenomena among adult Americans', *Skeptical Inquirer*, 15, 137–46; Erlendur Haraldsson (1985), 'Representative national surveys of psychic phenomena: Iceland, Great Britain, Sweden, USA and Gallup's Multinational Survey', *Journal of the Society for Psychical Research*, 53, 145–58; John Palmer (1979), 'A community mail survey of psychic experiences', *Journal of the American Society for Psychical Research*, 73, 221–51.
5 Jennifer Brown (1987), 'A survey of the public's belief in and experience of paranormal phenomena', based on face to face home interviews with a representative sample of 218 people in Reading, England; unpublished Report no. 101, Brown & Campbell, Guildford. The survey was commissioned by Channel 4 Television in connection with the making of 'Is There Anybody There?', transmitted 30 October 1987.
6 Cited by Erlendur Haraldsson (1985), 'Representative national surveys of psychic phenomena: Iceland, Great Britain, Sweden, USA and Gallup's Multinational Survey', *Journal of the Society for Psychical Research*, 53, 145–58.
7 Sigmund Freud (1933), *New Introductory Lectures on Psychoanalysis*, trans. W. J. H. Sprott, pp. 45–77, London: Hogarth Press.
8 O. Costa de Beauregard, R. D. Mattuck, B. D. Josephson, E. H. Walker (1980), letter to the *New York Review of Books*, June 26 1980.
9 John E. Mack (1992), Foreword to *Secret Life* by David M. Jacobs, New York: Simon & Schuster.

10 Advertisement for the Perrott-Warrick Fellowship, Darwin College, Cambridge, 1991.
11 Stewart Brand, quoted by John Brockman (1995), *The Third Culture*, p. 18, New York: Simon & Schuster.
12 Sergei Kapitza (1991), 'Antiscience trends in the U.S.S.R.', *Scientific American*, August 1991.
13 John Keats (1819), 'Lamia', II, 229.
14 Vaclav Havel, *The End of the Modern Era*, quoted by Francis Slakey (1993), 'When the lights of reason go out', *New Scientist*, 11 September 1993.
15 Adolf Hitler, from *Gespräche mit Hitler* by Herman Raschning, quoted in ibid.
16 John Dos Passos (1936/1966), *The Big Money*, in *USA*, p. 1080, Harmondsworth: Penguin.
17 Albert Camus (1942/1955), *The Myth of Sisyphus*, trans. J. O'Brien, p. 4, New York: Random House.
18 Susan Sontag (1992), *The Volcano Lover*, p. 116, London: Cape.
19 Comte d'Argenson, quoted by Voltaire (1759), *Alzire, Discours Préliminaire*.
20 Ann F. Garland and Edward Zigler (1993), 'Adolescent suicide prevention', *American Psychologist*, 48, 169–82.
21 Blaise Pascal (1669/1966), *Pensées*, trans. A. J. Krailsheimer, 68 (206), Harmondsworth: Penguin.
22 Alfred Tennyson (1850/1971), *In Memoriam A. H. H.*, stanza 54, in *Tennyson: Poems and Plays*, ed. T. H. Warren, Oxford: Oxford University Press.
23 Daniel N. Stern (1990), *Diary of a Baby*, p. 36, New York: Basic Books.
24 Carl Jung (1933/1984), *Modern Man in Search of a Soul*, p. 264, London: Routledge.
25 Karen Armstrong (1993), interviewed in *Financial Times*, 3 March 1993.
26 Sheena Ashford and Noel Timms (1992), *What Europe Thinks*, p. 45, Aldershot: Dartmouth.
27 Elizabeth Barrett (1846), letter to Robert Browning, 7 May 1846.
28 Søren Kierkegaard (1843), *The Journals of Søren Kierkegaard*, ed. and trans. A. Dru, Oxford: Oxford University Press.
29 Robert Burns (1794/1991), letter to Alexander Cunningham, 25 February 1794, quoted by Roy Porter in *The Faber Book of Madness*, p. 68, London: Faber.
30 Martin R. Grimmer (1992), 'Searching for security in the mystical', *Skeptical Inquirer*, 16, 173–76; John Palmer (1979), 'A community mail survey of psychic experiences', *Journal of the American Society for Psychical Research*, 73, 221–51; John F. Schumaker (1990), *Wings of Illusion*, Cambridge: Polity Press.

31 John F. Schumaker (1992), 'Mental health consequences of irreligion', pp. 54–69 in *Religion and Mental Health*, ed. John F. Schumaker, Oxford: Oxford University Press.

32 Carl Jung (1933/1984), *Modern Man in Search of a Soul*, London: Routledge.

33 Søren Kierkegaard (1843/1938), *The Journals of Søren Kierkegaard*, ed. and trans. A. Dru, p. 127, Oxford: Oxford University Press.

34 Blaise Pascal (1669/1966), *Pensées*, trans. A. J. Krailsheimer, 47, Harmondsworth: Penguin.

35 Plato (380 BC/1955), *The Republic*, trans. H. D. P. Lee, 415, Harmondsworth: Penguin.

36 Elizabeth F. Loftus (1993), 'The reality of repressed memories', *American Psychologist*, 48, 518–37, 1993.

37 Charles Darwin, *More Letters of Charles Darwin*, ed. F. Darwin and A. C. Seward, vol. I, p. 176, 1903.

38 Immanuel Kant (1787/1933), *Critique of Pure Reason*, 2nd edition, B xiii, trans. Norman Kemp Smith, p. 20, London: Macmillan.

39 *Punch*, 79, 63, 1880.

40 Isaac Newton, quoted by Richard S. Westfall (1993), *The Life of Isaac Newton*, p. 303, Cambridge: Cambridge University Press.

41 Francis Bacon (1625/1973), 'Of Atheism', *Essays*, XVI, London: Dent.

42 David Brewster (1855), *Memoirs of the Life, Writings, and Discoveries of Sir Isaac Newton*, Edinburgh: Constable.

43 Bertrand Russell (1967), *The Autobiography of Bertrand Russell*, vol. I, Prologue, London: Allen & Unwin.

44 Ivan Pavlov (1936/1941), 'A Letter to the Youth', *Lectures on Conditioned Reflexes*, ed. W. Horsley Gantt, vol II, p. 189, London: Lawrence & Wishart.

45 Humphrey Newton, quoted by Richard S. Westfall (1993), *The Life of Isaac Newton*, p. 141, Cambridge: Cambridge University Press.

46 William Derham (1723), *Physico-Theology: or, a Demonstration of the Being and Attributes of God from his Works of Creation*, p. 427, London: W. & J. Innys.

47 Albert Einstein (1965), quoted in *New Statesman*, 16 April 1965.

48 Isaac Newton (1700), quoted by David Castillejo (1981), *The Expanding Force in Newton's Cosmos*, p. 116, Madrid: Ediciones de Arte y Bibliofilia.

49 Rupert Sheldrake (1990), *The Rebirth of Nature*, London: Century.

50 Frank Tipler (1989), 'The Omega point as *Eschaton*', *Zygon*, 24 (quoted by Martin Gardner (1991), *Skeptical Inquirer*, 15, 128).

51 William Blake (1794/1967), 'The Sick Rose', *Songs of Experience*, ed. Geoffrey Keynes, Oxford: Oxford University Press.

52 Example taken from David MacKay (1993), 'Probability theory and Occam's Razor', *Darwin College Magazine*, 8, 81–5.

53 E. A. Burtt (1924), *The Metaphysical Foundations of Modern Physical Science*, quoted by Arthur Koestler (1959), *The Sleepwalkers*, p. 538, London: Hutchinson.

54 Henry More (1648), quoted by Bernard Williams (1978), *Descartes*, p. 282, Harmondsworth: Penguin.

55 Henry More (1659), *The Immortality of the Soule*, in F. I. MacKinnon (1925), *Philosophical Writings of Henry More*, London.

56 William Derham (1723), *Physico-Theology: or, a Demonstration of the Being and Attributes of God from his Works of Creation*, pp. 428–30, London: W. & J. Innys.

57 Friedrich Nietzsche (1882), *The Gay Science*, 319, in R. J. Hollingdale (1977), *A Nietzsche Reader*, p. 36, Harmondsworth: Penguin.

58 Franz Joseph Gall (1825/1835), *Sur les fonctions du cerveau et sur celles de chacune de ses parties*, in *Gall's Works*, trans. Winslow Lewis, vol. VI, p. 310, Boston.

59 Arthur Koestler (1959), *The Sleepwalkers*, p. 539, London: Hutchinson.

60 See Foreword by Nicholas Humphrey to E. P. Evans (1906/1987), *The Criminal Prosecution and Capital Punishment of Animals*, London: Faber & Faber.

61 The text is given by Joseph Hemingway (1831), *History of Chester*, vol. I, p. 360, Chester: J. Fletcher. I am grateful to Peter Howell for bringing it to my attention.

62 Reported in *Fortean Times*, 72, p. 18, 1994.

63 Jacques Monod (1972), *Chance and Necessity*, p. 160, London: Collins.

64 Bertrand Russell (1918), quoted by E. A. Burtt (1924), *The Metaphysical Foundations of Modern Physical Science*, p. 9, London: Kegan Paul, French and Trubner.

65 Jonathan Swift (1731), *Cassinus and Peter*.

66 Frederick Reynolds (1775), Letter written on his second day at Westminster School, quoted by J. D. Carleton (1954), *Westminster*, London.

67 Bertrand Russell (1967), *The Autobiography of Bertrand Russell*, vol. I, Prologue, London: Allen & Unwin.

68 Harry F. Harlow (1959), 'Love in Infant Monkeys', *Scientific American*, July 1959.

69 Blaise Pascal (1654/1966), *Pensées*, trans. A. J. Krailsheimer, p. 309, Harmondsworth: Penguin.

Notes

70 William Blake (1804/1988) 'To the Deists', in *William Blake: Selected Poetry and Prose*, ed. David Punter, p. 211, London: Routledge.

71 William Blake (1803/1988) 'Mock on, Mock on', in ibid., p. 152.

72 Osip Mandelstam (1913/1973), 'Stone', no. 5, in *Osip Mandelstam: Selected Poems*, trans. David McDuff, Cambridge: Rivers Press.

73 Ralph Waldo Emerson (1867), 'Brahma'.

74 Andrew Lang (1905), 'Brahma', in *New Collected Rhymes*, London: Longman.

75 John Clare (1844/1950), 'I Am', in *Selected Poems of John Clare*, ed. Geoffrey Grigson, London: Routledge.

76 John Searle (1987), 'Minds and brains without programs', in *Mindwaves*, ed. Colin Blakemore and Susan Greenfield, pp. 209–34, Oxford: Blackwell.

77 Francis Crick (1994), *The Astonishing Hypothesis*, p. 3, New York: Simon & Schuster.

78 Alfred Tennyson (1850/1971), *In Memoriam A. H. H.*, stanza 120, in *Tennyson: Poems and Plays*, ed. T. H. Warren, Oxford: Oxford University Press.

79 Charles Babbage, quoted by B. V. Bowden (1964), 'Thought and machine processes', in *Readings in Psychology*, ed. John Cohen, pp. 195–213, London: Allen & Unwin.

80 *Jesus Revolution Streetpaper*, no. 31, Third Quarter 1993, Northampton.

81 Paul Feyerabend (1975), *Against Method*, pp. 25, 27, London: Verso.

82 Alfred Tennyson (1850/1971), 'The Village Wife', II, in *Tennyson: Poems and Plays*, ed. T. H. Warren, Oxford: Oxford University Press. (Dialect spelling has been modernised.)

83 Denis Diderot (1749/1982), *Letter on the Blind*, in *The Irresistible Diderot*, trans. and ed. John Hope Mason, p. 47, London: Quartet.

84 John Beloff (1980/1990), 'Is normal memory a "paranormal phenomenon?" ', in *The Relentless Question*, pp. 110–22, London: McFarland.

85 Rupert Sheldrake (1988), *The Presence of the Past*, New York: Times Books.

86 J. B. S. Haldane (1934), *Fact and Faith*, quoted in personal communication by C. H. Waddington.

87 Thomas Henry Huxley (1866), quoted by Adrian Desmond and James Moore (1991) *Darwin*, p. 533, London: Michael Joseph.

88 Denis Diderot (1754/1982), *On the Interpretation of Nature*, XXX, in *The Irresistible Diderot*, trans. and ed. John Hope Mason, p. 66, London: Quartet.

89 Gillian Bennett (1987), *Traditions of Belief*, p. 32, London: Penguin; Harvey J. Irwin (1993), 'Belief in the paranormal: A

review of the empirical literature', *Journal of the American Society for Psychical Research*, 87, 7–39.

90 Andrew Lang (1894), *Cock Lane and Common-Sense*, pp. 338, 356, London: Longman.

91 Lewis Wolpert (1992), *The Unnatural Nature of Science*, London: Faber & Faber.

92 Mark Ridley (1993), 'Infected with science', *New Scientist*, 25 December 1993.

93 Brian Appleyard (1992), *Understanding the Present*, London: Pan Books.

94 *Chambers Twentieth Century Dictionary* (1972), Edinburgh: Chambers.

95 St Paul, I Corinthians 15:39.

96 Joseph Heller (1961), *Catch-22*, p. 450, New York: Simon & Schuster.

97 H. M. Wellman and D. Estes (1986), 'Early understanding of mental entities: A re-examination of childhood realism', *Child Development*, 57, 910–23.

98 Paul L. Harris, Emma Brown, Crispin Marriott, Semantha Whittall, and Sarah Harmer (1991), 'Monsters, ghosts and witches: Testing the limits of the fantasy-reality distinction in young children', *British Journal of Developmental Psychology*, 9, 105–23.

99 Pascal Boyer (1994), *The Naturalness of Religious Ideas*, p. 21, Berkeley: University of California Press.

100 ibid., p. 76.

101 David Hume (1748/1985), *Essay on Miracles*, Part 2, La Salle: Open Court Classics.

102 Blaise Pascal (1669/1966), *Pensées*, trans. A. J. Krailsheimer, 859 (852), Harmondsworth: Penguin.

103 Thomas Hardy (1915/1979), 'The Oxen', in *Poems by Thomas Hardy*, ed. Trevor Johnson, London: Folio.

104 Dan Sperber (1990), 'The epidemiology of beliefs', in *The Social Psychological Study of Widespread Beliefs*, ed. Colin Fraser and George Gaskell, pp. 25–44, Oxford: Clarendon Press.

105 Claude Rivière (1989), 'Concepts of the soul in tribal communities', pp. 232–9, in *Death, Afterlife, and the Soul*, ed. L. E. Sullivan, New York: Macmillan.

106 Denis Diderot (1774/1937), *Elements of Physiology*, in *Diderot, Interpreter of Nature*, trans. J. Stewart and J. Kemp, p. 139, London: Lawrence & Wishart.

107 ibid., p. 136.

108 Père Bougeant (1739), *Amusement Philosophique sur le Langage des Bestes*, p. 7, Paris.

109 Uri Geller (1975) quoted by David Marks and Richard Kammann

(1980), *The Psychology of the Psychic*, pp. 91-2, Buffalo: Prometheus Books.

110 Alan Turing (1950), 'Computing machinery and intelligence', *Mind*, 59, 433-60.

111 John Beloff (1977), 'Historical overview', in *Handbook of Parapsychology*, p. 21, ed. B. B. Wolman, New York: Van Nostrand Reinhold.

112 Claude Rivière (1989), op. cit.

113 Pascal Boyer (1994), *The Naturalness of Religious Ideas*, p. 25, Berkeley: University of California Press.

114 Blaise Pascal (1669/1966), *Pensées*, trans. A. J. Krailsheimer, 830, 865 (Appendix XIII, 832), Harmondsworth: Penguin.

115 Frederick Myers (1885), *Proceedings of the Society for Psychical Research*, 3, 30.

116 Isaac Newton (1700), quoted by David Castillejo (1981), *The Expanding Force in Newton's Cosmos*, p. 116, Madrid: Ediciones de Arte y Bibliofilia.

117 John Donne (1640/1953), Sermon xxii, Easter Day, 25 March 1627, in *The Sermons of John Donne*, ed. G. R. Potter and Evelyn M. Simpson, Berkeley: University of California Press.

118 St Paul, I Corinthians 15:17-19.

119 Ruth Brandon (1993) has made the parallel explicit in her book *The Life and Many Deaths of Harry Houdini*, London: Secker & Warburg.

120 Roseanne Arnold, quoted by Jane Walmsley (1994), *Independent Magazine*, p. 46, 29 January 1994.

121 David Hume (1748/1985), *Essay on Miracles*, Part I, p. 32, La Salle: Open Court Classics.

122 ibid., Part II, p. 52.

123 A good discussion of Hume's argument is provided by C. A. J. Coady (1992), *Testimony: A Philosophical Study*, Oxford: Clarendon Press.

124 Hilaire Belloc (1907), 'Matilda', in *Cautionary Tales for Children*, London: Eveleigh Nash.

125 John Locke (1690/1975), *An Essay Concerning Human Understanding*, Book IV, ch. 15, 5, ed. Peter H. Nidditch, Oxford: Clarendon Press.

126 The hidden reference to Shakespeare in Psalm 46 has apparently long been known to people who research this kind of thing; but the anagrams are my own addition.

127 John Stuart Mill (1843), *A System of Logic*, 630, quoted by C. A. J. Coady (1992), *Testimony: A Philosophical Study*, Oxford: Clarendon Press.

128 Arthur Conan Doyle (1890), *The Sign of Four*, ch. 6.

129 Nicholas Humphrey (1980/1983), 'Straw ghosts', in *Consciousness Regained*, pp. 168–75, Oxford: Oxford University Press.

130 See Martin Gardner (1983), *Science: Good, Bad and Bogus*, pp. 406–8, Oxford: Oxford University Press.

131 William Vandereycken and Ron van Deth (1994), *From Fasting Saints to Anorexic Girls*, London: Athlone.

132 Thomas Mann (1932), 'An experience in the occult', *Three Essays*, quoted by Brian Inglis (1984), *Science and Parascience*, London: Hodder & Stoughton.

133 Brian Inglis in ibid., p. 339.

134 William James (1909/1961), 'The final impressions of a psychical researcher', in *William James on Psychical Research*, ed. G. Murphy and R. O. Ballou, London: Chatto & Windus.

135 Albert Einstein's words, spoken in 1921, are carved above the fireplace in a Common Room at Princeton University.

136 Matthew 4:3.

137 John 4:48.

138 See accounts in Morton Smith (1978), *Jesus the Magician*, London: Gollancz; Paul Kurtz (1986), *The Transcendental Temptation*, Buffalo: Prometheus Books.

139 Celsus (2nd century AD), in Origen, *Against Celsus*, I. 68, quoted by Morton Smith (1978), *Jesus the Magician*, p. 83, London: Gollancz.

140 ibid., pp. 92–3.

141 Origen, *Against Celsus*, I. 68, quoted in ibid., p. 83.

142 Luke 4:23.

143 Mark 6:5.

144 Morton Smith (1978), *Jesus the Magician*, p. 141, London: Gollancz.

145 Matthew 13:58.

146 Matthew 27:40, 42.

147 Ernst Becker (1973), *The Denial of Death*, p. 18, New York: Free Press.

148 Romans 1:3.

149 Isaiah 7:14.

150 Micah 5:2.

151 Numbers 24:17.

152 Robin Lane Fox (1991), *The Unauthorized Version*, London: Viking; A. N. Wilson (1992), *Jesus*, London: Sinclair-Stevenson; also sources cited in note 138 above.

153 J. Mayo, O. White, and H. J. Eysenck (1978), 'An empirical study of the relation between astrological factors and personality', *Journal of Social Psychology*, 105, 229–36.

154 Hans Eysenck and D. K. B. Nias (1982), *Astrology: Science or Superstition?*, London.

Notes

155 A. N. Wilson (1992), *Jesus*, pp. 73–86, London: Sinclair-Stevenson.
156 Luke 2:48, 49.
157 Nicholas Humphrey (1987), 'Folie à deux', *Guardian*, 8 April 1987. (The boy's name has been changed to preserve anonymity.)
158 Uri Geller (1975), quoted by David Marks and Richard Kammann (1980), *The Psychology of the Psychic*, p. 90, Buffalo: Prometheus Books; see also Uri Geller (1975), *My Story*, New York: Praeger.
159 Arthur Koestler (1952), *Arrow in the Blue: An Autobiography*, p. 36, New York: Macmillan.
160 Arthur Koestler (1976), quoted by Adam Smith in *New York* magazine, 27 December 1976.
161 Uri Geller, quoted by Merrily Harpur (1994), 'Uri Geller and the warp factor', *Fortean Times*, 78, 34.
162 Cited by Martin Gardner (1983), *Science: Good, Bad and Bogus*, p. 163, Oxford: Oxford University Press.
163 A good review is given in Robert Buckman and Karl Sabbagh (1993), *Magic or Medicine?: An Investigation of Healing and Healers*, London: Macmillan.
164 Uri Geller (1975), quoted by David Marks and Richard Kammann (1980), op. cit., p. 92.
165 ibid., pp. 107–9.
166 Psalm 22:1, 9–10.
167 John Beloff (1993), *Parapsychology: a Concise History*, London: Athlone.
168 Stephen E. Braude (1986), *The Limits of Influence*, pp. 66, 222, London: Routledge.
169 Matthew 7:7.
170 Further details of these and other cases that I refer to may be found, for example, in John Beloff (1992) *Parapsychology: a Concise History*, London: Athlone, and in Brian Inglis (1984) *Science and Parascience*, London: Hodder & Stoughton. The particular allusions are as follows: 'Italian monk', Joseph of Copertino, 17th c.; 'rabbit births', Mary Tofts, 18th c.; 'Scottish gentleman', D. D. Home, 19th c.; 'French maiden', Marthe Béraud, 19th c.; 'Russian grandmother', Nina Kulagina, 20th c.; 'twenty-stone matron', Mrs Guppy, 19th c.; 'Indian yogi', Sai Baba, 20th c.; 'Polish journalist', Franek Kluski, 20th c.; 'Chicago bellhop', Ted Serios, 20th c.; 'young Israeli', Uri Geller, 20th c.
171 Herodotus, *Histories*.
172 Thomas Henry Huxley (1871), Letter to the Committee of the London Dialectical Society, *Daily News*, London, 17 November 1871.
173 Charles Honorton et al. (1990), 'Psi communication in the ganzfeld', *Journal of Parapsychology*, 54, 99–139; Daryl J. Bem and Charles Honorton (1994), 'Does psi exist? Replicable evidence for

an anomalous process of information transfer', *Psychological Bulletin*, 115, 4–18.

174 Richard Wiseman, Matthew Smith, Diana Kornbrot (1995), 'The autoganzfeld: a critical reappraisal', in press.

175 A thorough critique of some of the recent experiments is provided by James E. Alcock (1990), *Science and Supernature*, Buffalo: Prometheus Books.

176 Sophia McFarlane and Nicholas Humphrey (1982), 'A Survey into the Perception of the Moon', unpublished dissertation, Cambridge.

177 Rupert Sheldrake (1993) nearly suggests so. See his chapter on 'The effect of experimenters' expectations', in *Seven Experiments that Could Change the World*, London: Fourth Estate.

178 David Hume (1748/1985), *Essay on Miracles*, Part II, p.34, La Salle: Open Court Classics.

179 Shestov, quoted by Colin Wilson, *The Listener*, 16 June 1988.

180 John Beloff (1986/1990), 'What is your counter-explanation?', in *The Relentless Question*, p. 151, London: McFarland.

181 G. R. Schmeidler (1971), 'Parapsychologists' opinions about parapsychology', *Journal of Parapsychology*, 35, 208–18, quoted by John Beloff (1990), *The Relentless Question*, p. 151, London: McFarland.

182 Jerry Fodor (1981), *Representations*, p. 316, Cambridge, Mass.: MIT Press.

183 John Beloff (1990) *The Relentless Question*, p. 151.

184 Baron von Schrenck-Notzing (1920), quoted by Ruth Brandon (1983), *The Spiritualists*, p. 149, London: Weidenfeld and Nicolson.

185 Donald McCabe and Linda Klebe, quoted by John Croucher (1994), 'The complete guide to exam cheating', *New Scientist*, 11 June 1994.

186 Stephen Newstead (1994), presentation at British Psychological Society Annual Conference, March 1994.

187 Nicholas Humphrey (1987), 'Tall stories from little acorns grow', *Guardian*, London, 1 July 1987.

188 Robert L. Trivers (1981), 'Sociobiology and politics', in *Sociobiology and Human Politics*, ed. Elliott White, p. 33, Lexington, Mass.: Lexington Books.

189 H. G. Wells (1903), *Love and Mr Lewisham*, ch. 23, London: Dent.

190 Jesuit divine (apocryphal).

191 Arthur Conan Doyle (1920), quoted by Ruth Brandon (1993), *The Life and Many Deaths of Harry Houdini*, p. 241, London: Secker & Warburg.

192 'James Randi: Psychic Investigator', Granada TV, 1991; quotation from review in *Daily Mail*, 18 July 1991.

193 J. M. Wober (1992), 'TV and the Supernatural: Resistance of Beliefs

to a Debunking Series', Independent Television Commission Research Paper, April 1992.

194 BBC Radio 4, Six o'clock news, 16 December 1993.

195 See, for example, my discussion of the language used about 'consciousness', in Nicholas Humphrey (1992), *A History of the Mind*, London: Chatto & Windus.

196 Laura A. Dale and Rhea A. White (1977), 'Glossary of terms found in the literature of psychical research and parapsychology', in *Handbook of Parapsychology*, ed. Benjamin B. Wolman, pp. 921–36, New York: van Nostrand Reinhold.

197 John Beloff (1990), *The Relentless Question*, p. 8.

198 Brian Josephson (1995), interviewed in *Varsity*, Cambridge University student newspaper, 17 February 1995.

199 Francis Bacon (1620), *Novum Organum*, Book I, aphorism 49.

200 James E. Alcock (1981), *Parapsychology: Science or Magic?*, p. 81, Oxford: Pergamon.

201 F. Ayeroff and R. P. Abelson (1976), 'ESP and ESB: Belief in personal success at mental telepathy', *Journal of Personality and Social Psychology*, 34, 240–7.

202 John 20: 25, 29.

203 John Locke (1690/1975), *An Essay Concerning Human Understanding*, Book 2, Oxford: Clarendon Press.

204 C. A. J. Coady (1992), *Testimony: A Philosophical Study*, Oxford: Clarendon Press.

205 Thomas Paine (1791), *The Rights of Man*, quoted by Alasdair MacIntyre (1960), 'Breaking the chains of reason', *Out of Apathy*, pp. 195–240, London: Stevens.

206 C. J. Jung (1933/1990), *Modern Man in Search of a Soul*, p. 240, London: Routledge.

207 Tony Pasquarello (1992), 'Humanism's thorn: the case of the bright believers', *Free Inquiry*, 13, 38–42, Winter 1992/93.

208 John Taylor (1973), quoted by Martin Gardner (1983), *Science: Good, Bad and Bogus*, p. 180, Oxford: Oxford University Press.

209 A. J. Ayer (1988/1990), 'That undiscovered country', in *The Meaning of Life*, p. 204, New York: Scribners. Ayer partly retracted these remarks in 'Postscript to a postmortem', ibid. p. 205.

210 Carl Sargent (1987), 'Sceptical fairytales from Bristol', *Journal of the Society for Psychical Research*, 54, 208–18.

211 Friedrich Nietzsche (1882), *The Gay Science*, 319, in R. J. Hollingdale (1977), *A Nietzsche Reader*, p. 36, Harmondsworth: Penguin.

212 Tony Pasquarello (1992), op.cit.

213 Michael Argyle and Benjamin Beit-Hallahmi (1975), *The Social Psychology of Religion*, p. 60, London: Routledge.

214 Jennifer Brown (1987), 'A Survey of the Public's Belief in and

Experience of Paranormal Phenomena', unpublished Report no. 101, Brown & Campbell, Guildford.

215 See, for example, Erlendur Haraldsson (1985), 'Representative national surveys of psychic phenomena: Iceland, Great Britain, Sweden, USA and Gallup's Multinational Survey', *Journal of the Society for Psychical Research*, 53, 145–58; J. M. Wober (1992), 'TV and the Supernatural: Resistance of Beliefs to a Debunking Series', Independent Television Commission Research Paper, April 1992.

216 R. A. McConnell and T. K. Clark (1980), 'Training, belief and mental conflict within the Parapsychological Association', *Journal of Parapsychology*, 44, 245–67.

217 John Beloff (1990), *The Relentless Question*, p.1, London: McFarland.

218 Thomas Browne (1635/1943), *Religio Medici*, Part I, Sect. XV, London: Macmillan.

219 Graham Reed (1972), *The Psychology of Anomalous Experience*, p. 162, London: Hutchinson.

220 James E. Alcock (1985), 'Parapsychology as a "spiritual" science', in *A Skeptic's Handbook of Parapsychology*, ed. Paul Kurtz, pp. 537–68, Buffalo: Prometheus Books.

221 William Grey (1993), 'Philosophy and the paranormal', *Skeptical Inquirer*, 18, 142–9.

222 Susan Blackmore (1992), 'Psychic experiences: Psychic illusions', *Skeptical Inquirer*, 16, 367–76.

223 J. M. Wober (1992), 'TV and the Supernatural: Resistance of Beliefs to a Debunking Series', Independent Television Commission Research Paper, April 1992.

224 George H. Gallup and Frank Newport (1991), 'Belief in paranormal phenomena among adult Americans', *Skeptical Inquirer*, 15, 137–46.

225 Jean Piaget (1929/1973), *The Child's Conception of the World*, trans. J. and A. Tomlinson, p. 193, London: Granada.

226 H. M. Wellman and D. Estes (1986), 'Early understanding of mental entities: A re-examination of childhood realism', *Child Development*, 57, 910–23.

227 Jean Piaget (1929/1973), op. cit., p. 193.

228 Alan Cromer (1993), *Uncommon Sense: The Heretical Nature of Science*, cited in *Skeptical Inquirer*, Winter 1994.

229 Walter Scott (1828), Journal, 16 February, quoted by Neal Ascherson, *Independent on Sunday*, 17 October 1993.

230 Matthew 13:57.

231 Matthew 13:55.

232 Samuel Taylor Coleridge (1817), *Biographia Literaria*, ch. 14.

233 cf. William Shakespeare (1595), *The Merchant of Venice*, III, i, 63.

234 William James (1896/1956), *The Will to Believe*, p. 9, New York: Dover.

235 Solomon Asch (1956), *Studies of Independence and Conformity*, Psychological Monographs, 70, 416.

236 R. S. Crutchfield (1955), 'Conformity and character', *American Psychologist*, 10, 191–8.

237 John Maynard Keynes (1926), *The End of Laissez-Faire*, p. 3, London: Hogarth Press.

238 Charles MacKay (1852), *Memoirs of Extraordinary Popular Delusions and the Madness of Crowds*, vol 1, p. 225, London: National Illustrated Library.

239 See the original discussion by Gregory Bateson (1972), *Steps to an Ecology of Mind*, New York: Ballantine.

240 Jonathan Miller (1992), in *A Profile of Jonathan Miller*, by Michael Roman, p. 36, Cambridge: Cambridge University Press.

241 Bertrand Russell (1928), *Sceptical Essays*, opening paragraph, London: Allen & Unwin.

242 In the Reading survey (1987), 79 per cent of women and 57 per cent of men said they believed in at least three of the paranormal phenomena in question.

243 Ken Feder (1988), 'Trends in popular media: Credulity still reigns', *Skeptical Inquirer*, 12, 124–6.

244 James Lett (1992), 'The persistent popularity of the paranormal', *Skeptical Inquirer*, 16, 381–8.

245 Julian Brown (1994), 'Martial arts students influence the past', *New Scientist*, p. 14, 27 August 1994.

246 James E. Alcock (1990), *Science and Supernature*, p. 104, Buffalo: Prometheus Books.

247 See the discussion by Glenn G. Sparks, Tricia Hansen, and Rani Shah (1994), 'Do televised depictions of paranormal events influence viewers' beliefs?', *Skeptical Inquirer*, 18, 386–95.

248 Edward Tylor (1851), *Primitive Culture*, quoted by Brian Morris (1987), *Anthropological Studies of Religion*, p. 100, Cambridge: Cambridge University Press.

249 Leonard Zusne (1985), 'Magical thinking and parapsychology', p. 690, in *A Skeptic's Handbook of Parapsychology*, ed. Paul Kurtz, pp. 685–700, Buffalo: Prometheus Books.

250 Colin McGinn (1993), 'Consciousness and cosmology: hyperdualism ventilated', in *Consciousness*, ed. Martin Davies and Glyn W. Humphreys, pp. 155–77, Oxford: Blackwell.

251 My own most recent contribution to the debate is: Nicholas Humphrey (1992), *A History of the Mind*, London: Chatto & Windus.

252 M. A. Thalbourne (1984), quoted by James E. Alcock (1985), 'Parapsychology as a "spiritual" science', in *A Sceptic's Handbook*

of Parapsychology, ed. Paul Kurtz, pp. 537–68, Buffalo: Prometheus Books.

253 John Beloff (1987), review of *The Adventures of a Parapsychologist* by Susan Blackmore, *Journal of the Society for Psychical Research*, 54, 219–21.

254 John Beloff, letter to NH, 11 February 1993.

255 Blaise Pascal (1669/1966), *Pensées*, trans. A. J. Krailsheimer, 882 (222), Harmondsworth: Penguin.

256 The possibility that Shakespeare himself was involved with the translation of the Psalms is raised by Anthony Burgess (1970), *Shakespeare*, p. 233, London: Cape.

257 Blaise Pascal (1669/1966), *Pensées*, 830.

258 Robert L. Morris (1990), 'The parapsychology challenge', in *Frontiers of Science*, ed. A. Scott, pp. 50–65, Oxford: Blackwell.

259 True, it has occasionally been claimed by parapsychologists that they have evidence of psychic interactions where, although a correlation does indeed exist, the input is *not* a straightforward copy of the output. For example, a person's attempts to influence a random number generator may consistently have the opposite effect of that intended, or their guesses in a card-guessing experiment may prove to be significantly worse than chance. Even in these cases of 'psi-missing', however, we can take it that the mapping remains semantically transparent.

260 Sigmund Freud (1933), *New Introductory Lectures on Psychoanalysis*, p. 75, London: Hogarth Press.

261 Looking back, I see I may be more indebted to Beloff for my own discussion than I realise. The issues are raised in several of his essays in John Beloff (1990), *The Relentless Question*, London: McFarland.

262 Albertus Magnus (citing Avicenna), *Metaphysica vera*, Part III, quoted by C. J. Jung (1951/1985), *Synchronicity*, p. 45, London: Routledge.

263 Helmut Schmidt (1974), quoted by John Beloff (1990), *The Relentless Question*, p. 93.

264 I have discussed this question of 'bodily ownership' in much more detail in Nicholas Humphrey (1992), *A History of the Mind*, London: Chatto & Windus.

265 Friedrich Nietzsche (1885/1961), *Thus Spake Zarathustra*, trans. R. J. Hollingdale, p. 61, Harmondsworth: Penguin.

266 For irresistible arguments see Richard Dawkins (1986), *The Blind Watchmaker*, London: Longman; Daniel C. Dennett (1995), *Darwin's Dangerous Idea*, New York: Simon & Schuster.

267 William Shakespeare (1594), *Hamlet*, I, ii, 129.

268 Thomas Traherne (1670/1908), *Centuries of Meditation*, Century i, 29, London: Dent.

269 Bertrand Russell (1952), quoted by Ray Monk, *Independent*, 24 November 1993.

270 Igor Stravinsky (1942), *The Poetics of Music*, p. 62, Cambridge, Mass.: Harvard University Press.

271 Immanuel Kant (1787/1933), *Critique of Pure Reason*, 2nd edition, trans. Norman Kemp Smith, Introduction A5, p. 47, London: Macmillan.

272 The painting was made in 1768, predating Kant's metaphor. The identity of the bird is not entirely clear: if not a dove then probably a white cockatoo.

Index

Index

Index

paranormal fundamentalism
143–4, 153–4, 155
Parapsychological Association
(American), The 143, 164,
165, 189
Pascal, Blaise 11, 12, 19,
41–2, 46, 58, 66, 159, 199–200,
203–5, 220
Pasquarello, Tony 160, 162
Paul, St 54, 69
Pavlov, Ivan 25
personal experience
faith in 156, 158–66, 167–74
illusions and 167–71
Petronius 35
Pfungst, Otto 84
phantom body 123–5, 137, 190
phrenology 34
Piaget, Jean 170
PK *see* psychokinesis
Plato 20, 93, 158–9
poltergeists 88, 117, 126
'primitive peoples' *see* savage
mind
psi-inhibitors 152
psychokinesis (PK) 5, 116,
117–27, 128, 131, 198–9, 206,
207, 208, 210, 211–12, 214,
215
laboratory studies 138, 140
public figures: and the paranormal 181–2, 185–6

rainbows 156–7, 188
Randi, James 86, 150
random number generators 5,
184, 216
Reading survey (1987) 3–4,
162–3, 164, 165, 189
Reed, Graham 167–8
reincarnation 3, 73, 167, 191
religion (*see also* Christianity;
God) 9, 40, 181
human need for 10–16

internal logic of 17–22, 29
mental health and 15
and materialism 58
and miracles 57–8
as parent substitute 12–16
science and 1–3, 23–8, 29–36,
40, 41–4, 47–8, 224
resurrection 200–1
Rhine, J. B. 152
Ridley, Mark 52–3
Rivière, Claude 61, 65
'Robert' 107–8
Rousseau, Jean-Jacques 42
Russell, Bertrand 24–5, 38, 40,
182, 220, 222–3

Saint-Cyran, Abbot de 203
Saint Veronica Giulani 89
Sargent, Carl 161
'savage mind' 51, 52–7, 61, 66,
170–1, 190–1
Schmidt, Helmut 184–5, 215–16
Schrenck-Notzing, Baron von
145
Schumaker, John 15
science 4–5, 7–8, 9, 45–51
and common sense
explanatory style of 21–2,
23–7, 30–1
lawfulness of 65–6 67–9
and religion 1–3, 23–8, 29–36,
40, 41–4, 47–8, 224
see also materialism
Scott, Sir Walter 171
Searle, John 43–4
self-image, development of
100–1, 103–4
Shakespeare, William 78–9, 201–3
Sheldrake, Rupert 26–7, 49–50
Shestov (Russian philosopher)
143
Socrates 20
Sontag, Susan *Lover* 11
soul,
belief in existence of 3